Computers in Education

To Linda,
thought you might,
want to look at this!
Good luck in all your
plans for the new year.

Bob Smith
Oct 2017

CSLI
Lecture Notes
No. 215

Computers in Education
A Half-Century of
Innovation

Patrick Suppes & Robert Smith

CSLI
PUBLICATIONS
Center for the Study of
Language and Information
Stanford, California

Library of Congress Cataloging-in-Publication Data

Names: Suppes, Patrick, 1922–2014, author.

Title: Computers in education : a half century of innovation / Patrick
  Suppes and Robert Smith.

Description: Stanford, California : CSLI Publications, Center for the
  Study of Language and Information, [2016] | Series: CSLI Lecture
  Notes ; number 215 | Includes bibliographical references and index.

Identifiers: LCCN 2016038577 |
  ISBN 9781575868707 (hardcover : acid-free paper) |
  ISBN 1575868709 (hardcover : acid-free paper) |
  ISBN 9781575868684 (paperback : acid-free paper) |
  ISBN 1575868687 (paperback : acid-free paper)

Subjects: LCSH: Education–Data processing–History. | Educational
  technology–History. | Education–Effect of technological innovations on.

Classification: LCC LB1028.43 .S86 2016 | DDC 371.33/4–dc23

LC record available at https://lccn.loc.gov/2016038577

CIP

∞ The acid-free paper used in this book meets the minimum requirements
of the American National Standard for Information Sciences—Permanence
of Paper for Printed Library Materials, ANSI Z39.48-1984.

CSLI was founded in 1983 by researchers from Stanford University, SRI
International, and Xerox PARC to further the research and development of
integrated theories of language, information, and computation. CSLI headquarters
and CSLI Publications are located on the campus of Stanford University.

Visit our web site at
http://cslipublications.stanford.edu/
for comments on this and other titles, as well as for changes
and corrections by the author and publisher.

Contents

List of Tables

List of Figures

Preface

Remembering Patrick Suppes's Contributions

Patrick Suppes worked for over a half century on the uses of computers in education. When he started in January of 1963, computers were large, expensive machines mainly used for business and scientific computing and almost never interacted directly with people and certainly not in education. When he finally left the field in July of 2013, people were carrying networked computers in their pockets and almost everyone had taken training online.

Suppes and his teams carried this work out mainly at Stanford University, where he was a professor, and at Computer Curriculum Corporation (CCC), founded in 1967. This book is a telling of those times, the efforts, some of the mistakes, and many of the consequences of the work.

Not coincidentally, Patrick Suppes mastered many fields, often making substantial contributions to areas he knew little about until he started studying them. His overall goal can be described as systematizing human knowledge: how it is discovered, codified, transmitted, and applied. His academic fields included classical philosophy, logic and set theory, statistics, the foundations of measurement, the philosophy of science, psychology, education, parts of economics, physics, and brain science. He held appointments in philosophy, statistics, education, and psychology. He also knew a lot about food, painting, high fashion, and dozens of other subjects, and would gladly engage in a good argument about almost anything. Happily, we are not going to be responsible for all of these topics in this book, but are confined to computers in education!

Suppes was a successful entrepreneur who understood the deep connections between economics and research. He was a strong advocate of the free marketplace to the point of calling himself a "radical libertarian," but he also appreciated much of the scientific research funded by the government, including his own research funded by the National Science Foundation, the Department of Education, the Agency for International Development, and other government agencies. Often, in his own business efforts, he preferred science over profit, but he did know when he had to take measures to ensure survival and growth of a business.

Pat and I got the idea for this book in late 2013 during several discussions. The previous July, Stanford had licensed to a startup the courseware that Pat had developed from 1990 to 2013 at Stanford under the name Educational Program for Gifted Youth (EPGY). This meant that he no longer had any educational projects to work on, and hence he was thinking about a summation of his work in this field.

In 2013, at Stanford—as at other educational institutions—there was a lot of discussion about the future of online instruction and what it meant for the future of the university. A startup incubated at Stanford, Coursera, had just become a noted new company presenting university-level courses from many universities.[1] Stanford had created the position of the vice-president for online instruction. In all this excitement, it seemed as though Pat's original contributions beginning fifty years earlier were being forgotten.

Pat was somewhat relaxed about this, considering it a natural consequence of the passage of time. But we did feel that a summary of the record should be set down while many of the people who worked with him were still available for interviews so we could assemble a book.

Sadly, Patrick Colonel Suppes passed on November 17, 2014 after a sudden illness. We had been meeting most Fridays at 4pm to go over the material. Pat had recovered from a serious illness in late 2012 and was extremely busy trying to finish all of his myriad projects. He hated to leave unfinished anything he had begun, and his secretary's chalkboard was full of project notes. While he wasn't giving up on finishing things he was already committed to doing, he kept thinking of new projects—some very expansive—that he would like to undertake. Dan Flickinger noted that they had mapped out another twenty years worth of work on the language arts course.

Nancy Smith, my wife and another of Pat's co-workers, and I were still trying to unearth documents, find and interview collaborators, and assemble this history at the time of his passing.

Pat never had the opportunity to view much of this volume in its finished state. If he had reviewed it critically or written more of it, it would, I think, be a deeper and more insightful book. I have, however,

---

[1] See https://www.coursera.org/ and Wikipedia "Coursera" [177].

tried to give a sense of the people who worked with Pat, the connections between groups at Stanford and Computer Curriculum Corporation, and the excitement in those early days when interactive computing, artificial intelligence, networking, and dozens of applications (educational and otherwise) were invented or at least dreamt of. It was a heady time, and working with Pat was always a challenge and a delight. He wanted the sense of those times to be preserved.

The photo in Figure 1 shows his office in Ventura Hall shortly after his passing. It was filled with artifacts of his interests—books, papers, notes about work in progress. Many of them were there for decades. Now the office is empty for the first time in over fifty years.[2]

FIGURE 1: Pat Suppes's Office in Ventura Hall, Stanford University

What Was Patrick Suppes Like Personally?

Since Pat's passing in November of 2014, there have been many articles and obituaries that focused on his work, especially the work relating to computers in education, together with the usual demographic information. See for example the following obituaries: the New York Times [72]; the Los Angeles Times [236]; Alistair Isaac [53]; and Michael Friedman at Stanford University [41].

The following is a more personal portrait that can perhaps illuminate many of the anecdotes in the book.

---

[2]Upon seeing this picture, Sil Sanders noted that the office looks just like it looked decades ago.

I have known Patrick Suppes since 1967, when I came to Stanford; we were working on this volume a few weeks before he passed. Both my wife, Nancy Smith, and I were two of his PhD students, and both worked for him in a number of capacities over the years. I was a vice president of Computer Curriculum Corporation and became Executive Vice President upon the sale to Simon and Schuster; Nancy was the head of the entire EPGY group at Stanford that moved to join Redbird Advanced Learning when the EPGY courseware was licensed. Pat knew our family and we knew his, and Pat introduced us to many of his friends and colleagues over the years, which was an education in itself.

It is an understatement to say that he is the most important person to us outside of our immediate families.

Pat was a person who was most effective in teams that he formed and led. This is different than many academics, especially philosophers, who tend to work alone or with colleagues at other universities. Pat did a lot of individual work, but much of it was stimulated by the work with his teams.

Pat began at Stanford in 1950 and was a professor there until 2014, a duration of 64 years. He was at his office almost every day working on his many projects. Pat had been offered many opportunities to leave over the years (only once being tempted, he allowed). He was loyal to Stanford. He was especially proud to have been a part of the big surge in activity that Stanford made in the 1950s and 1960s, giving it the blueprint for success that led Stanford into world prominence in the following decades.

Loyalty was very important for Pat. He was loyal to institutions, ideas, and people. He worked with many of the same people over the years, helping them to retool for new tasks. He stayed in close touch to a broad range of people, whom he asked for advice on various matters.

Pat was an empire builder. He loved to create teams of people, to get funding, and work on new problems. He was in this way like his Stanford compatriots John McCarthy, Joshua Lederberg, and Edward Feigenbaum. He was also able to commercialize his work successfully.

Pat was friendly and engaging. He was an exciting person to be around (most of the time!) and always full of new ideas. He would borrow things from others, generally with attribution, but add his own spin to them. While seldom overtly funny, he was amused with the world and communicated his enthusiasm for things. He could brighten the disposition and lighten the load of his collaborators.

Many people remember how much Pat helped them in their careers. He had a knack for seeing how effective people could be doing something different than what they had been trained to do. Often but not always, the new position was with one of his groups, and the person got a chance to try it out for a few years. He was ahead of his time on advancing the careers of women and minorities in every capacity.

Pat traveled widely and lectured at many places in the earlier years. Often he would meet someone interesting and bring them back to Stanford or CCC and find something for them to do. He would build disparate teams of people with different backgrounds, give them something to do and "stir the pot" occasionally. If it worked, he would do more, otherwise try something else. (One of the reviews of a funded proposal from the 1960s contained a criticism that Pat should hire more established workers and managers and relied too much on students and people with no specific experience. There is no evidence that he followed this advice.)

Pat was always learning new things. He would attend a meeting and hear some new terms or ideas, and within a few days he would have familiarized himself with the basics. Sometimes he would go on to make original contributions.

The only thing he never seemed to pick up was the practical issues of computer programming, although he wrote on the mathematical theory of computation. This may be because he had no patience with the arcane and sometimes inconsistent details of software development. I once saw him puzzle for some time over the grammar for the LISP programming language and the anomaly of the "dotted pair" in LISP's syntax.

He was remarkably consistent on a given topic but completely willing to change his mind given new evidence. It was the arguments and evidence that mattered. Some people were a bit intimidated by his strong assertions, not realizing that he loved a good argument and was often waiting for someone to contradict him. Many days I would apparently lose an argument only to go home and work all night on a better set of debating points. Hopefully, in a day or two, he would ask if I had capitulated, and then I could give it another try.

The longest-lasting argument I ever had with him and actually won was about the importance of color graphics in CCC's courseware. He did not so much agree that I was right as he simply co-opted my position!

Dean Jamison used to say that the way to win an argument with Pat was to be the first person to ask for "hard data" about some claim for which there was no hard data.

In work, he was relentless and expected other people to put in effort as well. He remembered his days in World War II (with a fine patina of romance embellishing his memories), and especially remembered how much was accomplished in so little time by the United States in those years. He was always impatient.

When the basic concepts for any project were laid out, he expected the actual work to be finished immediately, and could not tolerate delays. I remember when I figured out that some course had been developed in only a few months in 1979, I asked Pat how it could have been done so quickly. He said, "Because we had to." Pat always "had to." He refused to believe that software could be hard to produce on a schedule, and was even less tolerant of delays in curriculum development and would say that he could do it faster himself.

Pat hated to not finish a project. He was always bringing something out from his catalog of unfinished things, trying to think of a way to rejuvenate it. His award-winning book on the philosophy of science, *Representation and Invariance of Scientific Structures* [133], was originally a paper-bound textbook he developed in the 1960s called *Set-Theoretical Structures in Science*. He took many decades to finish it to his satisfaction.[3]

To many people, Pat was an enigma because of the breadth of academic areas that he contributed to as well as being a pragmatic and effective business man. However, knowing something about his academic work as well as his work with computers, it seems to me that he was remarkably consistent throughout. For example, when Pat would do an about face and change his mind about something, he framed it in terms of his ideas about decision-making under uncertainty and the need to use new evidence to update previous opinions.

His mind could work at several levels at the same time, and even communicate different things to different members of his audience. He always adjusted to every member of his audience and was equally at home with a room of school children and a lecture hall of academicians at a conference.

Pat certainly had a strong emotional side that was not always the first thing that you would notice. John Perry pointed out that he felt his interest in computers in education was largely motivated by the desire to help children, especially disadvantaged ones.[4]

Overall, he was a rational and objective observer on the landscape of life, as well as being a kind, benevolent, and persistent mover and shaker for a better world.

---

[3]I think Pat has been haunting me for the last year to finish this book that we started!

[4]Private communication.

Acknowledgments

Nancy Smith and I would like to thank all of the many people who worked with Pat over the years at Stanford and Computer Curriculum Corporation on computers in education, as well as the many other collaborators from whom he drew inspiration. Nancy herself has served as researcher pouring through Pat's archives and proof editor, as well as writing two sections.

The following people helped with this volume, many with several interviews and materials that they supplied, as well as reviews of various drafts: Kathleen Adkins, Tryg Ager, Ted Alper, Alice Bauder, Lee Blaine, Jeff Boenig, Jeanette Cook, Randy Edwards, Carolyn Fairman, Matthew Mugo Fields, Dan Flickinger, Ronald Fortune, Sandy Hestes, Dean Jamison, Pentti Kanerva, Larry Markosian, David McMath, Betty Menacher, David Munson, Michelle Nguyen, John Perry, Ray Ravaglia, Lea Roberts, Marianna Rozenfeld, Barbara Searle, Marc Sanders, William R. "Sil" Sanders, Rainer Schultz, Richard Schupbach, Richard Shavelson, Kim Sheehan, Wilfried Sieg, Rick Sommer, Trish Suppes, Anne Trumbore, and Mary Wallace.

Our special thanks go to Kenneth J. Arrow[5] for writing the foreword. We also thank our publisher Dikran Karagueuzian for his advice and patience, Amita Kumar for facilities and support, Lauri Kanerva, Quinn Barker-Plummer and Emma Pease for technical assistance with LATEX, and Sarah Weaver for copy editing.

Robert Smith, October, 2016

---

[5] As this was going to press, Kenneth Arrow died on February 21, 2017. He will be sadly missed.

Foreword by Kenneth J. Arrow

I joined the Stanford University faculty in the fall of 1949; Pat Suppes came a year later. Stanford University was at that time a relatively poorly endowed university; its initially large body of assets had been dissipated by unwise restrictions on their investment. But it still retained a good reputation, especially for undergraduate students, and several departments were still outstanding (psychology, electrical engineering, in particular). There was no room for expansion of the faculty, but there were many vacancies created by wartime departures. The support for education of veterans created an increase in potential graduate students, and there was a considerable crop of new doctorates, whose careers had been delayed by the war, available for hire. Both Pat and I, for example, had served as weather officers. A department which wanted to raise its research level and was willing to work to that end had opportunities. While not all departments took advantage of these opportunities, the Economics and Philosophy departments had leaders who were committed to improvement, even in new directions.

I do not now recall exactly how we met, though it was not long after Pat's arrival. Of course, we had a great deal in common. We were both trained in mathematics and found it a useful way of expressing hypotheses clearly and drawing inferences, so that empirical evidence could be used more precisely to test and illuminate hypotheses about human behavior. Closely related was a more careful understanding of the meaning of measurements. Economists had come to ask when preferences could be measured as numbers or only as orderings, a problem made still more complex by developments in the theory of risk-bearing, where John von Neumann and Oskar Morgenstern had shown that a cardinal representation (expected utility) could be derived from some assumptions of rationality in behavior. We also were joined in a sense of the unity of the behavioral and social sciences; the individual making decisions in the market was the same as the person who could be learning to behave differently in response to rewards, according to the then-new Bush-Mosteller model, a model which gave rise to extensive experimental study. I was indeed surprised to find a philosopher engaged in large-scale experimentation. I soon learned of the remarkable range of his concerns. The breadth of his interests was not compromised by any diminution in depth. When Pat went into a subject, like learning, he went in thoroughly, frequently raising issues which changed the direction of the field he was working in.

Though we thought alike when it came to methodology and to the set of topics we found fruitful, there was one aspect in which we differed. He had the patience and the sense of organization to carry out large projects, a talent which I entirely lacked. (I have compensated by a substitute talent, finding someone else to whom to attach to help me run things; Pat was one of my major discoveries along this line.) The period in which we set out was also the beginning of government-supported research, and, at first, we worked through a group designed for applied mathematicians and statisticians. It supplied help in the form of typing pools (this is a pre-PC world that I am describing) and handling the administration of grants.

After a few years, Pat suggested to me that we form our own administrative unit. More precisely, he had already formulated his idea and even found a physical location, the now legendary Serra House, which was in fact the house which David Starr Jordan, the first president of Stanford University, had built for his retirement. Thus was created the Institute for Mathematical Studies in the Social Sciences (IMSSS). Around this nucleus, there was rapid growth, economists that I drew as well as those drawn by Pat's ever-widening set of interests. Pat was Director, fortunately.

Both of us were expanding our activities and drawing more young scholars into our work. The mathematician, Samuel Karlin, joined in many of our activities. We organized a major conference of the use of mathematical methods in the social sciences, which led to a major volume. I began to draw some graduate students and outside scholars, such as Hirofumi Uzawa, Herbert Scarf, and Harvey Wagner, into our orbit and our building. But Pat was expanding his activities and personnel even more rapidly.

Indeed, while Pat was always juggling several intellectual balls, his early interest in refutable models of learning had expanded into what became a lifelong concern with improving the process of education at every level. In particular, the rapid developments in electronic computation meant, among other things, that logical operations were just another kind of computation, and therefore computers could be used to transmit knowledge. All the complications of trial and error, feedback to correct errors in understanding, and the sheer bulk of facts and ideas new to the student, could be built into the computer program. Pat began to conduct his courses with larger enrollment, such as basic logic or set theory through the use of mini-computers with work stations (remember, the personal computer was not yet with us). He also began to concern himself with the uses of computers for elementary and high school education.

As may be supposed, the demands for space outran the size of Serra House within a few years. Serra House was devoted to economists, while Pat moved to the larger quarters of Ventura Hall. The separation was formalized by designating an Economics Wing of IMSSS, for which I was Associate Director, while Pat remained overall Director.

This separation, though in one sense a sign of success, since it reflected the greater interest in mathematical methods, also was in line with a nationwide decrease in interest in the unity of the social sciences. Traditional disciplinary lines reasserted themselves, though one new field, operations research, had been added in the process (it became a department in the School of Engineering).

I think we are in a period in which the disciplinary lines are again weakening, but this is hardly the place to develop this idea. In any case, Pat has always worked outside standard patterns, so that, if my surmise is correct, the importance of his work will be rated even more highly than it is now

I left Stanford for eleven years but returned in 1979. Though no longer in an organizational relation with Pat, we resumed our friendship, more and more intensely as time went on. We exchanged thoughts on many aspects of human society, not indeed always agreeing but always learning from each other.

Kenneth J. Arrow, June 2016, Stanford, CA

1

The Beginnings Before 1963

It all began when Patrick Suppes joined the Stanford University faculty in 1950 as an assistant professor of philosophy. In the next few years, he branched out into areas that were outside of traditional philosophy.[1]

One of his activities was the Institute for Mathematical Studies in the Social Sciences (IMSSS), founded in 1959 by Suppes and Kenneth Arrow, to formulate and test mathematical theories associated with the social sciences, especially psychology, learning theory, and economics.[2] In an unpublished (and funded) proposal sent to the Ford Foundation in 1955 to start a similar earlier effort, Suppes and Arrow provided the following description of the interdisciplinary character of the work and the underlying mathematical knowledge required:

> Without doubt the most difficult obstacle to the development of these research possibilities [across fields] is that few behavioral scientists (pure or applied) have any substantial knowledge of mathematics, and few mathematicians have extensive knowledge of any one of the behavioral sciences. One way of removing this obstacle is to give mathematical training to behavior scientists; another is to educate interested mathematicians in a given behavioral science. Although both these approaches are desirable and to some degree necessary, they are subject to the objection that it is not sufficient to make poor mathematicians out of good scientists nor poor economists, psychologists or industrial engineers out of good mathematicians. There are several reasons for believing that the most fruitful possibilities lie in an organizational set-up which both initiates and stabilizes permanent research teams of behavioral scientists and mathematicians. ([137])

At IMSSS, Suppes worked with Richard Atkinson, William Estes, Duncan Luce, and others. Increasingly devoting himself to the work

---

[1] Suppes's autobiography can be found in [112].

[2] Eventually, the economics group operated quite independently from the psychology and learning theory group.

1

at IMSSS, Suppes learned enough about statistics and psychology to make original contributions in those fields. He also received courtesy appointments in statistics, education, and psychology.[3]

1.1 Historical Antecedents to Computers in Education

Suppes had a long interest in educational technology, broadly construed; examples follow.

1.1.1 Libraries

He often referred to the construction of libraries as a key event in the maintenance and dissemination of knowledge. He was fond of telling stories about the Alexandrian library that stored the manuscripts of Aristotle and was destroyed accidentally by the armies of Julius Caesar. In American history, he noted philanthropist Andrew Carnegie's donations of "Carnegie libraries" across the country as being a seminal event in American education and the democratization of learning.

1.1.2 Correspondence Courses

Suppes often noted that correspondence courses were an important and early kind of "distance learning" using the transportation network and mail system that evolved in the late 1800s. In such a course, the school would mail work to the student; the student would do the readings and associated homework and send it back; finally, the correspondence school would correct and return the assignments along with new materials.[4]

Suppes himself took a number of correspondence courses while stationed in the Solomon Islands during World War II; he enjoyed the self-pacing and finished courses quickly.

1.1.3 Simple Scoring Machinery

During his undergraduate days at the University of Chicago at the beginning of World War II, Suppes recalled that classes such as calculus had to use machine-graded tests due to a lack of staff to grade tests. He noted, however, that the multiple-choice questions were very subtle and in his opinion did a good job of measuring the students' progress. He used this as a counter-example to those who argued that simple computational devices could not teach sophisticated content.

---

[3]The Stanford Department of Psychology finally made its courtesy appointment after Suppes had won the American Psychology Association's award for scientific research in 1972.

[4]See Wikipedia "Distance education" [178] for a review of the history of distance learning, including correspondence courses.

1.1.4 John Dewey

Suppes was impressed with the work and attitude of American philosopher and educator John Dewey.[5] Dewey held that students should be considered as individuals in the learning process and should expand their horizons beyond vocational skills. Dewey's interest in professionalizing teachers and expecting them to understand how their students were thinking and learning had an impact on the role that computers should have in education. Suppes always rejected the idea that computers might "replace" teachers, arguing instead that computers would allow teachers to spend more time mentoring and interacting with their students.

Suppes was able to hear Dewey speak near the end of Dewey's life and always mentioned this as a formative moment.

1.1.5 Programmed Instruction

"Programmed instruction" (PI) is the presentation of educational content by breaking it down into small pieces with one or a few questions in each small piece. The student would evaluate his/her own work, and then "branch" to the next piece of content depending on whether or not the student answered the questions correctly. PI often used books or brochures with instructions at the bottom of a page telling the student where to branch to. Simple machines were built on the same principle.[6]

Suppes was aware of PI and knew B. F. Skinner, but he was not at all impressed by the operation of PI materials, considering them to be superficial and awkward. He claimed that PI had little influence on his own work, although some critics might have thought differently. Suppes later wrote critically of Skinner's ideas of teaching arithmetic in a report entitled *Facts and Fantasies of Education* [126] pp. 12–14.

1.1.6 Educational Television

Suppes followed the developments in educational television. One example was the "Continental Classroom" programs presented in 1960–61 on NBC television at 6:00AM. Funded by the National Science Foundation, Continental Classroom presented a course in modern algebra taught by John Kelley and a course in probability taught by Frederick Mosteller. Students watched the lectures, did homework, and took exams at nearby colleges for credit.[7]

---

[5]See Wikipedia "John Dewey" [187].

[6]See [30]

[7]Suppes's associate Robert Smith took Mosteller's course for credit when he was in high school. He went to Iowa State University in Ames to sit for the exams. He remembers vividly Mosteller's use of a computer simulation of the central limit

1.1.7 Mathematical Psychology

At IMSSS, working with Atkinson, Estes, and others, Suppes developed mathematical learning theories and then tested them using stimulus-response experimental methods. For example, an experiment might consist of forming a hypothesis and then finding a group of student subjects to use in testing the hypothesis.[8] The subjects would be randomly assigned to treatment and control groups, and the experimenter would present stimuli (for example, cards containing symbols) to the subjects, and then measure the recall rates as a function of different protocols. Finally, the results would be compared statistically to the predictions of the mathematical model.[9]

This work was very prolific and well-funded. Some articles of interest follow:

- Concept formation in children with or without correction; with Rose Ginsberg, *Journal of Experimental Psychology*. See [142]. There were several follow-up studies.[10]

- Modern learning theory and the elementary-school curriculum. This study, published in 1964 in the *American Educational Research Journal*, showed a connection to the move to technology that Suppes was in the process of making. See [116].

- Discussion of the learning theory of William K. Estes. This article, published in 1992 in a volume in honor of Estes, describes the evolution in learning theory that was in part connected to Suppes's work with online instruction (see [132]).[11]

There were any number of ways in which computers, interactive or not, could be used in such research including:

- *Analysis*: By the middle 1950s, much statistical analysis was done via computers; some was still done by hand calculations.

- *Presentation*: The task of presenting the stimuli to the subjects could clearly be done by interactive computers. Suppes realized this, but there were no such computers available at the time.

---

theorem. Smith eventually met Mosteller at Stanford.

[8]Sometimes these experiments actually used rats rather than students.

[9]See for example [138].

[10]It should be noted that in the last years of his life, Suppes sponsored a great deal of research into the brain and how we can identify cognitive activities in the brain.

[11]Suppes said, "Once Bill began explaining to me the details of statistical learning theory I took to it like a duck to water, because I soon became convinced that here was an approach that was both experimentally and mathematically viable" (p. 3).

- *Actual instructional delivery*: The prospects of actually using computers for instruction apparently did not occur to Suppes until about 1960 or 1961.

1.2 Conference on Programmed Learning and Computer-Based Instruction

In the fall of 1961, the Office of Naval Research conducted a conference in Washington on the growing interest in using computers in education. The conference included programmed instruction researchers now rethinking their approaches, theoreticians dealing with learning models, and computer scientists and engineers building equipment and doing experiments. The conference proceedings were published in [27]. Some speakers at the conference included the following:

- Richard C. Atkinson of Stanford University gave a theoretical paper with Richard Dear of Systems Development Corporation, one of the sponsors of the conference, on the allocation of items in a two-concept teaching model (see [27] pp. 25–45). The paper referenced a number of articles by Suppes and others associated with IMSSS.[12]

- Donald Bitzer together with P. G. Braunfeld and W. W. Lichtenberger of the University of Illinois gave a paper on their Plato II instructional system (see [27] pp. 205–216).[13] The computer used a CRT to display slides with instructional and question frames; students used a separate, custom-built keyboard. The programming was intended to represent a framework similar to classic programmed instruction. The paper notes operational difficulties with timesharing when multiple students used the system simultaneously.[14]

- J. C. R. Licklider of Bolt Beranek and Newman discussed a computer program for teaching and reviewing German vocabulary (see [27] pp. 217–239).[15] The system was implemented on the Digital Equipment Corporation PDP-1 and used a Teletype terminal for conversation with the student.[16] The program would display a German word, e.g., *arbeiten*, and expect the student to type the associ-

---

[12] Atkinson was to become Suppes's key associate at Stanford and also one of the founders of Computer Curriculum Corporation. See chapters 2, 3, and 4.

[13] Bitzer went on to run the Plato project into the 1970s; see page 96.

[14] Bitzer may well get the credit for the first computer-assisted instruction demonstration with his Plato I and Plato II systems, but clearly a number of people were thinking about it at the same time.

[15] Licklider went on to be a key supporter of artificial intelligence research and the development of the ARPANET. He was a legendary figure. See Wikipedia "J. C. R. Licklider" [186] for more details.

[16] There is more about the PDP-1 on page 15.

ated English, in this case *to work*. The paper is noteworthy for the number of experiments conducted about the program design and input/output. For example, Licklider also programmed the display screen of the PDP-1 instead of printing on the Teletype, and discovered that this modification did not help very much in terms of the learning. The article is noteworthy because the first true interrupt system on a computer—an essential capability for interactive computing—was done for this project; see page 11. This paper appears to have the strongest connection of any of the work done at the conference to Suppes's efforts at Stanford two years later.

1.3   The Influence of John McCarthy

McCarthy had received his PhD from Princeton University. He had taught in the Mathematics Department at Stanford, then went to MIT where he started his groundbreaking work in computer science. He returned to Stanford in the new computer science department. McCarthy coined the phrase "artificial intelligence," which has entered the public consciousness as one of the key ideas of the last century.

McCarthy was also known as the "father of timesharing." This concept was the first practical approach to interactive computing. The idea was that a computer (an expensive machine!) could interact with multiple human users on terminals "at the same time" by switching between "processes" so quickly that all users believed they were getting "instantaneous" response. McCarthy argued that timesharing was making interactive computing cost-effective.

It should be noted that Suppes was never hugely interested in computer hardware or software *per se*, even though his team created many artifacts and some innovations. Suppes's interest was always in learning. He realized that such an approach, now called "computer-assisted instruction," would not only change learning theory research, but also the practice of education itself.

1.4   Some Target Areas for Curriculum Development

During the 1950s and 1960s, Suppes had already been developing curriculum materials as traditional textbooks. These included:

- *Introduction to Logic*: Suppes had taught logic at Stanford for years by 1962, and allowed that he was getting tired of it. He had written a standard textbook in the field, *Introduction to Logic* (see [113]), and implementing it on the computer was one of his first priorities. In the next five decades, about six versions of logic courses were done under Suppes's direction.

- *Axiomatic Set Theory*: Another textbook Suppes wrote was *Axiomatic Set Theory* (see [114]). This was built as a CAI course in the 1970s at Stanford and used by Stanford students for about five years.

- *Elementary Classroom Materials*: Working with Associate Professor Newton Hawley of the Stanford math department, Suppes had written in 1959 a proposal for the experimental teaching of math in the elementary schools, asking for about $67,000 ([145]). He and Hawley also did some experimental teaching in the Palo Alto schools, as described in the *San Francisco Chronicle* [88]. As he explained in the proposal, they had realized that arithmetic was "ordinarily the principal (if not the sole) branch of mathematics currently taught." They wanted to expand this to geometry and had experimented with 28 students to study "pupil interest, problems of vocabulary, and even the muscular coordination required to operate compasses." Suppes later commented that he learned there was a lot to do to make improvements in mathematics instruction and learning, and was looking for technology to help with this.

- *Sets and Numbers*: This was a grade-school text in mathematics written as a part of the "new math" movement that emphasized logic and set theory in teaching. The first edition came out in 1961. Suppes always wanted to computerize this entire text series, but later allowed that he had never done so to his satisfaction.

Now, it was necessary to find money to pay for the next developments.

2

The Dawn of Computers in Education: 1963–1971

2.1 A Modest Proposal to the Carnegie Corporation

Proposals were a very different matter in 1962 than they are today! On December 21, 1962, *Proposal for a Computer-Based Learning and Teaching Laboratory* was sent from Stanford University to the Carnegie Corporation of New York.[1] Suppes likely wrote all of this proposal that had already been worked out with Carnegie, making the proposal itself mostly a formality. A few weeks later, on January 4, 1963, Stanford president J. E. W. Sterling sent a letter encouraging approval of the proposal to John Gardner, president of the Carnegie Corporation.[2]

Looking back on this experience and its simplicity compared to current Stanford proposal policies, Suppes marveled at the change. For example, staff benefits in 1962 were only 7% of the salaries with no Stanford University overhead. In 2016, the staff benefits would be 32.45%, and the university overhead would be 58.45%. Proposals could focus on the substance of the work then, rather than getting bogged down in a maze of bureaucracy. At least that was his view.

2.1.1 Main Purpose of the Proposal

The proposal described the purchase of computer equipment and staff salaries for five years, for a total amount of $1,009,700 for the founding and operation of the Computer-Based Learning and Teaching Laboratory. As the proposal said:

---

[1] This "corporation" was actually a foundation. The proposal is unpublished but noted as [115].

[2] Gardner became Secretary of Health, Education, and Welfare under President Lyndon Johnson and helped redefine the role of the Federal Government in education. Further, this department later provided significant support for projects at IMSSS.

It is envisaged that the laboratory would be used for three major kinds of research: the investigation in a depth and intensity not heretofore possible of fundamental processes in human learning; the development of a normative theory of the learning process with intended quantitative applications to the sequential organization of instructional material; and the detailed study and analysis, from the standpoint of learning theory, of certain bodies of instructional material, e.g., elementary mathematics and foreign languages. ([115] p. 1)

The laboratory would be focused on learning research, as well as actual delivery of education using a computer and evaluating the feasibility or efficacy of such delivery. The laboratory would provide facilities not otherwise available at Stanford and would facilitate learning experiments on a large number of subjects, recording both responses and response times automatically. In time, the laboratory focused more on building and evaluating actual courses.

The proposal emphasized that including a computer would "permit a much higher order of flexibility in programming experiments than is possible within the framework of the traditional learning laboratory" ([115] p. 1). In addition to needing a computer for interacting with the subjects, the computer would also allow for the statistical computations for analysis. The Institute at that time employed two full-time programmers for the analysis of experimental data, submitting punch cards to the IBM 7090 located at Pine Hall. The proposal still stated that the central Computation Center at Stanford would have an "intimate connection" in the research work ([115] p. 16).

2.1.2 Detailed Objectives

The following areas were identified for this research into learning:

- *Language Learning:* Research on the role of a computer-based laboratory for the automated teaching of a second language. The proposal mentions that existing language labs were "handicapped" ([115] p. 6) by not providing behavioral criteria for stating student growth and not allowing random access to instructional materials. Here we have the two key issues of measuring learning and providing individualized instruction. At that time, Stanford's best equipment used IBM punch cards to control the movement of an audio tape to a specified position.
- *Mathematical Proofs:* Research on teaching students mathematical proofs. Suppes believed that proofs were a significant part of mathematics, and logic was one of his central interests. The proposal notes the fact that there are many correct proofs for a given mathematical statement, and the computer can check a proposed proof in a way that cannot be done with any lesser technology such as workbooks.

- *Concepts of Elementary Mathematics:* Research into the learning of the great variety of concepts in elementary (grades 1–6) mathematics. The proposal says "a central problem is the optimal sequencing of mathematical concepts. A typical scheme for using the learning laboratory with rapid random access to instructional materials is to organize the sequence of concepts to be learned in such a way that at each stage of development the student is required to satisfy a behavioral criterion of learning" ([115] p. 9). The proposal also references Suppes's prior authoring of workbooks for elementary school mathematics.

Learning experiments that Suppes and others had conducted during the 1950s often dealt with only one aspect of the work at a time (e.g., the effect of reinforcement on learning). Suppes had never believed it was that simple, seeing the computer implementation of instruction as a way to combine many different parameters and aspects to test the overall space of options more fully. The proposal states: "It seems likely that the next major step will be to introduce teaching routines in which the branching is based not simply on raw measures of performance, but upon the current state of the learning with respect to theoretically significant parameters of the learning process." It promises that the computer would "carry out theoretical calculations during the course of the experiment" ([115] p. 12).

2.1.3 Computer Equipment

The proposal budget included $440,700 for a computer (a Digital Equipment PDP-1[3] pre-selected by McCarthy) and associated equipment, headlined by $120,000 for the computer with 4K of core memory. An additional 4K of memory cost $40,000. The proposal states "the selection of this computer is based upon extensive consultations with Professor John McCarthy of the Stanford Computation Center. Professor McCarthy is familiar with the range of computers available and has had extensive experience with the PDP-1 at Massachusetts Institute of Technology (MIT). It is his judgment that this is the best computer available for research of the sort proposed here" ([115] p. 15).

However, this view of the time-sharing software on the PDP-1 was overly optimistic. Fortunately, Digital supplied the source files for the operating system; so late at night the programmers could make necessary modifications and use the opportunity for improvements as well. For example, the commitment had initially been to run 6 stations simultaneously, but "tweaking" allowed much larger projects on the PDP-1.[4]

---

[3]See Wikipedia "PDP-1" [205].

[4]Edward Fredkin, working at Bolt Beranek and Newman, added the interrupt

2.1.4 The Role of John McCarthy–Timesharing and Artificial Intelligence

Obviously, Professor McCarthy was a key person in helping select and program the computer system, but his importance to Suppes goes beyond that.

McCarthy is known as the inventor of timesharing. The conceptual importance of this for computer science cannot be overstated. Longtime McCarthy associate Les Earnest said: "The Internet would not have happened nearly as soon as it did except for the fact that John initiated the development of time-sharing systems. We keep inventing new names for time-sharing. It came to be called servers.... Now we call it cloud computing. That is still just time-sharing. John started it" ([235]). At the very least, time-sharing was an enabling technology that made computers in education feasible.

Suppes did not recall the details of the total influence McCarthy had on him. He did observe that ideas traveled between the two very quickly, and they always talked a lot. It is possible that the idea of using computers for research in learning took some inspiration from McCarthy.

It is also well known that McCarthy was the great evangelist that computers could take on any task. He would point out to people how something could and should be automated.

As the father of the term "artificial intelligence," it is very likely that he argued to Pat that computers could be used to teach. McCarthy liked both computers and people, and felt that they would have a great future together.

McCarthy also had his own motives in wanting this PDP-1 computer for his work. He had had one at MIT and was happy to share Suppes's new PDP-1 until he could raise some money. As would be expected, the Stanford Artificial Intelligence Laboratory began operating in a few years with its own computers (see page 57).

2.2 The Laboratory and Its Equipment

2.2.1 The Physical Space and Equipment

In 1963, Pine Hall already housed the Computation Center, including the university's IBM 7090. The decision was made by Stanford to place the Computer-Based Learning and Teaching Laboratory in Pine. The computer was stored in a large room with air conditioning and raised floors while the adjacent space contained a number of small, sound-

---

system and did much of the timesharing work to increase the number of users. See [27] p. 236 and Wikipedia "Edward Fredkin" [181].

proof cubicles that were used for experiments. Figure 2 shows the signage that is still on this building identifying the laboratory, which itself has been gone for decades. The reflection is Polya Hall, formerly the home of the computer science department. Pine, Polya, and the other buildings in the area were built in the 1950s in the mid-century-modern style. The Pine space is now used for the Stanford Online High School.[5] These buildings are scheduled for demolition in a few years in order to use the land more efficiently.

FIGURE 2: Pine 192–6 Showing Location of Former Computer-based Lab (2015)

2.2.2 Terminals

The cubicles in Pine were outfitted with two terminals each for experiments. The first terminal was a random-access optical display device developed for the laboratory by IBM. It presented microfilmed content on a 10 by 13-inch screen. The student responded to the display by using a light pen on the screen itself. When the student pressed the light pen, a signal was sent to the computer indicating the coordinates to an accuracy of $1/4$ of an inch in each direction. These displays were predecessors of the IBM 1500 system, and were removed from Pine after a short time. See page 17 for details.

Each of the rooms also had a display terminal made by Philco, probably initially for a government agency. These were gigantic terminals with large metal frames and had to be located within 100 feet of the PDP-1 system. An interesting mechanical keyboard—these some-

---

[5]See page 264 for details about the Online High School.

times jammed—contained "meta" keys that could be programmed. The screens were huge CRT monitors that used vector graphics for everything including characters, so they could display primitive graphics. Their intended initial use was for the learning experiments. Figure 3 shows Patrick Suppes sitting with a subject of an experiment, probably around 1963–64.[6]

FIGURE 3: Philco Terminal in Pine Hall with Student and Patrick Suppes, ca. 1963

Teletypes were also used in order to have instructional delivery outside of the lab. Most of these were Model 33 Teletypes, manufactured by Teletype Corporation. They cost about $700 each, making them cost-effective for many years (see Wikipedia "Teletype Model 33" [227]).

2.2.3 Audio System

The audio system for use with the PDP-1 was a Westinghouse Corporation P50 computer which played sounds to the user through speakers in the sound-proof booths. The messages were recorded on a 6-inch-wide magnetic tape containing many tracks. An individual message could be retrieved in about 1 second. Two tape transports could be assigned to each student station, where each transport could hold up to 17 minutes of messages.

---

[6]See page 60 for details about using the Philco terminals for text editing.

Sil Sanders saw this commercial system in operation and observed that it was extremely unreliable, laying some of the groundwork for later experiments with digital sound at IMSSS and development of customized hardware at CCC.[7]

2.2.4   The PDP-1—A Famous Machine!

The computer was a Digital Equipment Corporation PDP-1. Figure 4 shows an operational PDP-1 now housed at the Computer History Museum in Mountain View, CA.[8] The PDP-1 is famous as the first interactive, time-shared computer. It also was programmed with the first video game, named *Spacewar!*, which ran on the monitor at the front of the picture. Ironically, *Spacewar!* did not run in timesharing mode, because it requires the entire computer in real-time. The Computer History Museum demonstrates *Spacewar!* periodically for visitors. It still operates by loading the program from a paper tape into main memory.[9]

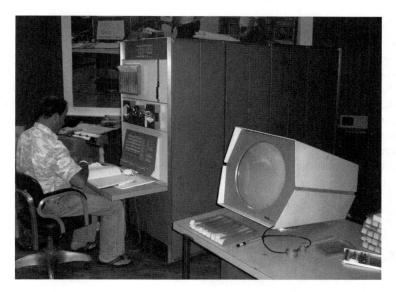

FIGURE 4: PDP-1 in Operation at the Computer History Museum

---

[7]Private communication.

[8]See Wikipedia "PDP-1" [205] for details of the PDP-1, and [85] for details about the restoration at the Computer History Museum.

[9]The July 1963 edition of the Stanford computation center's internal memo mentions Spacewar! thus: "Until the PDP arrived last March, Spacewar! didn't particularly excite us, but now that it's here, most of us have become hooked on the game."

The memory of the PDP-1 was initially 8K words but was expanded soon to 32K words plus a 4K core that could be swapped with any of the 32 bands of a 131K word swapping drum. Typically, a program was read into memory, allowed to run, and then swapped out. The swapping process took 32 milliseconds, and a program was allowed to run at least 64 milliseconds before being swapped back out.

The PDP-1 also boasted one of the first real "file systems," albeit a primitive one, on the IBM 1301 disk drive associated with the machine. Files had names and occupied certain physical regions of the disk. Files were used for storing programs, curriculum materials, and text documents.

2.3 First Courses Demonstrated on the PDP-1

The PDP-1 computer was delivered in May of 1963 but it took a while to setup the lab and all of the equipment as well as develop initial programming and courseware.

2.3.1 Elementary Mathematical Logic Course

The first instructional activity at the lab was the demonstration of a program for teaching elementary mathematical logic on December 12, 1963. Two lessons with 23 problems were run with four sixth-graders on December 20, and again with two fifth-graders on January 7, 1964. During the spring of 1964, 20 lessons in logic were programmed and used with two fifth-grade boys over the summer. These lessons were all presented on the Philco terminals in the lab.

During the spring of 1965, two second-grade boys worked through some of the logic course, and 26 second-grade students worked through a revision during the summer of 1965.

2.3.2 Elementary Mathematics Course

During the 1964–65 school year, 29 lessons of math were programmed, focusing on the first and fourth grades. During 1964–65, two groups of six first-grade children were given a preliminary version of the first-grade lessons.

2.4 School Locations Outside of Stanford

The Stanford Laboratory was becoming too confining. The lab was set up for psychology experiments that would be rather short, but the courses were now much too long for it to be feasible to bring students to the Stanford campus. Labs had to be set up in schools. In the summer of 1964, IMSSS received a contract with the United States Office of

Education to establish a computer-based instructional laboratory in a public school over a period of time.

2.4.1 Grant School—Overview

The Grant School in the Cupertino Union School District, Cupertino, CA, was chosen as the first school project. It ran from October 16, 1965 to June 8, 1966. Instruction was delivered on teletype terminals connected to the PDP-1 system at Stanford. 270 students from grades three through six participated in the program.

2.4.2 The Brentwood Project—Overview

The Stanford-Brentwood Computer-Assisted Instruction Laboratory was partly funded by the Office of Education and the National Science Foundation, but also supported by IBM Corporation somewhat indirectly. IBM had built the IBM 1500 Instructional System running on an IBM 1800 computer. It was installed at the Brentwood Elementary School in East Palo Alto, CA. There were 16 student stations, each of which had two visual displays and audio playback as well as audio recording.

The laboratory operated for two years, between 1966 and 1968. Courses in mathematics and reading were offered, generally to different sets of students. The reading course was the responsibility of Richard Atkinson, and the math courses were the responsibility of Patrick Suppes and his team.

2.4.3 Other Locations

During this period (1965–1968), many other schools had one or more terminals with some students. Here is a partial list:

- Ravenswood High School in the Sequoia Union High School District: one teletype, math course used by seven arithmetic classes with 60 students in total, in 1966.
- Costano School in Ravenswood City School District: four teletypes, spelling course, with audio provided by a second phone line.
- Oak Knoll School in Menlo Park, CA: first- and second-grade students in math drills, 1966.
- Walter Hays School, Palo Alto, CA: third- and sixth-grade students in math drills, in 1966.
- Breckenridge, the Morehead State University Laboratory School in Morehead, KY: two teletypes for fifth- and sixth-grade students in math drills, in 1966.
- More schools in Redwood City, CA; San Jose, CA.

2.5   The Grant School Project

Because of its size and duration, as well as the effort made to monitor the activity, the Grant School project was an important experimental laboratory. For example, student response times were measured to an effective accuracy of $1/10$ of a second.[10]

There were eight teletype terminals using telephone lines to the PDP-1 at Pine Hall on the Stanford campus. The teletypes were noisy and were therefore baffled by placing them in large, ventilated closets.

There were about 270 students in grades three through six in the Grant School program, which was the entire school population except for the handicapped students. The school was located in Cupertino, CA, a middle-class community about 12 miles from Stanford.

2.5.1   Curriculum Structure and Content

The math curriculum was organized into 41 *blocks*. Each block presented a concept or skill from the elementary curriculum. The material itself was adapted from *Sets and Numbers*, written by Patrick Suppes [118].

The same content block appeared at all grade levels 3–6, with increasing difficulty. For example, the first block covered simple sums. For the third grade, sums from 0 to 20 were covered. For the fourth grade, 0 to 40; for the fifth, 11 to 61; for the sixth, a "mixed drill" included all sums. Most of the blocks contained variations of the elementary operations with some word problems and other topics.

Each block had a specified amount of time it was expected to take, between three to twelve days. The teacher was mostly able to set the block for all students in order to match the material the teacher was covering in class. The online drills did not contain any tutorials or expository material since it was assumed that the teacher had already covered this material.

Internally, each block was composed of material organized into five levels. Level one was the least difficult, and level five was the most difficult. The middle level, three, was used as the starting point on the first day of using the block. For subsequent days, the material would go up by one level if the student achieved a score of 79% or better on the previous day; if the score was less than 60% on the previous day, then the student moved down a level. See Figure 5 for a graphical example of how the motion within the block worked over several days.

---

[10]The interest in measuring latencies—a large issue in psychology experiments—did seem to be reduced over time and as the courseware and programming became more complicated. Suppes also moved from primitive stimulus-response models to more cognitive and algorithmic models of learning.

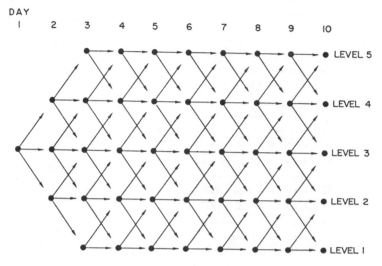

FIGURE 5: Motion for Math Drills

This approach was effective for teachers who wanted the drills to correlate to what the teacher was teaching in the classroom. Individualization within the selected block was implemented by having each student receive problems at the difficulty level appropriate for that student based on previous performance. All students in the class were working on the same material, but at different levels of difficulty.

2.5.2 Presentation of Math Problems

Problems were presented on the less expensive Model 33 Teletype terminals, which used paper from a large roll in the machine instead of having the newer CRT displays. Printing exercises on paper was a challenge that programmers had worked out. The PDP-1 serviced the terminals using "full-duplex mode," which means that a character typed on the keyboard would not be printed until it was sent back from the computer. This allowed more flexibility in creating displays on the paper, but was harder to achieve on the computer and associated telecommunications.

The blocks were organized so that a daily session would take about 4–6 minutes, delivering about 20 drill problems per session. Students would file into and out of the classroom on a schedule so that all enrolled students could have a lesson every day. Figure 6 shows a scroll of paper for a student on a given day.

PLEASE TYPE YOUR NAME

MIKE ODELL

DRILL NUMBER 509013

(42 + 63) / 7 = (42 / _7_) + (63 / _7_)

48 - 38 = 38 - _48_
WRONG

48 - 38 = 38 - _4_
WRONG, ANSWER IS 28

48 - 38 = 38 - _28_

76 - (26 - 10) = (76 - 26) + _10_

4 X (7 + 13) = (4 X _7_) + (4 X _13_)

(53 - 20) - 11 = 53 - (20 + _11_)

32 + (74 + 18) = (_32_ + 74) + 18

51 X (36 X 12) = (_51_ X 36) X 12

17 X (14 + 34) = (17 X 14) + (17 X _34_)

362 + 943 = 943 + _362_

(5 + 8) X 7 = (_5_ X 7) + (_8_ X 7)

(90 / 10) / 3 = _90_ / (10 X 3)

(72 / 9) / 4 = 72 / (_9_ X 4)

(54 + 18) / 6 = (54 / 6) + (18 / ___)
TIME IS UP

(54 + 18) / 6 = (54 / 6) + (18 / _6_)

60 - (19 - 12) = (60 - _19_) + 12

72 X (43 X 11) = (72 X 43) X _11_

(63 / 7) + (56 / 7) = (_63_ + _7_) / 7
WRONG

(63 / 7) + (56 / 7) = (_63_ + _56_) / 7

END OF DRILL NUMBER 509013

13 MAY 1966
16 PROBLEMS

	NUMBER	PERCENT
CORRECT	13	81
WRONG	2	12
TIMEOUTS	1	6

WRONG
2
16

TIMEOUTS
13

222.7 SECONDS THIS DRILL

CORRECT THIS CONCEPT - 81 PERCENT, CORRECT TO DATE - 59 PERCENT

4 HOURS, 46 MINUTES, 59 SECONDS OVERALL

GOODBYE MIKE.

FIGURE 6: Scroll of Paper with Math Drill for a Student

In addition, there were a few tricks that Teletypes could do. The printer head could be moved back one position with a "backspace" character sent from the computer. There were also separate operations for moving the head all the way back to the beginning of the line ("carriage return"), and for moving to the next line ("line feed"). These features could be used to display a "blank" and then position the head for the student to type there. See Figure 7 for a long-division exercise. This was accomplished by having the student fill in the partial results on the right-hand side. So the answer is "300 + 70 + 1," or 371. Back-spaces were used so that the student would fill out the partial addends from right to left (i.e., the student would type one character, and then the teletype would backspace two columns).

$$
\begin{array}{r}
123\overline{)45678} \\
36900 \\
\hline
8778 \\
8610 \\
\hline
168 \\
123 \\
\hline
45
\end{array}
\qquad
\begin{array}{r}
\underline{300} \\
\\
\underline{70} \\
\\
\\
\underline{1}
\end{array}
$$

Thus $123 \times \underline{371} = 45678 + 45$

FIGURE 7: Example of a Long-Division Problem

A variety of reports were provided for use by the teacher. For example, Figure 8 shows the number of problems correct, wrong, and timed-out for a given student. The reports were quite sophisticated, including data such as mean latencies. However, teachers were not actually able to take full advantage of the information available while information that teachers did need was sometimes not included, for example the student's name on some reports.

2.5.3   Reactions to the Experience at the Grant School

The project was well received despite many technical issues. In fact, the book reporting on this project included an "edited" daily log of about forty pages length that recorded the problems. Technical terms like "igl op" (the computer executed an illegal operation) abound. See [148] pp. 41–91.

There was a staff member on duty at the school most of the time to watch over things and help the students. As in later years at CCC, it was clear that the operation of the laboratory—the sheer logistics of having the students come to the lab, sign on, then get up and leave

```
PLEASE TYPE STUDENTS NAME.   FRED SMITH
   DRILL - 506045
NUMBER OF PROBLEMS THIS DRILL     20
          NUMBER   PERCENT
CORRECT     18       90
WRONG        0        0
TIMEOUT      2       10

TIMEOUTS
   10
   15


TOTAL ELAPSED TIME     205 SECONDS

PERCENT OF PROBLEMS CORRECT TO DATE IN CONCEPT BLOCK     90

PERCENT OF ALL PROBLEMS CORRECT TO DATE     90

TOTAL TIME     1 HOURS     2 MINUTES     0 SECONDS

END OF REPORT
```

FIGURE 8: Example of a Daily Student Report for Math Drills

at the end—was of primary concern. There were also people back at Stanford to address problems with the system and telecommunications.

Problems that would not be accepted today were dealt with cheerfully. The clunking sound of the partially-baffled teletypes was considered charming. The down-time and errors on the system were taken in stride.

Questionnaires were given to the students, teachers, and parents about their reactions to the project. A few results follow.[11]

- *Popularity among students.* 71% of the surveyed students liked the drills, while less than 2% did not.
- *Younger vs. older students.* Younger students liked the drills more than older ones. Older students were more likely than younger ones to emphasize how they performed rather than whether they liked the experience or not.
- *Criticism of technical problems.* The students did not seem to mind the many technical problems, while the teachers were more likely to complain about them. Parents also were slightly more concerned about breakdowns and also the noise.
- *Reactions to timeout timing.* The computer was programmed to timeout rather quickly. The idea was to improve focus and reduce latencies. Most students, and their parents, did not like this feature. At the time, Suppes said that "this problem needs more attention."

---

[11] This list is summarized from [148] 93–154.

However, it should be noted that later products allowed the time-out time to be set within the management system, and that timeout times were often defaulted to a very long time. This practice meant that abandoned stations might cause very long measured latencies, so the data had to be reviewed carefully.

- *Parent reactions.* Parents liked the program, but it was clear that communications with the parents had not been optimal. Parents requested more information, and their responses indicated that the nature of the program had not been adequately communicated. Parent comments included: "it certainly takes the role of the teacher out of the school" and "it does not increase knowledge of concepts."

- *Printouts for parents.* About 90% of the students took printouts to parents, and parents liked these printed reports. Many parents reviewed the printouts with their students.

- *Students not receiving 100%.* Many parents also wanted their children to receive 100% correct on the drills, perhaps not realizing that students who were doing well were deliberately given more challenging problems, and that the drill was supposed to be a learning experience and not a test.

- *Teachers' general reaction.* Teachers generally saw this for what it was: a way to provide more drill for students and not a replacement for the teachers. Some felt that students who did not focus on drills in class were more attentive to the computer-based drills.

- *Teachers' concerns.* They expressed concerns about the break-downs. Noise made some students nervous. Teachers believed that the time-outs were too fast. Some teachers felt that contact with parents had been insufficient.

2.5.4 Performance Models for the Elementary Operations

As was originally planned, the Grant School Mathematics program was also used to test models of student performance. The system collected, for each instance of a student taking an exercise, data about both the correctness of the final result and also the latency. Only the blocks dealing with the elementary operations were used for this analysis.

The performance model used was based on the number of primitive memory operations the student would have to perform, with both a probability of an error for each operation and an amount of time. The model basically predicted that the more human memory operations a given exercise required, the higher the probability of a final error, and the higher the latency would be for completing the problem. The theoretical difficulty of a problem could easily be counted from the problem itself.

To test this model, linear regressions were run (on Stanford's IBM 7090, next door to the PDP-1) and the goodness of fit of the model was determined. Figure 9 shows the predicted and observed errors on fourth-grade addition, and Figure 10 shows the predicted and observed latencies on the same fourth-grade addition sample. Suppes claimed that both of these correlations were reasonably good.[12] The other elementary operations (and also the commutative, associative, and distributive laws) were handled in a similar manner.

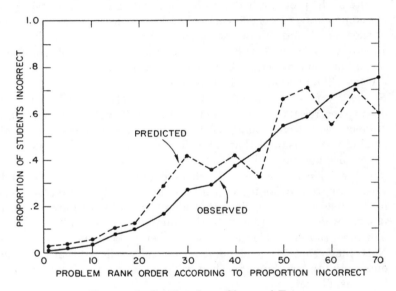

FIGURE 9: Predicted vs. Observed Errors

Considering that the original purpose of the learning laboratory was to use the computer for testing learning models, this is at least a convincing example of research that would not have been feasible without the computer.

2.5.5   Handling of Technical Issues

Terminals

The lab leased 32 telephone lines for use by schools in the area. In the lab itself, patch-panels allowed connections to the PDP-1 to be altered. This also enabled direct contact between the lab and a teletype in the field.

---

[12]See [148] pp. 187–255.

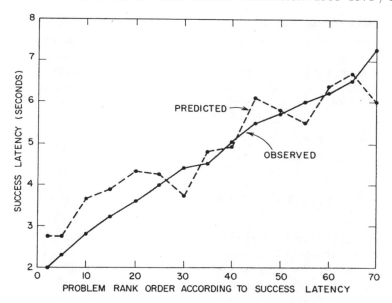

FIGURE 10: Predicted vs. Observed Latencies

Modifications had to be made to obtain accurate latencies on a character-by-character basis. These were considered to be accurate to 1/10th of a second after all considerations were accounted for. One problem was that the computer would still be sending a lengthy message (at 10 characters per second) to the teletype for a period of time after the program would have thought that it was ready. To solve this, special non-printing characters were used between the computer and the terminal. Using these, the instructional program was able to more accurately compute when the student was actually able to start a response; hence the latency would be more accurate.

"Micro Time Sharing"

The PDP-1 was only designed to have a small number of users, about 12. However, this was increased to about 31 by having the operating system run four programs, called drivers: the math driver, the spelling driver, logic-algebra driver, and monitor. Each driver could attend to more than one student at a time, with separate data for each student within a driver. Hence, the number of programs running, from the point of view of the operating system, was acceptable.[13]

---

[13]Later techniques that compare to this are operating systems that allowed shared code segments, and later still systems with multi-threaded programs.

Authoring Languages

The math drills were coded in a special-purpose language that was intended to be easy for non-programmers to use. This language was input using a text editor on the CRT screens of the Philco terminals and saved onto disk files.[14] The language was then directly interpreted by the driver. Here is one simple example:

```
PR
PS 2 + ZZ = 5
RT
SP 2
ANS 3
```

This encodes an addition exercise which displays as the following:

```
2 + __ = 5
```

The student then fills out the blank (the print head moves to the blank); the correct answer is 3; the computer then evaluates the student's input.

Suppes's approach to curriculum coding was generally *ad hoc*, inventing small, easy-to-use languages with terse commands for the most common exercise types in a course. The actual programming was inside the course driver, where decisions about evaluation and motion to the next exercises were made. This simplicity generally remained until the 1970s, when more complex language elements were developed.

Error Handling

There were many errors in the courses, but methods of detection and repair were primitive. The system was programmed to log all errors on a teletype in the computer room. If a program had an error, it was flushed from memory and restarted. This could lose work for some students.

2.5.6   Automata Models of Student Performance

Suppes was rapidly moving on from simple stimulus-response models of learning. He felt that the phenomena were too complex, and cognitive models were needed. He therefore took the basic algorithms for elementary math operations and expressed them as finite-state automata, such as the one shown in Figure 11 that represents column addition of two numbers.

The "correct" algorithm is to add the two digits in the right-most column, output the answer, and remember whether there was a carry. Then, proceed to the next column on the left, adding 1 more if there was a carry. Repeat this until there are no more columns.

---

[14]See page 60 for a description of TVEDIT.

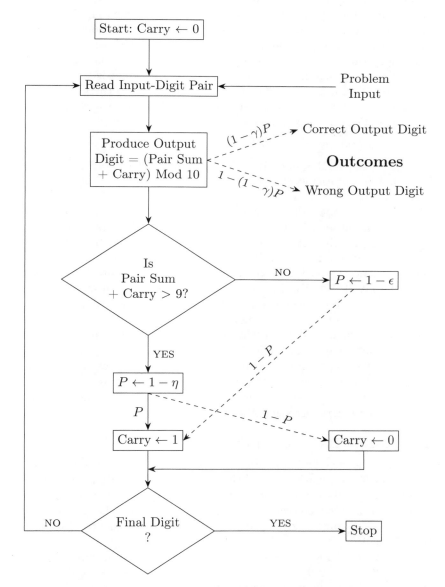

FIGURE 11: Probabilistic Automaton for Predicting Errors In Addition

The automaton has been altered from its normal form to include three kinds of error situations, one for outputting the wrong digit, one for generating a spurious carry, and one for forgetting a previous carry. Each of these has a probability of error associated with the error situation; for example, the probability of generating the wrong digit is γ, and hence the probability of generating the correct digit is $(1 - \gamma)$. η is the probability of generating a spurious carry, and ϵ is the probability of forgetting a previous carry. The model predicts that the probability that the entire answer will be correct is:

$$P(correct) = (1 - \gamma)^D * (1 - \eta)^C * (1 - \epsilon)^{(D-C-1)}$$

where D is the number of digits if the problem is solved correctly and C is the number of carries that will be generated if the problem is solved correctly.

Using this model, the predicted probability of errors can be compared to the observed results, which Suppes did in detail. See [151] pp. 133–206 for the details and also the analysis of data from children using his courses during 1967–68. Also see [122] for a more mathematical treatment together with the defense of using automata in this way.

In the late 1970s, BBN researchers John Seely Brown and Richard Burton built a program called "BUGGY" based on an automaton model of arithmetic errors to define diagnostic procedures for helping students improve their skills at doing arithmetic problems. Data from IMSSS was used for their project. See [16].

In the 1980s at Computer Curriculum Corporation, revisions to the main math course Math Concepts and Skills (MCS) were made using components of this model to give tutorial suggestions to students who were making errors. See page 214.

2.6   Logic—Its Place in the 1960s

Logic was the very first course started at IMSSS in December of 1963. While math was clearly the priority course overall, logic held a great interest for Suppes, who had written a college textbook in logic in 1956.[15] So, in 1964–65, the first of many courses in logic that Suppes and his collaborators developed was presented to students. See [148] pp. 342–349.

Mathematical logic as a subject for instruction came into its own in the 1960s. The subject had matured during the 1930s, and by the 1960s, it had entered public interest. The "new math" that was popular in that period was based on logic and set theory. Suppes himself had

---

[15]See [113].

contributed with his basal mathematics series *Sets and Numbers* [118]. Stanford had a large group devoted to "new math" called the School Mathematics Study Group (SMSG).[16] Suppes was active in supporting this effort. The Stanford mathematics and philosophy departments had a large program in logic. Many logicians-in-training took various roles in Suppes's courses.

Today, logic has largely moved into theoretical computer science, and does not garner the interest in mathematics and philosophy that it once did.[17]

2.6.1   Propositional Logic, Sentences, Rules of Inference

The course taught simple propositional logic in which entire sentences are combined using logical connectives. For example, consider the following English *atomic sentences*:

```
John is here.
Mary is at home.
```

Atomic sentences can be combined using *logical connectives* such as the words *and*, *or*, *not*, and *if... then*. Some examples of *molecular sentences* are:

```
John is here and Mary is at home.
If John is here then Mary is at home.
```

Rules of inference allow larger sentences to be created from smaller ones, and allow smaller sentences to be extracted. Suppose we have the following *premises* displayed by the computer. The line numbers are used to allow commands to be applied to the statements on the lines.

```
1.  John is here.
2.  If John is here then Mary is at home.
```

The task for the student is to prove *Mary is at home.* from the premises. To do this, the student would type "1,2 AA" and the computer would print:

```
1,2AA    3.  Mary is at home.
```

The "AA" stands for "affirm the antecedent," one of the classical names for this rule of inference.

In addition to English sentences, mathematical sentences could be included. For example, the student could be asked to type the commands that perform the following derivation. (Student input is shown in bold; the "FC" command forms a conjunction from two other lines.)

---

[16]See Wikipedia "School Mathematics Study Group" [166] and also "Edward G. Begle" [182].

[17]See Wikipedia "Logic in computer science" [192].

```
Derive:   y + 8 < 12

Premise:    1. if x = 4 and z = 3 then y + 8 < 12
Premise:    2. x = 4
Premise:    3. z = 3
```

To do the proof, the student would type the following:

- **2,3 FC** 4. x = 4 and z = 3

- **1,4 AA** 5. y + 8 < 12

- CORRECT!

After the student has given the last command, the computer would observe that the student has completed the proof, and would type "CORRECT!" If the student made a conceptual error (or a typo), the program would print out the reason for the error and wait for the student to type another command. For example, an error in the above could be the command "2,3AA." This is wrong because line 2 is not an "if... then" sentence and hence the AA command cannot be used.

This simple example has an obvious solution, but it is by no means the only correct solution. In practice, students discover very different approaches to proving the derivations, and the computer program handles them all up to the limits of available memory, of course.

2.6.2   Curriculum Content and Programming

By the spring of 1965, the logic course had 29 lessons covering proposition rules, creating derivations, and semantic concepts such as truth tables, tautologies, and the notion of validity. Now the course utilized another special-purpose authoring language for the lesson text, the derivations to be performed, and some other exercise types.

This course was continually modified based on analyses of student data, and from the desire to handle more topics in more sophisticated ways.

2.6.3   Logic Course in a Local Elementary School

The pictures in Figures 12, 13, and 14 are from a film entitled "Please Type your Name" showing the logic course (probably about 1967) being taught in a Palo Alto, CA school. Figure 12 shows an instructor (from Stanford) explaining the AR rule ("associate right" for addition) to a group of students. Figure 13 shows a student at the keyboard of a Model 33 teletype, and Figure 14 shows the scroll of the student's work on the teletype.

FIGURE 12: Logic Instructor in a Palo Alto School

FIGURE 13: Student Using the Logic Course on a Model 33 Teletype

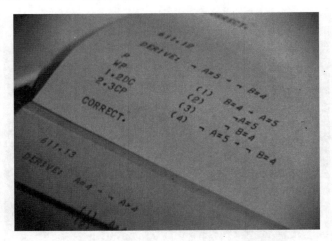

FIGURE 14: Scroll of Logic Course on a Teletype

2.6.4   Suppes's Comments about the Logic Course

Suppes noted that the "computer program accepts any logically valid response of the student. The student is not restricted to a few multiple-choice answers, or more generally, there is not a unique constructed answer that must be given" ([148] p. 344). Suppes felt that the computer implementation of the proof checker as the underlying engine for the logic course was an innovation in educational technology that needed to be emulated in other domains. While recognizing the theoretical problems of doing this, he envisioned many areas where it would be possible. This has indeed happened in educational programs and other areas.

2.7   *Scientific American* Article: "The Uses of Computers in Education"

In September, 1966, *Scientific American* magazine published a special issue on computers. The issue is remarkable for the number of key contributors to computer science who exposed seminal ideas in a single magazine. Among others, John McCarthy wrote the introduction, Ivan Sutherland wrote on user interaction and graphics, Marvin Minsky wrote on artificial intelligence, and Christopher Strachey wrote on computer software. Patrick Suppes wrote on the uses of computers in education.[18]

---

[18]See [117]. The entire issue of the magazine can be purchased from *Scientific American* and is recommended for providing both a time capsule of the current thinking in 1966, but also a wealth of ideas that remain current. The advertisements also provide a time capsule of companies then marketing in the computer field.

The article recapitulates the work that was done for the Grant School project at Stanford. Photos and some descriptions also relate to the Brentwood Project, which was not actually operational until a few months later, in November, 1966. See page 37 below.

Suppes repeats and crystallizes many of his previous arguments for using computers in education. But the fame and lasting importance of the article derives from his characterization of three levels of CAI, caricatured as "drill, tutorial, and dialogue" when people refer to this oft-cited article.

Suppes begins with an optimistic prediction of the future of CAI:

> Not only are machines now able to deal with many kinds of information at high speed and in large quantities but also it is possible to manipulate these quantities of information so as to benefit from them in entirely novel ways. This is perhaps nowhere truer than in the field of education. *One can predict that in a few more years millions of school children will have access to what Philip of Macedon's son Alexander enjoyed as a royal prerogative: the personal services of a tutor as well-informed and responsive as Aristotle.* (p. 207; emphasis added)

It was not typical of Suppes to promise too much too soon in the field of CAI, and for most of his career, he emphasized the difficulties as well as the opportunities. This exuberance was an exception.

2.7.1 Benefits of CAI

Suppes acknowledged the growing importance of computers in school administration, but did not cover this in the article, instead focusing on computers in educational delivery.

Individualization

Suppes claimed that "the truly revolutionary function of computers in education, however, lies in the novel area of computer-assisted instruction" (p. 207). He noted that individualized tutorial instruction was one of the glories of ancient Greece and Rome and is carried on at universities like Cambridge and Oxford. The main objection to such individualization is, however, cost, and he speculated that the computer may address this. "It is widely agreed that the more an educational curriculum can adapt in a unique fashion to individual learners –each of whom has his own characteristic initial ability, rate and even 'style' of learning–the better the chance is of providing the student with a successful learning experience" (p. 208). McCarthy, in his introduction in the same magazine issue, presents some of these ideas in a more general way by arguing that "computers, far from robbing man of his individuality, enable technology to adapt to human diversity" ([74] p. 65).

Suppes's work on individualization has often been associated with motion schemes that give students more or less of certain kinds of material based on their mastery of the content. While this is an important feature of individualization, he went much further in this article to consider individualization based on cognitive styles of different students. He said, "A body of evidence exists that attempts to show that children have different cognitive styles. For example, they may be either impulsive or reflective in their basic approach to learning" (p. 220). He offered the possibility of accommodating different learning styles, though he admitted difficulties in doing this.

- *Can we address differences in cognitive styles?* Suppes wrote, "It is not at all clear how evidence for the existence of different cognitive styles can be used to guide the design and organization of individualized curriculum materials adapted to these different styles" (p. 220).
- *How far should we go to accommodate different cognitive styles?* Suppes reflected, "what we face is a fundamental question of educational philosophy: To what extent does society want to commit itself to accentuating differences in cognitive style by individualized techniques of teaching that cater to these differences? The introduction of computers in education raises this question in a new and pressing way. The present economics of education is such that, whatever we may think about the desirability of having a diverse curriculum for children of different cognitive styles, such diversity is not possible because of the expense. But as computers become widely used to offer instruction in the ways I have described here, it will indeed be possible to offer a highly diversified body of curriculum material" (p. 220).

Here, Suppes himself has raised the objection that his detractors have focused on for decades, namely, that rather than constructing curricula of skills and concepts for students to master, we should be accommodating individual styles by encouraging discovery and creativity. See Chapter 8 for further discussions of this issue.

Data Collection for Learning Research and Evaluation of Curriculum

In *Scientific American*, Suppes said, "Before the advent of computers it was extremely difficult to collect systematic data on how children succeed in the process of learning a given subject.... A computer, on the other hand, can provide daily information about how students are performing on each part of the curriculum as it is presented, making it possible to evaluate not only individual pages but also individual exercises" (p. 208).

Data for Teachers and Administrators

Suppes noted that by having the computer create and store data, an "extensive summary of student results is available to the teacher. By typing in a simple code the teacher can receive a summary of the work by the class on a given day, of the class's work on a given concept, of the work of any pupil and of a number of other descriptive statistics" (p. 217). Suppes allowed that such data can easily be overwhelming and research was needed to determine what data teachers could use. For example, one of the observations at the Grant School was that too much data was available in the reports.

This was certainly a problem at CCC years later, which was partially addressed by creating a report-generation system for teachers, administrators, and others to make their own reports, but seed the report generator with a large number of commonly requested reports. See page 175 for a discussion of the IPS system, which dealt with individual student trajectories.

2.7.2 Levels of Computer-Assisted Instruction

Suppes recognized the three distinct levels of CAI which would each have, to some degree, the advantages listed above: drill, tutorial, and dialogue.

Drill

Suppes felt that drill and practice was "at the most superficial level (and accordingly the most economical one)" (p. 214–215) and that such programs are "merely supplements to a regular curriculum taught by a teacher" (p. 215). As an example, he pointed to the drill programs he had thus far developed.

However, he argued that drill was an important part of almost any educational process. In teaching arithmetic skills, he argued that "*there seems to be no way to avoid a good deal of practice in learning to execute the basic algorithms with speed and accuracy*" (p. 215, emphasis added).

The value of drill has been an especially controversial issue in mathematics instruction and particularly in evaluating Suppes's contribution. See Chapter 8 for more discussion of the role of drill.

Tutorial

The second level of complexity of an instructional computer system was the tutorial level. Tutorials could provide introduction to new concepts and skills, working through sample solutions.

Another function of a tutorial program would be deciding that a student had mastered a concept and moving the student along at an accelerated rate, or deciding that a student needed additional or remedial practice. This function is something of an adjustment to drill and practice, and in the future, this was considered a part of drill itself.

More importantly, tutorials could provide assistance to students having difficulty by diagnosing problems and activating assistance customized to the student. One simple example is that the computer could notice that a student was failing to "carry" when attempting to do a column addition problem. The tutorial could show the student the nature of his mistake and provide more exercises.

Later programs for elementary mathematics at both Computer Curriculum Corporation and EPGY had many such tutorials built into the system (see page 218). It should be noted that care must be taken in designing such tutorials: it is easy to give the student too much advice or to be mistaken about the diagnosis. Suppes anticipated this problem, noting that it is important "to keep the deprived child from developing a sense of failure or defeat at the start of his schooling. Tutorial 'branches' must be provided that move downward to very simple presentations, just as a good tutor will use an increasingly simplified approach..." ([117] p. 217).

Dialogue

Suppes believed that the most sophisticated level of interaction would be the dialogue level. This is intended to be a free-wheeling, open discussion between teacher and student.

Suppes gives the following example of a dialogue. "Suppose in a program on economic theory at the college level the student types the question: 'WHY ARE DEMAND CURVES ALWAYS CONVEX WITH RESPECT TO THE ORIGIN?'" (p. 219). The computer would have to be capable of parsing and processing the natural-language input. If this were spoken, the harder problems of "speech recognition" would also need to be solved. Understanding that both of these computer functionalities were at the time beyond the state of the art, Suppes nevertheless believed that it was possible and desirable to solve them.

2.7.3 Issues with Suppes's Levels of CAI

The three levels have stayed with us as part of the lore of CAI. Suppes always kept the paradigms in mind and held that true tutorial and dialogue capabilities remained the fundamental goal for the future. Reaching this goal is, however, complicated. The ideas of tutorial and dialogue are very deep, difficult to achieve, and not even agreed upon in theory as to what constitutes a successful example of achievement.

Suppes argued that the ability of the logic course to recognize and accept arbitrarily many correct proofs of a theorem, while rejecting all incorrect proofs, was a tutorial capability of his logic course. However, it might be noted that this was simply a property of the domain of the curriculum. A truly "tutorial" proof checker would also help a student or provide advice to the student based on the current proof under construction. Adele Goldberg, in her thesis written at Suppes's lab, did something like this, carrying the notion of tutorial much further. Still, her approach also worked because of properties of the domain (see page 102).

Speech recognition and natural-language parsing capabilities are also important; great progress has been made on these areas in the last fifty years. It is also correct that a "knowledge base" that can store knowledge in general ways and an "inference engine" that can make inferences from the knowledge base will also be required in order to support dialogue.

We have seen many programs that legitimately have provided tutorial and dialogue within limited domains. Modern-day cell phones can answer spoken questions about the location of the nearest pizza restaurant. Suppes later realized (and made sure to publish his revised view) that it might well be over a hundred years before a computer would be a tutor "as well-informed and responsive as Aristotle" ([117] p. 207).

2.8   The Stanford-Brentwood Project

For those who saw it, the CAI project at Brentwood Elementary School in East Palo Alto between 1966 and 1968 was an extraordinary experience and view into the future.

Suppes remembers that IBM came to him in about 1964 and expressed great interest in entering the educational market. They were impressed with his progress using Digital Equipment Corporation's PDP-1, and they wanted to be a big part of what they thought would be a growing market. Together with funding from the National Science Foundation and the United States Office of Education, IBM expressed a willingness to underwrite many of the costs by supplying their system (see [151] p. 263).

2.8.1   The System and Student Stations

The hardware was an IBM 1800 computer running what they called the IBM 1500 Instructional System.[19]

> The IBM 1500 Instructional System was the only commercial system produced by a single manufacturer that had an integrated student terminal configuration providing a keyboard and light pen response mode,

---

[19]See Wikipedia "IBM 1500" [185] for details about this system, including its use at Brentwood. They cite 1967 as the year, which is incorrect. Also, see [18] for a retrospective of the system, including samples of Coursewriter code.

CRT-based graphics, audio, and static film projection. Experimental instructional systems had been developed by IBM prior to a prototype version of the 1500 Instructional System, which was tested at Stanford University. A production version of the 1500 System with changes in the CPU and the audio system and having the capability to run a maximum of 32 student stations was installed in over 30 sites beginning in the late 1960s. IBM's commitment to the development of this system was extensive but short-lived, as most sites were unable to maintain funding support for the system. In retrospect, *the IBM 1500 System had capabilities yet to be supported on the microcomputer systems of the 1990s.* ([18], emphasis added)

This system included the following:

- An IBM 1800 computer with a timeshared operating system.

- 17 student stations, one for the lab manager and the rest for the students.

- Each station consisted of a CRT terminal with a keyboard, a film projector (for still color images), a light pen, all in a modern custom-built station.

- Audio was supplied from a special device that had tapes loaded into it for random-access sounds. The audio unit had 10 separate tape drives, each with four tracks: three for sounds and one for digital control codes. The tapes could fast forward or reverse at a speed of 70 inches per second, which reduced delays to a minimum. An operator could change the tapes for each reading class. Each station had two headphone sets, one for the proctor to listen in on the student session when desired. See [18] p. 24 for details.

- The headset also had a microphone. Recordings of student responses could be made and then played back for evaluation.

- A building with 3200 sq.ft. was constructed on the Brentwood parking lot and staffed by IMSSS.

Figure 15 shows a photo of the IBM 1500 student station with the two displays, lightpen, and headphones. Figure 16 shows a diagram of the entire 1500 system, including the CPU, hard disks, audio equipment, and other peripherals.

There were two courses used at Brentwood. The math course was the responsibility of Suppes's team, and the reading course was designed and operated by Richard Atkinson's team. The school had 800 students. Each class was divided to allow 13–15 students to come to the laboratory at the same time for half-hour periods. Reading was given in the morning and math in the afternoon. Students worked at their

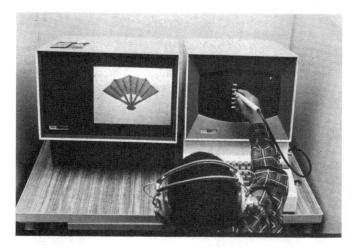

Figure 15: IBM 1500 Student Station

own pace, and by the end of the year, some students had covered three times as much of the basic material as others.

The assumption was that the classrooms were being taught in a manner that correlated to the work on the computer system. Indeed, Stanford staff gave all of the mathematics instruction to make sure that this was the case. The reading instruction was done by the school's regular teachers, as described below.

2.8.2 The Math Course

The math course was much more extensive than the Grant School "blocks" program but had a similar structure. The availability of displayed pictures and audio messages, as well as a CRT terminal, allowed much more variety of activity. The discussion here focuses on the first-grade curriculum. The entire curriculum and all features are described in [151], especially Appendix D.

The first-grade curriculum had a number of content areas (or topics) spread out through the sequence: sets, numerals and counting, addition, subtraction, geometry, games, and miscellaneous topics. The topics were further divided into units, and then internally there were five levels of difficulty that individualized the instruction. In general, all students would take the same content on a given day, but individualized by difficulty. Since Stanford employees were responsible for all math instruction, they could keep the classroom instruction and the computer synchronized.

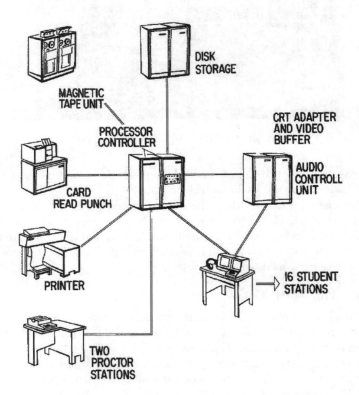

FIGURE 16: IBM 1500 Instructional System

(b) Union of sets with the union operation
     symbol in the stimulus

   {duck} ∪ {   } ∪ {cat bird} = _____

   ☐   {   }   Audio: Find the set that goes
   ☐   {duck bird}   on the line.
 →☐   {duck cat bird}

FIGURE 17: Set Exercise from the Brentwood Math Course

Audio: Point to the circle.

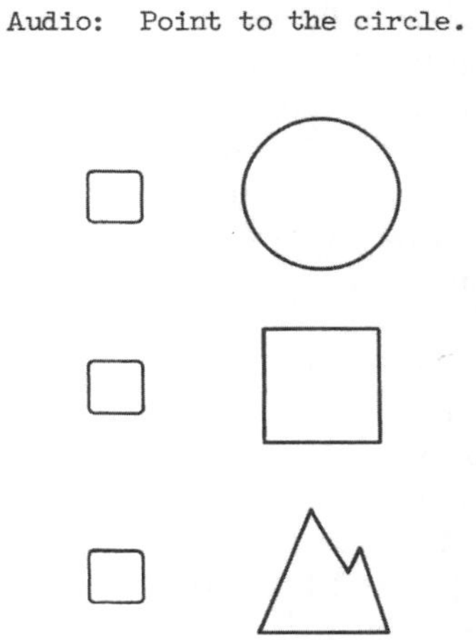

FIGURE 18: Geometry Exercise from the Brentwood Math Course

Figure 17 displays the content from an exercise from the sets topic; Figure 18 from the geometry topic, and Figure 19 from the numerals and counting topic. The exercises adroitly used the still-film display and the CRT display together. The CRT had the keyboard and the light pen, so sometimes the student would answer on the CRT but read the choices from the film display screen. Obviously, the designers of the IBM 1500 had in mind the kinds of computer displays that we have had for the last 30 years, but were far from being feasible in 1966.

The content was largely taken from that used in the Grant School program. A group of Stanford employees and graduate students in Stanford's Cedar Hall apparently made the drawings for the film screens and drafted the content. They sent the content to IBM's Science Research Associates subsidiary, where it was programmed in Coursewriter, IBM's new curriculum programming language, for the project. Programming could also be done on-site at the lab itself at Brentwood School when needed.

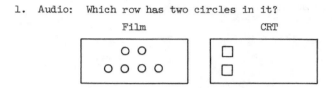

FIGURE 19: Counting Exercise from the Brentwood Math Course

2.8.3   Initial Reading Course at Brentwood

The Brentwood Initial Reading program was created by a team supervised by Professor Richard C. Atkinson of the Psychology Department who was also the Associate Director of IMSSS. Atkinson and Suppes worked together on many projects and were in constant communication, but tended to run their own CAI experiments. Suppes had general responsibility for the infrastructure and operation of IMSSS as a whole. Some of Atkinson's key team members over the years (including after the Brentwood project) were Hal Wilson, Dexter Fletcher, Duncan Hansen, Carolyn Stauffer, Avron Barr, Marian Beard, and Olin Campbell. The Initial Reading at Brentwood is more completely described in [234]. This also contains a detailed description of the lab. Research at IMSSS into psycholinguistics played a role in this work, including Hansen and Rodgers [48] and Rodgers [93].

Wilson and Atkinson felt that audio was essential for Initial Reading, graphics were highly desirable, and the tutorial capabilities of the IBM 1500 Instructional System were very important, as were the text analysis facilities of the Coursewriter II language. Wilson and Atkinson reviewed the benefits of CAI and felt that, in their case at least, the principle argument for CAI was individualization. It also was a powerful research tool because of the ability to control independent variables precisely as well as the environment and style of interaction. Finally, CAI was a valuable new tool for curriculum evaluation.

The Initial Reading course used the existing reading teachers at Brentwood, unlike the Brentwood Math course. No attempt was made to intervene with the normal classroom instruction. For the 1966–67 school year, only the first-grade students used Initial Reading. There were two classes of first-grade reading; each class was divided into two subsets since only 16 terminals were available for students.

The course assumed that students knew English, so it was largely designed to teach them the orthographic code using drills and some tutorials. As Rodgers said in [93], "give students enough drill and self-confidence to involve them in that confrontation known as beginning reading" (p. 22).

The course contained four major elements: decoding skills, comprehension, games and other motivational devices, and review. The overall flow of a session is shown in Figure 20.

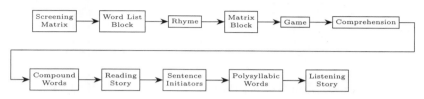

FIGURE 20: Session Structure for Brentwood Initial Reading

Decoding Skills

This content included showing a list of words and asking students to select the correct word. Cues were provided by audio, images on the film display, or other words on the CRT display. The lists for any given lesson were composed of words generated by the rhyming and alliterative patterns being presented in that lesson (for example, "ran," "fan," and "can" for rhyming).

Another kind of exercise was the "reduplication and initiator" exercise. For example, the student would be provided the initial phrase "It's a," and asked to fill in "dog" from a word list. Exercises of this kind were in the "matrix" blocks in the session.

Comprehension

Meanings were taught using audio and/or images on the film display to compare to the word. The meanings taught were selected from standard word lists and dictionaries for students.

A sample exercise is shown in Figure 21 below; in the sample, the student is asked which of four words fit into the sentence. The audio message asks the student to make a selection. "CA" labels the response if the student answers correctly, and "WA" if the student answers incorrectly.

Another sample comprehension exercise is shown in Figure 22 below; in this exercise, a sentence is presented on the CRT and the student is asked to answer two questions about the sentence.

Stories were used for comprehension instruction. The student reads the story to himself. If he does not know a word, he touches the word and the entire sentence is read. Illustrations are displayed on the film screen. After the child has completed the story, a series of questions is provided. These questions deal with direct recall of facts, generalizations about an idea, inferential questions relating information in the

	tan	
Dan saw the	fat	hat.
	man	
	run	

Only one of the words in the column will make sense in the sentence. Touch and say the word that belongs in the sentence.

CA: Yes, Dan saw the tan hat.
Do the next one.
↓CA

WA: No, tan is the word that makes sense. Dan saw the tan hat. Touch and say tan.

FIGURE 21: Sample Comprehension Exercise—Fill in the Blank

story to things the student already knows, and also subjective questions.

Games and Motivational Devices

Rhymes were sequenced into a lesson as a listening activity to help the child develop competency in the discrimination of the rhyming and alliterative sounds of words and to demonstrate to the child the rhythmic use of language. The selection of rhymes for each lesson was based upon the sound patterns found in the matrix section of the lesson.

Games were sequenced into each lesson primarily to encourage continued attention to the lesson materials. The games were similar to those played in the classroom and utilized the terminology common to game-like situations such as baseball.

Review

Review was continuous throughout each lesson since the same words and patterns were used continually.

The review lessons varied as the vocabulary and skills of the student progressively developed. In the simplest level, the review lessons consisted primarily of straightforward matrix review; that is, the words which had been introduced in the preceding five to seven matrices were reordered and presented in new matrix formats. The later review lessons focused on the recently acquired vocabulary items, prepositions, and inflectional variations of the base word.

2.8.4   Production, Operation, and Analysis

There were ten members of the staff, including programmers, authors, artists, and voice artists. Most of the content work was done at Ventura Hall at Stanford or at the Brentwood facility. Programming was also done at IBM.

The content was coded in Coursewriter II. Each lesson required about 9000 commands for its execution. All pieces had to be assem-

```
┌─────────────────────┐
│ John hit the ball.  │
└─────────────────────┘
```

Touch and say the word that
answers the question.

RR 1   Who hit the ball?

CA: Yes, the word "John" tells
       us who hit the ball.
            ↓CA
WA: No, John tells us who hit the
       ball. Touch and say John.

RR 2   What did John hit?

CA: Yes, the word "ball" tell us
       what John hit.
            ↓CA
WA: No, ball tells us what John hit.
       Touch and say ball.

FIGURE 22: Sample Comprehension Exercise—Answer Questions about a
         Sentence

bled together, including program, text, artwork displayed on the film
screen, and audio messages, making a large job out of integration, testing, and debugging. Keeping track of the media assets was a huge chore,
one that would be done by a content-management database today but
had to be done by hand in 1966.

There were about 160 lessons written for the first year of the curriculum. Each lesson had about 125 "mainline" problems. The researchers
expected that the median number of lessons done by each student would
be about 120. This proved to be overly optimistic; the median proved
to be 16–19 lessons being done by each student.

Data analysis was done on the IBM 1800 on-location at Brentwood.
Data was dumped to tape during each day because there was not
enough disk space to store the item-level data. The task was very labor-
intensive.

The analysis was done by using the first-grade math students as the
"control" group because they were not using the computer for reading
instruction; the students who took Initial Reading were the "treatment"
group. The results showed that the differences in means and standard
deviations of the treatment group were statistically significant over a
range of measures, including both the tests administered and the sections of the course completed.

2.9   Brentwood Remembered

2.9.1   A Tour of Brentwood

Several color 16mm films exist about the Brentwood Project. These
films have been partially restored by Stanford University and are being

FIGURE 23: Brentwood Elementary School in East Palo Alto

included in an online archive. Recent screenings of the films, apparently the first time they have been seen in decades, elicited much surprise from the audiences because of the apparent sophistication of the instructional setting. The following shows a tour of the project using stills made from those films.

Figure 23 shows the film narrator in front of the school. The structure to the right is the 3,200-sq-ft building constructed for the project.

Figure 24 shows the lab with the teacher and students filing in. Note the cubicles separating the students.

Figure 25 shows a math exercise on the CRT screen. The exercise asks the student to select another name for the number 2, which is the cardinality of a set with two elements.

Figure 26 shows one of the many images the film screen could display. Figure 27 shows the exercise on both screens. The photo of Sam is on the left, and the exercise is on the right.

Figure 28 shows the student using the light pen to select the correct answer, the word "Sam."

Finally, Figure 29 has a photo of Patrick Suppes in the Brentwood computer lab, explaining about individualization using computer-assisted instruction.

2.9.2 A Reaction to the Reading Course

In 1967, Professor George D. Spache of the University of Florida published an article critical of the reading course ([106]). Spache based

FIGURE 24: Computer-based Laboratory at Brentwood

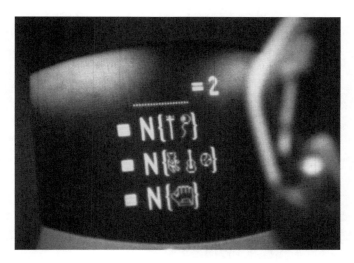

FIGURE 25: Math Exercise on the CRT

FIGURE 26: Cartoon Image of "Sam" on the Film Screen

FIGURE 27: Exercise with "Sam" on the Film Screen

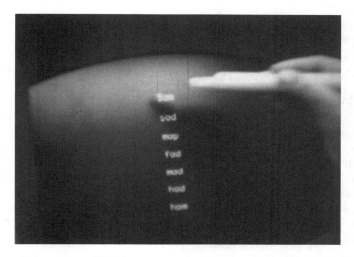

FIGURE 28: CRT Screen and Student Using the Lightpen

FIGURE 29: Patrick Suppes in the Brentwood Lab

his concerns on Atkinson and Hansen's paper describing the Reading Course ([7]).

A bulk of Spache's criticisms are focused on the dehumanizing aspects of Atkinson's presentation which he felt ignored the teacher. "It is rather disconcerting that Atkinson and Hansen never refer to a classroom teacher nor imply her presence in this complete program for teaching reading in the first grade" ([106] p. 101).

Atkinson published a response [5] in which he finds that the objections "can only be understood in the context of a fear of automation replacing live teachers, coupled with a rather low regards for the average teacher's ability to utilize information about her students" ([5] pp. 418–419).

We will not go through the list of Spache's objections and Atkinson's responses. But it seems relevant that the objections seem rooted in a fear of automation and dehumanization. Spache even invokes the image of "Rossum's Universal Robots" from Capek's play *R.U.R*; see Wikipedia [219]. Objections of this kind have been very common in the last fifty years to many applications of computers and perhaps especially those in education.

2.9.3 Articles in Popular Magazines

The Brentwood project and previous work at Grant School brought many articles into the popular press. *Life* magazine published a nine-page spread with photos in January 1967 about Brentwood.[20] The article describes the lab thus: "The children were seated at the terminals and the computer quickly took them in hand. 'Well, hello, Jimmy' the machine said into an astounded 6-year-old's earphones. 'I've been waiting for you.' Thus began the most eerie and perhaps the most promising dialogue ever carried on in a United States grade school." The article continues with a mostly effusive account of the effort. One thing no one can argue with is the following observation: "Whatever happens in the executive suite [of companies like IBM], is, in any case, of only minor concern to tough and independent learning specialists like Suppes and Atkinson, who are clearly in command of their research-and-development ship." See Figure 30 for a photo of the two captains in Suppes's Ventura Hall office at Stanford.

Other popular magazines to publish articles include: *Science* in the fall of 1968 (Atkinson and Hal Wilson in [8]) and *Psychology Today* in early 1968 (Atkinson in [4]).

---

[20]See [14] for a reference containing a URL to this interesting artifact.

FIGURE 30: Richard Atkinson and Patrick Suppes (*Life* photo by Ralph Crane, January 1, 1967, used by permission from Getty Image)

2.9.4 The End of Brentwood

Suppes recalled that IBM executives came to visit him in his office in Ventura Hall. Sitting "right in that very spot" he said, pointing to the chair still in his office almost fifty years later, they told him that IBM was not able to continue the project beyond academic year 1967–68.

The costs were simply too huge, they explained. The hardware was expensive to manufacture, maintenance was difficult, curriculum costs and media costs were higher than they had expected, and the operations cost was very high for the people to keep changing the disk packs and magnetic tapes.

Suppes said that they were still very enthusiastic about what he was doing and felt that it actually worked and had a future. The IBM folks encouraged him to try commercializing it—as he was actually already doing—but recommended that he keep an eye on costs and system reliability. These lessons were well-taken, as we shall see on page 73.

2.10 Russian Language Course

One of the commitments that Suppes made in the original Carnegie grant was to explore the role of the computer in teaching languages. In this regard, he had a great ally in Joseph Van Campen, Professor of Slavic Languages and Literatures. Van Campen threw himself into the project for many years and became one of the most effective proponents of computer-assisted instruction.[21]

A Russian-language course was programmed on the PDP-1, which still required that instruction in different courses be scheduled at different times of the day due to memory limitations on the number of course drivers that could run simultaneously.

This course was very important in the history of IMSSS because it was the first time that a for-credit college course had been taught using a computer, and likely the first time that a college course had been taught solely by a computer without any lectures or classroom activities. In the 1970s, Suppes went on to make a great effort at university-level instruction. See Chapter 4.

There are also many stories about this course that have been repeated over the years. Barbara Searle, who worked at IMSSS at the time, had a Russian-equipped Teletype installed in the closet of her son's room. He learned some Russian, and later majored in Russian in college. His PhD dissertation compared patterns of friendship of Russians and Americans. He is now a Professor of Psychology at Allegheny

---

[21] See [128] pp. 603–646 for a description of this course.

University, and credits the Stanford Russian course with getting him started.[22]

A group at Harvard University, in discussing MOOCs on their blog, noted the following:

> For several years, U.S. colleges and universities extensively and effectively provided credit and non-credit online courses. The first online for-credit course was offered by Stanford University for the 1966–67 school year. At that time Principal Investigator Patrick Suppes predicted 15% of colleges and university students would be taking online courses by 1980; this actually occurred in 2005. ([35])

See also Chapter 4 and Chapter 8.

2.10.1 Special Equipment

The terminals for the Russian course were Model 35 Teletype machines, a different model than the uppercase-only Model 33 that was otherwise used. The Model 35 normally had both upper- and lower-case Roman characters. There also existed a special version of the print head that had upper-case Roman along with the Cyrillic character set used for Russian, so both English and Russian could be printed. However, the keyboard of these Model 35s only had Russian characters, thus all responses by the student were input in Russian.[23] Six of these machines were installed in a room in Ventura Hall.

Audio was generated by special Ampex tape drives, one for each Teletype. These tape drives were connected to the relays in the Model 35 Teletype so that special character codes were sent to the teletype from the PDP-1, which triggered operations such as play, stop, and rewind on the audio tape drive.[24] This can be described as "semi-random access" since any sound on the tape could be played back at any time, but the amount of time that the "seek" took would vary and could be very large. This created some constraints on the curriculum design since the program had to select the next exercise for the student from a part of the tape that was near the present position in order to keep the seek times small. In addition, the correct tape had to be loaded for each student, which was the duty of a teaching assistant.

---

[22]Private communication.

[23]Suppes recalled that these Model 35 machines with Russian were classified by the U.S. Government and permission had to be obtained in order for Stanford to buy them. This has not been verified.

[24]Private communication from Sanders. See also [94] for Sanders's recollections of his work in multimedia over the years.

2.10.2 Student Selection and Activity

During 1966–67, students who enrolled in first-year Russian were asked on the first day of class if they wanted to volunteer for a computer-based course. There were 30 slots for this course, and more than 30 students volunteered.

The computer students came to Ventura Hall for scheduled 15-minute sessions between 1:15pm and 5:30pm, and also at 7:15pm. Students were scheduled for five sessions per week. Students could sign up for makeup sessions on weekend hours.

While there was no classroom or instructor, there were some human interactions with the students. There was always a proctor in the lab who changed tapes and handled logistical issues, but no Russian instruction. Written homework and language-lab drills were corrected by a research associate and returned to the students. Some recordings were made and evaluated in private interviews with the students.

2.10.3 Russian Curriculum and Presentation

During the beginning of the course, both English and Russian audio were used. The first lessons familiarized the student with the keyboard and the Russian alphabet. As the instruction progressed, only Russian audio was used. English text was used for vocabulary introduction and drills. Students were only asked to translate into Russian since the keyboard only contained Russian characters.

The order of presentation, vocabulary, and syntactic constructions closely followed the regular classroom course that Prof. Van Campen had taught for some time. The curriculum was coded in another special-purpose coding language that Van Campen invented, which was somewhat similar to the math coding language (and likely programmed by the same programmer). See [128] pp. 622–642 for details about this language and the program environment for the course, called Boris.

For much of the first quarter, all students received the same material, although the pace varied somewhat depending on how much time each student actually worked. By Lesson 27, blocks of content would be omitted for a student depending on how well the student had done. Toward the end of the first quarter, some repetitive drills were cut from the course altogether.

Van Campen created a series of coding programs that generated many exercises from macro-like instructions. He encoded the inflections of words and generated many drill items that were grammatically correct combinations from small lists (see [128] pp. 647–655).

2.10.4   Evaluation

This is a short summary of the evaluation of the course, taken from [128] pp. 611–622.

First, students in the computer course were more likely to finish the course than those in the regular classroom. In the fall, 30 started the computer version and 29 finished; in the regular class, 38 started and 28 finished. The computer class was capped at 30, although more wanted to take it. This could have been for many reasons, but it was encouraging.

Second, based on the error rates on the midterm and especially the final examinations, students in the computer sections performed better. Van Campen says about the fall quarter: "The computer-assisted group greatly excelled the regular group on the final. Thus, the average number of errors for the regular group was three times greater than that for the computer-assisted group" ([128] p. 611).

In the spring quarter, about 80% of the final exam content was completely identical for both groups. The computer students' "performance on the final which covered the entire year's material was significantly superior to that of the regular students" ([128] p. 611).

Van Campen was interested in the difference between the midterm results and the final results, since the computer and classroom students were generally close together by midterm but the computer students were far ahead by the final exam. Van Campen's explanation was that the computer "constitutes a much better apparatus for the review of a large amount of previously learned material" than the classroom process provides ([128] p. 619).

In a 2014 symposium named after William K. Estes, Richard C. Atkinson told a story about Estes taking Van Campen's CAI Russian course in 1966. Thereafter, Estes attended an academic conference in Russia and was able to present his paper, and attributed his success to the CAI Russian course. See [96] for details.

2.10.5   Further Work

Van Campen continued this work into the 1970s in other forms; see page 133. Part of the work was his development of coding programs to generate exercises from grammatical and lexical constraints. In the 1980s, Van Campen worked for Computer Curriculum Corporation on the development of content for the ESL course.

2.10.6   Eye-witness Observations

Richard Schupbach, a professor emeritus of Slavic Languages and Literature at Stanford, worked with Joe Van Campen and created a course himself during the 1970s; see page 134. He remembers that the Russian course ran on the PDP-1 for several years but was then discontinued. He recalls that the students to whom he taught third-year Russian when he arrived had taken the computerized course, and he felt that these students were very good. He had some observations about the demise of the course.

The biggest problem, he thought, was the lack of "transportability." The course ran on a highly-modified PDP-1 (then obsolete) and required special keyboards and audio devices. He remembers that Van Campen spent some years in the early 1980s trying to put the course up on IBM PCs, with some success but never enough to mount a complete course. This problem is arguably "solved" today, he allows. From the perspective of the content itself, he felt that the inability to make small changes (e.g., add another verb to the list taught) made it very rigid. This of course would also be solved today by using tables and more generalized software.

Schupbach reconciled the documented success of the course with the fact that Stanford does not use such a course today. He felt that a problem that CAI must encounter is what he calls "Hans The Doxy Effect." Hans was his family's dachshund, and it only would do certain things if there were a human around when it did them. Analogously, Schupbach believes that students benefit from having human interaction.

Suppes did not comment on this, but would likely have considered this to be overly romantic, and that the benefits of computer courses more than justify their use. He would have pointed out that students do many things with their computers and cell phones, why not take lessons? However, in later years, Suppes became much more interested in human motivation, and would probably agree that there is still something to understand here.

2.11 Dial-A-Drill—The First Implementation

The other new program running on the PDP-1 in 1968 was Dial-A-Drill with 15 students in grades 2 through 6. This used new Touch-Tone dialing capabilities for a brand-new form of course. In discussing how this fit with IMSSS's current research goals in his 1968 progress report, Suppes explained, "The Dial-a-drill Program is testing branching criteria and the relative difficulty of fraction problems." It also fit with his long-time interests in serving students at home, experimenting with audio, and finding cost-effective ways of using current technology. Suppes continued:

> ... we telephone students in their homes and give them oral exercises in
> elementary mathematics by means of computer-generated speech. The

students respond by using a touch-tone dialing pad. These devices are now standard equipment on telephones in many parts of the United States and will soon be universal. We have been particularly interested in two features of the Dial-A-Drill program. First, we have been concerned to find a more flexible and more easily programmed approach to audio messages than is provided by standard tape or disk, with the full message stored in analog form. For many kinds of reasons it is desirable to store, at the most, the single vocabulary-items that will be used, and then to synthesize in program the individual sentences for delivery as audio messages. Along with many other people, we are experimenting with synthesizing words, but at the present time our operational efforts do begin with the recording of words with 6-bit sampling at 6-kilocycle frequency. In the case of the Dial-A-Drill arithmetic program we are able to synthesize literally thousands of messages from a vocabulary of not more than 100 words. The words that are recorded are the number names *zero, one, two, three . . . , ten, twenty . . . , hundred*, the standard names for the operations, a few verbs like *equals* and a few interrogatives and related words. The intelligibility of the speech we are producing is high. We are not yet satisfied with its total quality, but it is functioning in a serviceable and practical way. At the same time, we are gaining our first operational experience in bringing computer-based curriculum into the homes of students, rather than into the schools. ([119])

2.12   Summary of Usage 1967–68

Table 1 shows the student usage in the school year 1967–68. This includes Grant School, Brentwood, and the university-level Russian course, as reported in [147]. Nearly 300,000 arithmetic lessons were completed during the year.

2.13   The PDP-10 and Networking Era

By 1966, John McCarthy was Director of the Stanford Artificial Intelligence Laboratory, sometimes known as SAIL. Digital Equipment Corporation had shipped its new PDP-6 computer and McCarthy purchased one in 1966; the PDP-6 was in fact a prototype for the PDP-10, and in 1968, McCarthy purchased a PDP-10. Suppes had purchased a PDP-10 for the IMSSS laboratory in June of the same year.

The PDP-10, which had new models for the next 20 years, was a legendary computer in the world of computer science, and the *sine qua non* of artificial intelligence research and interactive computing in that era. The importance of the machine influenced the CAI research done at IMSSS throughout the 1970s.

Table 1: Stanford 1967–68 Programs in Computer Assisted Instruction
(The number of students shown is for May 15, 1968)

Program	# of Students		Terminals
	Jan.	May	
Drill-and-practice Mathematics, Grades 1–8			
California	985	1,441	TTY*
Kentucky	810	1,632	TTY
Mississippi	592	640	TTY
Tutorial Mathematics, Grade 2	76	76	CRT†+Audio+Film
Tutorial Reading, Grade 1	73	73	CRT+Audio+Film
Tutorial Logic and Algebra, Grades 5–8	195	195	TTY
Tutorial Russian, University level	30	30	TTY+Audio (Cyrillic Keyboard)
Dial-a-Drill	15	15	Telephone

*Teletype
†Cathode-ray tube

Various models of the hardware were the KA-10, KI-10, KS-10 and KL-10. Operating systems were known as Tops10, TENEX and its variant TOPS20. The Stanford AI Lab and the MIT AI Lab had their own versions of the TOPS10 operating system.[25]

2.13.1 The Influence of the PDP-10 Systems and the ARPANET

The various groups working with PDP-10s developed many software tools in the conduct of their funded missions. There was much sharing of people, programs, and ideas. SUMEX-AIM (see below) was even funded specifically for the purpose of encouraging collaboration in the area of AI in Medicine.

By 1974, the following PDP-10 systems were in place in the Stanford area:

- Stanford AI Lab: PDP-6 in 1966, PDP-10 in 1968. Work on general AI, vision, robotics, reasoning, natural-language and machine translation, music, and automated computer design.
- IMSSS: PDP-10 in 1968. Computer-assisted instruction in math, reading, logic, foreign languages, and a host of other curriculum areas.

---

[25]The authors will generically refer to them as "PDP-10s" throughout this book.

- Stanford Research Institute (SRI): Planning, reasoning, general artificial intelligence.[26]

- SRI Augmentation Research Center: Founded by Douglas Engelbart, this center focused on tools for human collaboration and information sharing. Achievements include the NLS system, an early system for browsing and exploring text, as well as the invention of the mouse. The first mouse ran on a PDP10. Famous for "the mother of all demos" in which Engelbart showed his ideas about man-machine interaction. See Wikipedia "Augmentation Research Center" [173].

- SUMEX-AIM had a KI-10 in 1974, expanded to a dual-processor system: AI in medicine, chemistry, and science. Collaboration among researchers using networking. The principals were Joshua Lederberg, Edward Feigenbaum, Edward Shortliffe, and Thomas Rindfleisch. See [36].

- Xerox Palo Alto Research Center: While not a part of Stanford, this famous group had many successes, including printing, Ethernet, graphical computing, and ideas about using computers in education that were distinctly different from Suppes and his group. Xerox had two PDP-10 clones connected to the ARPANET. Xerox Corporation apparently would not purchase a PDP-10 from Digital Equipment Corporation, but allowed the group to build their own PDP-10 clones, called MAXC.

Beginning in 1969, these systems were also connected with the ARPANET, the predecessor of the Internet; see [171]. Within a few years, computers at UCLA, Stanford, MIT, Carnegie-Mellon, and network center Bolt Beranek and Newman in Cambridge were all connected, and a nationwide "hacker" community formed.[27] A majority of the machines on the ARPANET were PDP-10 systems at this point. All research everywhere on this network changed as a result of the collaborative environment.

For the next few years, Suppes continued the research plan that he had already mapped out, but the availability of software tools, often being developed by multiple people at different sites, made some big changes. The most important example was the large Deaf Project that began in 1970 (see Section 2.16). This project connected schools for deaf and hearing-impaired students all over the country to IMSSS, a project clearly similar to the ARPANET. In addition, the research IMSSS did

---

[26]SRI became independent of Stanford University in 1970 but the ties remained strong.

[27]At this point, a "hacker" was someone who created things, not someone who was malicious.

in the 1970s on university-level CAI was greatly influenced by the AI research at the other groups, and much of the effort could be described as AI in education. However, Suppes was always reluctant to promise too much or to say that his work was AI. See for example [131].

Figure 31 shows the architecture of the system at IMSSS on the eve of the introduction of the ARPANET. It shows the new PDP-10 system, its main memory and disks, as well as the older PDP-1 system.

Note the schools on the right side. These schools were connected through leased telephone lines to their distant destinations. They used *terminal concentrators*, a technology that used small computers (mostly DEC PDP-8s) to mix characters intended for different terminals into the same data stream for a smaller number of telephone lines. The development of this technology at IMSSS is discussed on page 63.

2.14 General-Purpose Tools and Techniques Developed at IMSSS

Groups like the Stanford AI Lab and BBN had much more resources and a mandate to develop new tools, and IMSSS benefited from many of these. However, IMSSS also developed its own innovations.[28]

2.14.1 The THOR Operating System

The operating system for the PDP-1, as modified at IMSSS, was called THOR in its first version. Later this switched from Norse mythology to Greek with the name Zeus. Its main claim to fame was the incorporation of CRT displays (the Philco terminals initially). The displays could show audio speech patterns, an interactive debugger called RAID, and most importantly, the TVEDIT text editor. The entire system is documented in [75].

2.14.2 TVEDIT—The First Display Editor Came from IMSSS!

TVEDIT was the first text editing program that operated by providing a visual image of the file and allowing the editing to be done in what became known as a "WYSIWYG" manner. Up until then, input was done on punch cards or, for interactive systems, using editors that ran on teletype (or other "hardcopy") terminals and edited a line or a few

---

[28]Barbara Searle commented on this book that "I think it's wonderful [to have] this record of what went on at IMSSS. It was truly an amazing place!" in describing how strongly people felt about working at Ventura and with each other. The folks from the recent 50 year reunion were given a tour of the building and shared many memories. A common remark at that reunion was that working at IMSSS and/or CCC was the best job they ever had.

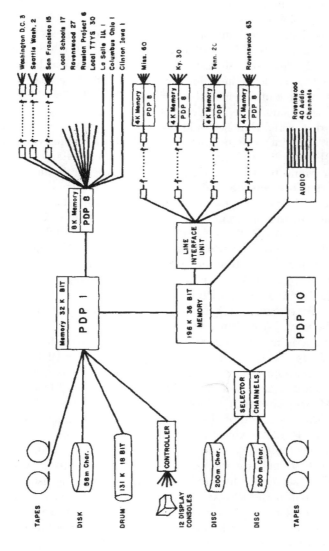

FIGURE 31: PDP-10/PDP-1 Configuration at IMSSS, ca. 1969

characters at a time, but without displaying the context of the editing session. TVEDIT inspired much of the new thinking about how people could actually interact with a computer. TVEDIT benefited from being used and seen by many people over a number of years.

The first version of TVEDIT was written by Brian Tolliver on the PDP-1 using the Philco terminals (see page 14). The Philcos used CRT tubes and displayed text from PDP-1 memory so characters and lines could be easily deleted and inserted. The Philco keyboards had two special keys that could be held down while other keys were typed. One was on the left side of the space bar, called "left-bucky," and the other was on the right side, called "right-bucky."

Tolliver discovered that he could place text on the screen, and then have a cursor point to a position in the text. "Left-bucky I" would put TVEDIT into "insert" mode, and the subsequent characters typed by the user would be inserted. Command sequences were devised that would insert and delete lines of text, scroll up and down ("left-bucky W" moved to the next chunk of text), and perform other operations. Anyone who saw this program wanted one for their house. According to Pentti Kanerva, TVEDIT had been suggested by Prof. Niklaus Wirth of Stanford's computer science department. Wirth also suggested the "bucky" keys for the custom-made Philco keyboards. See Wikipedia "Bucky bit" [176]. Such keys are now common on computer keyboards with names like ALT and APPLE.

The second version of TVEDIT came about because the Philcos could not be moved from Pine, where they were connected to the PDP-1, and more terminals were desperately needed at the other buildings such as Ventura. Also, an editor was needed for the new PDP-10. Kanerva recalls that Operations Manager John Ball responded to this demand by finding a minicomputer called the IMLAC and buying a set. The IMLAC was built into a desk, had a CRT monitor, and the CPU resided on the underside of the desk. It could communicate with the PDP-10 using RS-232 connections.

John Prebus built the second generation of TVEDIT using the IMLACs as workstations. He adopted a novel design that today would be called a "client-server" architecture. The entire editor and user interaction was built into the IMLAC. The program on the PDP-10 simply sent chunks of the file to the IMLAC and then received the chunks back and stored them on the disk. This minimized the computational load on the PDP-10, and also meant that user interaction was very fast and predictable since the user commands were processed directly by the IMLAC. Unfortunately, it occasionally would crash, so users learned to save their work frequently.

The third version of TVEDIT was arguably the best design given the direction the technology was headed. Pentti Kanerva had followed the evolution of text editing for several years. He was looking for inexpensive terminals that people could have both in their offices and at home. The first TVEDIT only used the expensive and bulky Philco terminals that had to be a few feet from their host PDP-1. The IMLACs were still bulky and too expensive for an individual user to have their own; instead, they were all setup together for sharing in a "terminal room." Kanerva saw that productivity would improve if terminals were small, inexpensive, and could be connected to their host computer via phone lines.

Suppes also wanted the IMSSS staff to be able to work at home on their projects, and wanted to get rid of the queues of people that sometimes developed around the existing terminals. Kanerva's wife, Diane, was one of Suppes's editors, and he wanted to speed up the editorial process for his papers and eliminate the IBM typewriters from his own publication process.

In about 1971, Kanerva started following the market for point-of-entry terminals used for various business applications, and tracking their features and prices. He defined a minimum set of features that would be required in the terminal's command language, including the ability to display characters sent from the host computer, clear the entire screen, and insert and delete characters and lines. The internal speeds of these operations also needed to be fast enough to support editing without "lagging."

By 1973, he started to find available terminals in the $2,000–$3,000 range and built the new TVEDIT to these specs. This TVEDIT did all of the editing in the programming on the PDP-10, with the terminal doing as little as possible in order to maximize the variety of terminals he could support and minimize their price. TVEDIT would recognize the type of terminal when it came up, and would interact with that terminal according to its own command language, which was still unique to each manufacturer in 1973. Kanerva used tables and code to specify the properties of the different terminals.[29] Eventually, this TVEDIT was very broadly distributed across the ARPANET for different PDP-10 operating systems.

2.14.3 Terminal Concentrators

The cost and inconvenience of using leased telephone lines was an impediment to CAI delivery from the outset. Computers like the IBM

---

[29]This anticipated Bill Joy's *termcap* of a few years later; see Wikipedia [228] for details about termcap.

1800 and the Digital PDP-10 were too large, operationally complex, and expensive to be located in many places. So, the delivery of CAI lessons to schools required phone lines in some form. However, analysis of the actual usage of the lines showed that bandwidth was going to waste. The idea was developed to *multiplex* the character streams from several terminals together.

Pentti Kanerva started working at IMSSS in the fall of 1967. His first assignment was to program the PDP-8 minicomputers to be used as terminal concentrators. He believes that prior to that, all terminals in schools were on individual leased telephone lines. The basic algorithm was to have a lead-in character identifying a series of characters for a given terminal. This tends to work for many of the terminals sharing the same phone line, because many terminals will not be doing active input/output while those students read the material and respond to the prompts. Efforts were made to optimize the algorithm by statistical analysis of actual student data.

By 1969, most of the schools connected to the computers at Stanford used PDP-8 concentrators. Figure 31 shows the PDP-8s along with another terminal concentrator. A similar technology was used at CCC with newer hardware into the 1990s, and was common throughout the industry. IMSSS's contribution was making it inexpensive enough to be used in CAI.

IMSSS pioneered the use of satellites to deliver instruction with some experiments. The hope was that satellite delivery could reduce the cost and improve distribution, especially in foreign countries; see page 68.

2.14.4 Other Areas

Teaching Computer Programming

The PDP-10 allowed building courseware that was simply not possible with the PDP-1. One early example was teaching computer programming using simplified versions of Logo, Basic, and a simple machine-language called SIMPER. This is described in [66]. More work was done in the 1970s; see page 138.

Systems Programming Development

IMSSS also pioneered many improvements to the various PDP-10 operating systems, especially for terminal interaction, latency timing, debuggers, and the port of the popular SAIL artificial intelligence programming language to run on the TENEX and TOPS20 operating systems; see [103]. Many of these innovations were widely distributed along with TVEDIT.

2.15   The Math Strands Course

In 1968, Suppes developed a new elementary mathematics course to replace the "blocks" program that had been used at the Grant School; see
page 18. The new design incorporated a *strand* structure. Each strand
dealt with a part of the scope of the curriculum, for example the skill
of vertical addition. Exercises were organized into *classes* with all of
the exercises in a class assumed to be equivalent. As the sequence progressed, the classes were of greater difficulty but still easily recognized
as belonging to the strand.

The adaptive algorithm had two key components: when to stop doing
one strand and switch to another, and when to consider that a given
class had been "mastered" and hence the program would move to the
next class.

Table 2 displays the original selection of strands for the math course,
as described in [141] pp. 7–11. The strands themselves, and to a great
degree the specific content, were developed by examining a number of
curriculum materials. Data from the previous projects at IMSSS were
also used, and the authors allow that there was some "normative" input
as well, where exercises were added or dropped based on the beliefs of
the authors. Note that not all strands range over the entire sequence
of the curriculum. Also see a handbook published in 1971 for use by
teachers [144], which contains a description of the math strands course
beginning on page 2.

A further consideration was the proportion of the student's time and
the proportion of the exercises to be devoted to each strand. This potentially changed at each half-year point. Table 3 displays these values.

In this version of the course, strand changes tended to be made in
order to balance out the strands in terms of time, as explained above.
The other important consideration was the determination of mastery.
Most of the approaches Suppes used for determining mastery did not
simply look at "percentage correct" but rather looked at the most recent
results within a class. This accounted for learning.

The strands approach was used extensively at CCC and later at
EPGY at Stanford; see page 216 for details of the last CCC version Suppes developed and page 252 for the K7 course at EPGY. The strands
approach was the most successful when the subject lent itself to an
orderly scope and sequence. Elementary mathematics was very well
suited, elementary reading and some parts of language arts were somewhat suited. Many other courses adopted a lessons approach but still
had adaptive elements in the sequence of material.

TABLE 2: Grade Level Spanned by Each Strand in the Elementary Mathematics Program

Strand	Content	Grade level
NUM	Number concepts	1.0–7.9
HAD	Horizontal addition	1.0–3.9
HSU	Horizontal subtraction	1.0–3.4
VAD	Vertical addition	1.0–5.9
VSU	Vertical subtraction	1.5–5.9
EQN	Equations	1.5–7.9
MEA	Measurements	1.5–7.9
HMU	Horizontal multiplication	2.5–5.4
LAW	Laws of arithmetic	3.0–7.9
VMU	Vertical multiplication	3.5–7.9
DIV	Division	3.5–7.9
FRA	Fractions	3.5–7.9
DEC	Decimals	4.0–7.9
NEG	Negative numbers	6.0–7.9

Later changes also included: new content to conform to new standards; additional strands; tutorial and gaming elements. Suppes saw the strands structure as a flexible design that could have many elements added in the future.

The math strands course was implemented on the PDP-10 and was used in the "deaf project" described below.

2.16   The Deaf Project

The "deaf project" at IMSSS provided CAI for hearing-impaired students. It was funded by the Office of Education for three years between July 1, 1970 and June 30, 1973, although preparations had been underway before with the PDP-10 deployment and developing a new math course as described on page 65.[30]

The use of computers accessed through Teletype terminals was an obvious way to teach hearing-impaired students. For some years, this population already had Teletype terminals in their homes using the machines instead of voice telephones with friends and family members (see [80]).

---

[30]The authors apologize for the term "deaf project" but that was the term used at the time.

TABLE 3: Proportion of Time and Proportion of Problems for Each Strand for Each Half Year

Strand		Half year													
		1.0	1.5	2.0	2.5	3.0	3.5	4.0	4.5	5.0	5.5	6.0	6.5	7.0	7.5
NUM	PT	50	24	24	17	10	5	7	7	8	11	14	10	15	15
	PP	36	18	16	12	10	4	8	8	10	14	20	10	19	19
HAD	PT	26	21	21	9	14	9								
	PP	32	28	26	10	14	8								
HSU	PT	14	10	16	9	4									
	PP	18	14	16	10	4									
VAD	PT	10	10	9	19	19	7	8	2	3	1				
	PP	14	12	12	22	20	6	10	2	4	2				
VSU	PT		9	8	15	22	10	13	3	3	1				
	PP		12	12	18	20	8	10	2	4	2				
EQN	PT		17	12	16	17	14	17	7	5	7	7	8	15	15
	PP		10	10	12	16	12	20	8	8	12	12	10	19	19
MEA	PT		9	10	8	8	11	7	7	5	5	5	5	5	5
	PP		6	8	6	6	6	8	8	8	8	8	6	6	6
HMU	PT				7	3	8	5	3	2					
	PP				10	6	14	10	6	8					
LAW	PT				3	5	5	3	3	3	1	1	8	8	
	PP				4	6	6	4	6	6	2	2	10	10	
VMU	PT					10	5	14	6	8	7	5	8	8	
	PP					14	6	16	8	4	4	2	4	4	
DIV	PT					15	22	34	48	33	40	13	14	14	
	PP					18	10	16	16	6	8	2	3	3	
FRA	PT					6	4	15	13	20	17	18	10	10	
	PP					4	4	24	22	32	32	26	10	10	
DEC	PT						7	5	4	11	7	36	10	10	
	PP						8	6	6	14	10	38	10	10	
NEG	PT											2	4	15	15
	PP											4	4	19	19

2.16.1 Students and Schools

During the early 1970s, there were many residential deaf schools where students were concentrated. This simplified the logistical and technical issues involved for the deaf project. More recently, there has been a movement to mainstream hearing-impaired students rather than have them in special schools, often away from their families.[31]

The Deaf Project had 15 residential deaf schools and up to 4,000 students involved at some point during the three years. Figure 32 shows the locations of the nodes of what was called the "deaf network." High-speed (at the time 4800 or 9600 baud) lines were connected to the schools from Stanford. Some of the nodes were connected through others in order to save money overall. There were about 180 terminals connected to the PDP-10 (a large number for that class of computer), and 90 could be used at any time for any subset of the available courses.

Particular note should be made of the connection to Isletta Pueblo, NM. This connection was made via satellite in conjunction with the Goddard Space Center.[32] This appears to be the first use of satellite communications for instruction in a school.

In 1971, Suppes and Dean Jamison made a proposal to the NSF for testing satellite delivery as a cost-effective solution for rural schools and students. The proposal also suggested using NASA satellites for demonstration purposes ([146]).

2.16.2 Courses and Programs for the Deaf Project

The math strands course that began in 1968 was the most important course. Obviously, courses such as Russian and reading were not used because of the audio requirements. A number of new courses were built to support the project, including Language Arts, Basic English, and two programming courses, BASIC and AID.[33] Table 4 shows the list of available courses for the deaf project. Work on the implementation of the AID course was supported by a NASA grant from 1968–71.[34]

Project director Jamesine Friend designed a somewhat general-purpose programming language, called INST, for developing the courses for the deaf project; see [42]. INST was used for the language-arts courses, the most important courses developed for this project and designed to help hearing-impaired students with their skills in written English. The programming courses were designed to give students something in-

---

[31]There is a large literature about this, see [82] for example.

[32]Private correspondence from John Ball to Goddard.

[33]AID was a simple programming language unique to the PDP-10, similar to BASIC but somewhat more structured.

[34]Unpublished grant documents [120].

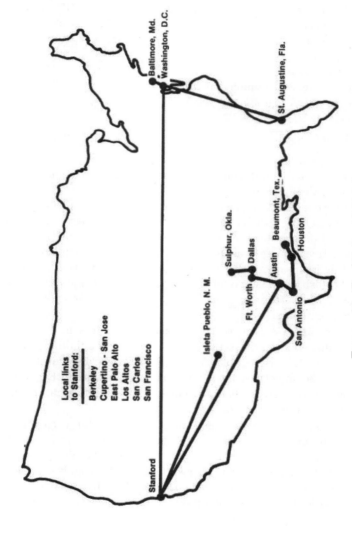

Local links
to Stanford:

Berkeley
Cupertino - San Jose
East Palo Alto
Los Altos
San Carlos
San Francisco

Stanford

Isleta Pueblo, N. M.

Sulphur, Okla.

Ft. Worth

Dallas

Austin

Beaumont, Tex.

Houston

San Antonio

Baltimore, Md.
Washington, D.C.

St. Augustine, Fla.

FIGURE 32: "Deaf Network" Topology

TABLE 4: Deaf Project Courses

Curriculum	Number of Students	
	1971–72	1972–73
Elementary Mathematics (Strands)	2146	1793
Arithmetic Word Problem Solving	107	520
Language Arts	1071	1058
Algebra	83	—
Basic English	165	64
Computer Programming in AID	93	34
Computer Programming in BASIC	124	—
Logic	216	77
Total Students	2279	2113

teresting to do that would combine understanding written instructions with mathematically-related exercises.[35]

Suppes noted, "The language arts course was designed to stress the structure of English, with particular emphasis on the roles of syntax and inflection and on the meaning of function words. An inductive rather than a deductive strategy was used. The course does not explicitly state 'rules' of English usage; rather it presents items illustrating aspects of standard English usage singly and in combination. Incidental learning of basic sentence patterns is enhanced by presenting curriculum items in complete sentences."

There were 218 lessons with 20–30 exercises per lesson. The course was built using a cumulative structure with concepts building on previous lessons; see [40] for example. A criterion test was also developed to measure only the objectives of the Language Arts course. Other courses such as logic were used in their current form with only small changes for wording to simplify the vocabulary.

One non-course program turned out to be a big hit with the students. Staff programmer Mike Raugh wrote a "TALK" program that students could use to communicate with their friends (old or new) on the Stanford Deaf Network. The program would be recognized today as a multi-person "chat" program. Students would gladly do their lessons to be able to use it. Many of them made friends at the other residential deaf schools.

---

[35]The AID course had an interface between the lessons and the AID interpreter that allowed partial programs to be passed in. This may be the first time such an interface was used.

2.16.3 Evaluation of the Deaf Project

With the largest number of CAI students that Suppes had ever had, his team tried a number of analyses on the data, including analysis models they had not previously attempted. For the Math Strands course, they created a modified version of the Stanford Achievement Test (MSAT) that was suitable for on-line use. Students were allowed to take only a specified number of sessions. The test measured grade placement (GP), allowing students' scores on the MSAT to be compared to published scores for hearing-impaired students.

Suppes summarizes this experiment: "if a student from this population takes about one mathematics strands session per day for at least two-thirds of a school year, a GP improvement of 1.0 to 1.5 years can be expected, depending on how it is measured. This improvement can be compared with an expected GP increase over a school year of 0.3 to 0.4 in the SAT computation subtest for hearing-impaired students receiving ordinary instruction."

Language Arts was also evaluated, with results that were less clear. Fletcher and Beard "concluded that the course is of significant value to students whose ratio of lessons completed to sessions taken is high but of much less value to students whose ratio of lessons completed to sessions taken is low." Other results were more complex.

Suppes, with frequent collaborators Mario Zanotti[36] and Dexter Fletcher,[37] also came up with an evaluation approach that was to become an important approach for the rest of his career in computers in education. Suppes had long been interested in individualization and how students learn differently. He was also somewhat frustrated by the typical pretest/posttest cycle and its attendant slowness. "A performance goal, defined in terms of GP, for progress over a predetermined time period was set for each of 297 subjects chosen from the entire population of students who were enrolled in three participating residential schools for the deaf in California, Texas, and Florida. Each subject was then assigned to one, two, or three daily CAI sessions for each of six two week periods depending on his progress toward his goal." The experimenters were able to show with great precision that one could predict the change in GP as a function of the amount of time spent for each student individually.

This work would later be productized as Individualized Prescriptive Strategy (IPS) at CCC; see page 175.

---

[36] Zanotti was a statistician at Stanford and later became Vice President of Research at Computer Curriculum Corporation

[37] Fletcher had become project director for the Deaf Project and later had a long career working on computers applied to training in various government positions.

2.16.4   Outcomes of the Deaf Project

The following are some of the key results of the project.

- The project confirmed the value of CAI in deaf education. As Suppes and Fletcher noted, "The proof of this project is in its impact on deaf education. Specifically, the willingness of the participating schools to support CAI from their own funding sources is the ultimate test of the project's impact. Thirteen of the fifteen schools that participated in this project committed funds to continuing their CAI activity in 1973–74."

- The project also demonstrated that a large number of students in disparate places could use CAI systematically and could communicate together with notable results.

- The deaf project was the first use of Suppes and Zanotti's ideas about predicting individual student growth.

- The cost-effectiveness of CAI was beginning to be seen as a future possibility. During the mid-1960s, the cost of an hour of CAI was estimated to be about $40 per hour. By 1973, IMSSS was delivering instruction for about $2.50 per hour.

- Graduate student Steve Weyer wrote an interactive graphics program that could spell out words with images of a hand using "finger spelling" to spell out the words. This was probably the first time this was done. Experiments were done with it to determine which characters seemed to confuse users the most. Weyer's work is reported in [164].

- An unexpected result was to prove the efficacy of computer networking for interactive users. The Stanford Deaf Network had about 15 nodes and over 4,000 users during its existence. The estimate is that this is more nodes and more users than the ARPANET had for about a year. While the architecture of the ARPANET was more scalable and robust, the Deaf Network had some features that would be seen in the ARPANET, including multiplexing of many users' data into a single telecommunications link and providing means of communication between users at different sites.

It was time to move on to commercialization of the basic ideas.

3

Commercialization at CCC:
1967–1981

3.1 Founding

Computer Curriculum Corporation. A very straightforward, even dull, name that describes what the company did for a late-1960s audience, unlike the names of Internet companies started in the twenty-first century.

Computer Curriculum Corporation (hereafter CCC) was founded on August 23, 1967. The founders were Patrick Suppes, Richard Atkinson, and Hal Wilson, each of whom invested $2,000 in the enterprise. This was just a bit more than four years after the founding of the computer-assisted instruction lab at Stanford on January 1, 1963, which was virtually the first effort to use computers in instruction. Typically, university research projects take (much) longer to achieve commercialization. Why the rush?

Suppes explains: "We wanted to take what we knew how to teach with computers and get it into commercial practice in order to get some real experience with it. We were using these techniques with hundreds of students in expensive equipment with a lot of support. We wanted to see what happened when we tried to make it into a cost-effective solution. We wanted the *data* we would get from tens of thousands of students using it for real instruction for a number of years." He added that the effort at Stanford would continue but would branch off into more advanced applications, leaving mainstream basic skills to CCC.

3.2 Lessons Learned 1963–1967

Suppes was now firmly convinced that the basic concept of using computers in education was sound. Especially for drill and practice, he felt that the program of research and development he had laid out would work and it was just a matter of execution. There were, however, any number of pragmatic and economic problems that had been uncovered at the Grant School and Brentwood projects, including the following:

- *Reliability:* People had tolerated the unreliability at the Grant School because of the sense of innovation and excitement. This cheerful acceptance of problems would obviously not last. The hardware and software would simply have to work.

- *Expense of the Computer System:* Computers were very expensive. One hope had been to share centralized facilities to spread costs, but this had communication problems. Another approach would be to build special-purpose equipment which would perform well for finely-tuned software applications. Suppes had seen that he could accommodate far more student users on the PDP-1 system than the manufacturer had ever intended, and knew that specialized programming techniques would increase the number of students supported on a given piece of hardware.

- *Expense of Display Terminals:* The CRT terminals, especially those at Brentwood, were very nice, but they were simply too expensive. For the next few years, he would use the Teletype terminals. A Model 33 cost about $700.

- *Expense of Leased Phone Lines:* The cost of leased telephone lines was virtually prohibitive. Centralized facilities certainly offered good features, including the ease of changing the software and ready access to student data for research, but for the present, the computer systems would have to be local in most cases.

- *Turnkey Systems:* Computer systems would have to be like appliances in order to function in schools. CCC would have to build and maintain the systems for installability, maintainability, and everyday use.

- *Labs Supporting a Whole Class:* Laboratories with enough stations for an entire class were needed. The Grant School and Brentwood laboratories didn't have enough student stations to hold an entire class, and this created logistical problems. Teachers wanted to take all of their students at the same time.

- *Courseware Should Be Individualized:* In the "blocks" math program at Grant School, all students were typically taking the same content (with individual variations). This sounded like a good idea because it would allow teachers control. In practice, however, the teachers didn't want to have to keep adjusting the settings for their students, and better individualization algorithms were possible with the strands approach he was then working on.

These things were much on Suppes's mind as he and his partners founded the company.

3.3 Curriculum and Systems Projects

CCC was shorter on usable computer platforms than educational ideas. If someone had a computer that they wanted to use for education with real students, CCC was likely interested in doing the work.

Hal Wilson supervised 11 Stanford University students in coding the curriculum using a simple curriculum coding language that he devised at an office at 800 Welch Road, Palo Alto. The computer was housed in Palo Alto, with phone lines to schools in Brentwood, CA.

At this point, CCC decided that they wanted to retain the naming rights and copyrights to any course that they created under contract. CCC signed a contract with IBM to create a seventh-grade language arts course which IBM allowed to remain with CCC.

CCC was basically inventing methods of processing and encoding content as it went along. Dave Munson remembers this effort: "In 1968, CCC hired me as a Systems Analyst to work on the conversion of curriculum for the IBM system. I was going to supervise 50 programmers, but we were able to develop a program that did this without much additional help. It was a time when people really had little idea how to do things or how much they would really cost."

3.3.1 The Univac in Chicago

Sometimes these were one-off projects, others involved major hardware manufacturers. For example, CCC implemented the math strands curriculum on a UNIVAC 418-III computer in Chicago, as reported by a district teacher in [64]. Suppes recalls that Chicago had purchased an expensive computer system for education but had no clear plan for its use. CCC was able to port their courseware for use on the system. Suppes always felt that Chicago was a large part of CCC's success.

The Chicago implementation was reported as a success, however, with the claim that CAI students showed more gains on the standardized test than non-CAI students.

3.3.2 RCA Instructional Systems

A potentially larger project was with RCA Instructional Systems. RCA had entered the computer industry in 1965 with the Spectra 70, a machine largely compatible with the IBM 360 non-privileged instruction set. One aspect of their business plan was computers for education, including both instructional and data-processing needs. See [92] and Wikipedia "RCA Spectra 70" [216].

RCA contracted with CCC and Patrick Suppes in 1967 for both a math course and a language arts course. The math curriculum was a version of the "blocks" program used at the Grant School, and was published by L. W. Singer. The language arts courses were developed by Computer Curriculum Corporation and were published by Harcourt, Brace, and World. See [19].

RCA Instructional Systems opened a storefront on University Avenue in Palo Alto with a complete Spectra 70 system including tape drives and blinking lights. They had over 130 employees working there on various aspects of the system. In addition to courses, a variety of administrative tools were envisioned, including class scheduling, attendance, and financial accounting. The Spectra 70 was built to support 196 terminals using telecommunications. The terminals appeared to be Model 33 Teletypes with a custom case. RCA set up two, one in New York and one in Palo Alto. A smaller system, the Spectra 71, was intended for 32 terminals only.

The business did not go very well. RCA sold their entire computer business to Sperry-Rand. This also included a large group of high-quality researchers at RCA's Sarnoff Labs in Princeton, N.J.[1]

Suppes felt that he had learned a lot from IBM and that they had built a forward-looking system with the IBM 1500. He did not see much innovation in the educational efforts of RCA.

3.4 Dial-A-Drill™ in New York City 1969

Dial-A-Drill was a system that used Touch-Tone telephones to deliver instruction to children at home from a computer connected to the telephone system.[2]

Western Electric had introduced their Touch-Tone system in 1963 as a faster and more efficient way of making connections, but also with the idea that computerized systems could use the tones.[3] However, by 1968, there were still few applications for the Touch-Tone technology, so the telephone company was very willing to assist in helping people use their system. CCC's Dial-A-Drill was one of the first such applications, and certainly the first commercial application for education. The first course was elementary math facts, although more curricula were added later. CCC returned to Dial-A-Drill more aggressively in 1982; see page 160.

---

[1]Private communication from computer scientist Saul Amarel.

[2]Experiments had already been run at Stanford delivering math exercises over Touch-Tone telephones in 1968 (see page 56). Suppes was always very interested in this idea.

[3]See Wikipedia "Push-button telephone" [215].

3.4.1 Dial-A-Drill Math Drill Example

The computer would call the student and would engage the student in a dialogue, something like the following:

> *Welcome to Dial-A-Drill. Please type your number followed by the pound key.*

> [Student types 1425#].

> *Hi Jon Jones. Let's continue your math lesson. Listen to the exercise, then type the answer, followed by the pound key.*
> *7 + 2 is ...*

> [Student types 9#]

> *Great!*
> *3 + 8 is ...*

> [Student types 10#]

> *Sorry, that is wrong. Please try again.*
> *3 + 8 is ...*

3.4.2 The Effectiveness of Dial-A-Drill

As with all of Suppes's projects, extensive evaluation and analysis of student learning was performed. Dean Jamison was at Educational Testing Service in 1973 and worked on a Research Bulletin entitled "The Effectiveness of Alternative Instructional Media." The results reported in [54] pp. 38–39 were not impressive due to lack of time on task by the students, as so often discouragingly happened with various products placed in schools as well. Nevertheless they were suggestive that the Dial-A-Drill product was worth pursuing:

> A different approach tried in the New York City Schools is the Dial-a-Drill program in which students are called at home and given five minutes' practice in oral arithmetic problems. The oral exercises are generated from digitized word recordings stored on a computer disk, and the students respond by using a touch-tone dial. Students in grades 2–6 participated in the demonstration project. Except at the third-grade level, students received the program at most three days a week. An intensive program for third graders required their receiving five minutes of drill and practice six days a week. Because the project was supported by an Urban Education Grant, the students participating were mainly from disadvantaged environments. Evaluation of the Dial-a-Drill is reported in Beech, McClelland, Horowitz, and Forlano [1970]. The results may be summarized briefly as follows. Experimental and control groups were both given the Metropolitan Achievement Test of Arithmetic Computation and a specially designed Oral Arithmetic Test in October 1969 and May 1970. A least squares analysis of covariance of the 1970 arithmetic achievement data failed to produce statistically

significant differences between the experimental and control students at any grade. Further analysis of the data showed that some students in the program did not actively participate. A separate analysis was performed on students in the experimental group who had more than 32 sessions (approximately one per week), and those selected students were matched with control group students. Three tests for correlated means were performed and only third-grade students exhibited a statistically significant difference. This difference was on the arithmetic test, in which the experimental students performed better than the control students. One inference to be made from this study is that 15 minutes a week, that is, three sessions a week of five minutes each, are not sufficient to produce a measurable difference. Beech et al. [1970] also investigated extensively the attitudes of parents and students to the program. The results are of some significance for two reasons. The terminals were located in the homes and not in the school, and the children were in all cases drawn from poverty areas. A survey of the attitudes of the parents toward this kind of program showed generally positive attitudes. The results of a questionnaire directed to the students also indicated a favorable response. While positive attitudinal responses to this experiment must be interpreted as preliminary, they do suggest that further research on bringing instruction into the home via telephone is worth investigating.

3.4.3 Recollections of the Dial-A-Drill System from Ron Roberts

Ron Roberts has clear and interesting recollections of the system implementation. Roberts became a Stanford undergraduate in 1966 and joined as an early member of the IMSSS team starting in 1967.[4]

In 1969, Roberts was asked to take a leave from Stanford and consult with CCC concerning the Dial-A-Drill project in New York. Dow Brian, the lead programmer at IMSSS also temporarily working for CCC, had been in New York for some time trying to make the system work, and was exhausted and needed to be relieved. Roberts remembers that Suppes asked him to fly to New York and fix the remaining problems by working on-site. He was admonished to "wear a tie," which complemented his late-'60s hippie-style appearance. Roberts recalls wearing the tie on his forehead, which he contends enhanced his technical reputation!

The system was written entirely on a PDP-8i computer with IBM hard drives. The audio used PCM (pulse-code modulation), and all

---

[4]Ron, now known as Lea Roberts, has had her entire career at Stanford University, and is now a network specialist. She has worked her way through generations of Stanford technology from 1968 on. Lea has asked to be referred to as "Ron" for the work done in the earlier years.

sounds were individually recorded. The system would support 16 simultaneous telephone calls. There were about 300 students using the system, all taking math lessons as described above. The hardware was located in the New York Telephone building in Manhattan, and the staff was very happy to see him and very proud of this use of Touch-Tone phone technology and gave it huge support.

Roberts remembers that the actual system worked pretty well. He does not remember that there were huge problems with the access of telephones, but Brian had left him a serious hardware problem: the first byte of a student's history was being trashed upon writing the history. Brian had developed a work-around of rewriting the histories each night.

After some weeks of monitoring the system (in the phone company building at all hours!), Roberts was able to figure out that there was a timing issue with the disk interface, which he was able to program around. Finally, he could go home.

3.4.4 Summary: Early Dial-A-Drill

The kind of experience recounted in the last section was typical in the early days of computing in all fields. Engineers often had to spend weeks with systems to fix issues that had developed. In the case of the work at CCC, the lack of the time and resources to do better engineering probably contributed to the need for such measures, but in this case, they were dealing with state-of-the-art IBM disk drives, and it appeared likely to Roberts that the timing issues were part of the IBM hardware itself.

The participants viewed the Dial-A-Drill project as successful educationally, but with some operational problems. One problem was that Touch-Tone phones were not ubiquitous then, and in many cases, the phones had to be installed in the homes of the students, adding extra expense.

Another issue was that calling the students was an awkward process, although it was supposed to be controlled by the computer.

Finally, the only course available was the math course. Clearly, other kinds of drills could be built using this technology. The project funding, however, was not renewed. CCC did not revisit Dial-A-Drill until 1982 when better systems and in particular more cost-effective speech solutions were available, and the other issues discovered in 1969 could be addressed.

Despite the limitations, CCC's Dial-A-Drill was heavily covered in the media, which looked at these efforts/experiments uncritically as representing progress. The wire services picked up the story, which was published throughout the country, with much of the publicity organized by the telephone company.

For example, Computerworld's June 3, 1970 edition had an article describing the project. Highlighting some of the advantages of CAI to students, the article quoted a student as follows:

> "If I don't get it right," he said, "I'm not on the spot. He (the computer) just says no, and no one can say, 'Ah, you're stupid,' and stuff like that. And it don't have to write everything down. There's no paper work." ([33] p. 27)

New York Telephone took out a 3-page advertisement in a *Saturday Review* edition that featured education. The ad detailed a number of projects using telephone communications in education, and also mentioned the use of computer terminals in Kentucky from Stanford's IMSSS laboratory. Here is an excerpt:

> For example: In New York City, more than 2000 elementary school pupils, using Touch-Tone® phones in their homes, are reinforcing math skills by 'talking' with a computer. The pupil hears the computer say, "What is four plus four?" He responds to the computer by pressing the buttons on his Touch-Tone phone. If he presses the right buttons, another problem will follow. If he is wrong, the question is repeated and if he is wrong again, the computer gives the correct answer and presents a different problem. The pupil's progress is recorded and future drills are structured to the student's achievement level. ([81] p. 42)

While telephone companies were obviously interested in CAI as another use of the phone system, they were also one of the key impediments to economic delivery of CAI. The first problem was that computer systems were too expensive and difficult to house and maintain in an individual school. But, if you tried to locate the computer at a shared facility (like Stanford's IMSSS laboratory), you then encountered the telephone company's high tariffs. CCC made inroads to both of these problems, as detailed below.

3.5   System Architectures for CAI 1967–1982

CCC's main goal was to provide cost-effective education by using computer technology. Throughout the years of its history, the technology evolved more quickly and in more directions than some of the basic conceptions of curriculum and effective instruction.

During this early period, all aspects of the systems were expensive. As the technology changed, it provided new opportunities both for richer products and also for more cost-effective delivery systems. It was a constant balancing of multivariate factors that changed about every 18 months, in tune with Moore's law.

Some of the constraints during this period included:

- **Computer processing units had to be "multi-user" with time-shared operation.** The expense of computers, including hard disks, multi-user/multi-process operating systems, and associated ports and power supplies, was too high to justify for only a single student. Before this time, some machines were designed for a single user but were on the order of $20,000 each.

- **Student terminals had to be "dumb" with no processing.** In 1967, the only cost-effective terminal was the Teletype. Model 33 Teletypes cost about $700 each depending on the configured features. Video terminals, with no processing, were available in 1970, but at an initial cost of about $10,000 each. (See Wikipedia "Teletype Model 33" [227] for details.) Gradually, video terminals became cheaper, and by about 1978 CCC was selling and later manufacturing them. Production on the Model 33 Teletype ceased in 1981, but CCC still had some in operation.

- **Connecting the terminals to the CPU was an issue and an expense.** The simplest approach was to have the CPU and the terminals in the same room and connect each terminal with a cable. If the CPU was to be in one place and terminals in another, then leased phone lines became necessary. These were very expensive, and it took time to requisition them from the phone companies. Hence, the design would have as few phone lines as needed. This created the need for terminal concentrators that would "multiplex" data for a number of terminals into a single serial line for use with a leased phone line. Suppes had already developed multiplexers at CCC. See page 63.

The continuing interplay of these factors caused changes to CCC's platforms while needing to retain some basic consistency to the underlying courses.

3.6 M8 System: Eight Terminals for Math Instruction

Released in 1971, the M8 system was probably the first "small" instructional computer system from any manufacturer or content provider and was CCC's first substantial product. It provided the Mathematics Strands, Grades 1–6 course and would support up to 8 students at a time using Model 33 Teletype terminals. The configuration was simple with the CPU, eight terminals, and a printer generally in the same room.

The benefits were a relatively clean installation not using any phone lines. However, some serious problems began to reveal the kinds of use cases people would want for instructional systems.

- People wanted enough terminals to allow an entire class to be scheduled into the lab at the same time. Eight was an interesting number, but 16 or 32 would have been a much better number for this purpose. In most schools, students from a given class would use the system at different times.

- One might expect that four M8 systems could supply 32 students at the same time, but this did not work as expected. Apart from the messiness of the installation, the records for each of the systems were not stored together, and teachers would want to run reports over all students in a class at the same time.

- Even 32 terminals was not ideal, since that would only represent one laboratory. Customers sometimes preferred to have one computer serving several labs in several schools as long as the telephone charges were reasonable.

- The M8 only supported a single course, the math course. Customers could only afford one computer system within the school, and wanted to have more courses on the same computer system.

The next generation of systems was to address some of these issues.

3.7   The A16 System

In 1971–73, CCC introduced the A16 system based on an existing minicomputer. This system initially ran 16 terminals, later 32 terminals, and could have more than the math course installed.

The minicomputer underlying the A16 was a process-control system manufactured by Cincinnati Milacron, a company that made a range of hardware for manufacturing.[5] The computer itself was relatively inexpensive yet powerful compared to other computers of its time. It originally used only paper tape for its memory, so the operating system had to be extended to handle hard disks and also multiple terminal connections.

Rainer Schulz recalls a good deal about this system. Schulz was the head of systems programming at IMSSS at Stanford starting in 1971. He did some brilliant work in converting the TENEX operating system to run on two Digital KI-10 processors at the same time, a feat that Digital Equipment Corporation and Bolt Beranek and Newman had thought impossible. This established his reputation as a high-end problem solver.

---

[5]See Wikipedia "Milacron" [199] for details about this company.

In early 1973, one of the first CCC A16 systems was installed at the Rikers Island Prison in New York City but was not working. Schulz came on as a consultant to help fix it. Schulz knew nothing about the CPU, but had an engineer who did, so Schulz directed the engineer. Schulz sat with the engineer and asked him to perform experiments. They hypothesized that the READ operations from the hard drive were simply not working. Schulz suggested putting all 1s in the buffer and using the heuristic that the data would never actually be all 1s to determine the success of the read. This led to the exact diagnosis, together with programming to retry until the operation succeeded. This increased the time the system would stay operational to about 1.5 hours, but there were more problems. So, they continued the iterative process until they had a reliable piece of equipment. After this Schulz was asked to join as a permanent consultant, and eventually as the head of software from 1976 to 1981.

A number of A16 systems were sold, mostly with 16 terminals, but the capacity of the machine to include more simultaneous terminals and courses was very limited, and the CPU was not very suitable for continuing work.

Nonetheless, the A16 had brisk sales representatives. In the fall of 1976, CCC completed its largest sale ever to the Compton, CA, school district. Seventeen A16 systems with 544 terminals were installed throughout the district in labs of 32 terminals each, allowing entire classes to go to the labs at the same time accompanied by the teachers. Together the systems could deliver about 20,000 lessons per day. To support this and other Southern California sites, a new office was opened at the same time.[6]

Milwaukee Public Schools was another large implementation of the A16. Milwaukee continued to be a customer through all of CCC's hardware iterations because Mr. Norm Rose believed in CCC's courseware and knew that it was making a difference for the disadvantaged students in the Milwaukee Public Schools.

3.8   CCC-17 System 1977–1984

The CCC-17 system was the first machine that began to match the actual use cases of its customers at that time. The CCC-17 was the primary system until 1984, and many machines were still in operation until the early 1990s. Eventually, special deals had to be offered to retire all of the CCC-17 systems. Schulz started development of the CCC-17 in 1976. He recalls that CCC decided to build a new machine using a

---

[6]Unpublished *News from CCC* document dated September 1976.

more powerful CPU and from a more mainstream manufacturer. CCC put out an RFP to Hewlett-Packard and Data General, among others. They preferred Hewlett-Packard, but Data General was more flexible with their terms, so Data General was selected. From 1977 up to 1984, CCC was one of Data General's largest accounts.[7]

DG had a 15-bit address space, reserving the 16th bit of a two-byte word. DG engineers were able to change this so that CCC had a 16-bit address space (about 65,000 words), which was substantial in 1977.

3.8.1 CCC-17 Operating System: HOMBRES

The operating system was called HOMBRES.[8] Schulz recalls the following design of the CCC-17 system.

1. The hardware integration was designed and built by CCC, which incorporated all peripherals, including ports and hard disks, with the CPU supplied by DG. The ability to attach 96 terminals was well beyond what DG had ever envisioned for their hardware.

2. HOMBRES and all application code was written in Data General assembly language with no high-level language support. CCC wrote all the device drivers from scratch in order to obtain the needed efficiency.

3. HOMBRES used many TENEX-like features even though it was much smaller. The terminal input and output code, so important in a CAI system, had features similar to those that Schulz had added to TENEX at Stanford.[9]

4. HOMBRES used dynamically linkable modules with shared program memory, again like TENEX. A given course might have a main module together with two library modules also used by other courses. The use of shared modules was critical to a CAI system where many students would be using the same course simultaneously.

5. Like TENEX, IO was generalized, so the user-level code did not need to be aware of the details of the hard disk or tape drive being used.

6. The operating system supported multiplexed lines and connections. Later versions used separate CPUs for IO.

7. The initial system had 10 MB of hard disk space. This was gradually expanded to 30 MB.

---

[7]Michael Gross, in sales support at Data General, recalls the uproar at DG when CCC announced that they would no longer be buying DG products. Private communication.

[8]The name is an acronym for the names of the principal engineers.

[9]Private communication.

8. The design was to run with up to 96 students simultaneously using multiple courses. One interesting statistic is that each student using the main math course, MK, used 90 bytes of memory in addition to the shared modules. Unfortunately, the complexity of courses increased, and the available memory was insufficient to allow all mixtures of available courses.[10]

3.8.2 CALC Authoring Language for the CCC-17

Suppes had never liked "authoring languages." Instead, at both IMSSS and CCC, he preferred *ad hoc* languages to encode content, languages that were largely declarative and without computational components. These coding languages looked a lot like XML or JSON which are used today to encode data.

Schulz thought differently about this. He believed that a language that included declarative elements for simple content together with general computation facilities would work the best, especially as time went by. In order to support the development of new courses, an authoring language was invented, using the experience of the curriculum and software groups. It was called CALC (for CCC Authoring Language Compiler) and contained features to accomplish the following:

- Specialized exercise templates for anticipated needs, such as multiple-choice exercises with many options
- General programming facilities
- Text presentation (no graphics were available)
- Answer processing
- Permanent storage of exercise status

Virtually anything that could be done with the terminals and keyboards could be done with this language.

The compiler for the CALC language was written for the Digital TOPS-20 system. For a while, facilities were rented from Stanford, until CCC bought its own TOPS-20 system.

3.9 Terminals for the CCC-17

CCC had previously used terminals built for general use. The M8 had used Model 33 Teletype terminals. The A16 had used Hazeltine terminals purchased under an OEM arrangement.

---

[10]This limitation caused no end of trouble until 1984 when a memory simulation program was written that allowed sales and service representatives to help customers schedule their courses. Some early customers had been promised that these overloads would never occur, and CCC had to make compensations in a few cases.

The Teletypes were very noisy. This had once been charming, but now it was unacceptable. And while inexpensive to purchase, the Teletypes were entirely mechanical and required considerable maintenance.

CCC decided it could build its own terminals, save money, and have equipment that would be more maintainable. Engineering designed a box to which eight terminals could connect. Called the MiniAce, it had the programming to do multiplexing of terminals and communicated with the eight terminals. The "terminals" were only video displays and keyboards. This both reduced the cost and made the overall system more maintainable.

This was particularly important for use with young students who could be very hard on the terminals. Ken Chin, who was head of engineering, liked to manufacture a terminal that had a simple clean design and could ideally be dropped on the floor without breaking! He could be seen sitting at child-height checking out prototypes and arguing with curriculum to minimize the number of keys on the keyboard.

Figure 33 shows a CCC-17 photographed in 1981 with multiple terminals (probably SLS10s). Some of the connections were hard-wired to the CCC-17; others were through leased phone lines.

3.10 CCC-17 Courses

Previous CCC systems focused on the math course and were limited in terms of additional courses. Now it was possible to create and deploy a large set of courses.

The CCC-17 had 10 MB of disk storage at launch, later 30 MB and more. This storage space included the operating system, the application software as dynamic modules, the courses, and the student data.

This sounds like very little space for large courses compared to modern (2016) computers that often have terabytes of storage.[11] However, most of the data was either text or numeric. In today's world, the massive storage space we are familiar with is needed to store sounds, pictures, and video. So the comparison is unfair. At this point, there were no such media involved in the CCC courses. (In 1981, audio was added, but the audio files were not located on the CCC-17; instead, they were stored on a separate device called the DSS. See page 157.)

With the introduction of the CCC-17 and the CALC authoring language, course development occurred very quickly. Using authors with subject-matter knowledge and curriculum-development experience, by 1981 the CCC-17 ran the courses listed in Table 5.

---

[11] 1 terabyte is approximately 1 million megabytes.

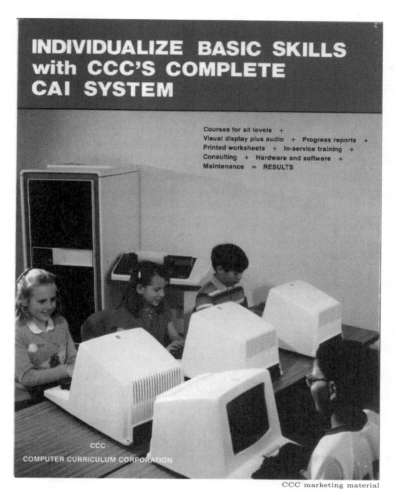

FIGURE 33: CCC-17 Installation with Terminals and Printer

TABLE 5: CCC-17 Courses by 1981

Code	Name	Notes
MA	Math Strands 1–6	The principal math course. Also available in Spanish at a later date. **About 55% of the usage of CCC-17.**
MM	Math Strands 7–8	Extension for grades 7 and 8.
PS	Problem Solving 3–6	Math problem solving for students in grades 3–6. Basically a number of topics. Some complicated CALC programming.
EM	Math Enrichment Modules 7–8	Assorted modules in mathematics intended for somewhat advanced students.
BS	Basic Sentences	Sentence structure. Not a popular course.
RD	Reading Grades 3–6	Older reading course, later dropped.
RC	Reading for Comprehension	The principal reading course. **About 30% of the usage.**
CRS	Critical Reading Skills	Large selections and paragraphs to read and answer questions about.
LS	Language Arts Strands 3–6	Writing skills broken into strands.
LT	Language Arts Topics 3–6	A topics course. Dropped after the CCC-17.
FUN	Fundamentals of English	English style.
BA	Basic Programming	Included a BASIC interpreter. Very consumptive of resources.
SS	Survival Skills	Functional skills for students. Largely topics.
AAS	Adult Arithmetic Skills	Similar to Math Strands 3–6 and 7–8 but with some changes to language for adults.
ARS	Adult Reading Skills	Similar to RC.
ALS	Adult Language Skills	Similar to LS, LT, CRS.
GED	GED Test Preparation	This course prepares the student for the GED exam. The course changed periodically to accommodate new exam requirements.
EX	Exploring Careers	A course that was an experiment in helping students define career goals and learn about career choices. Only on the CCC-17.

By 1981, the list of courses was now reasonably rich, including a variety of courses for each of the following areas: math for grades 1–8, reading for grades 3–6, language arts for grades 3–6, computer programming in Basic (generally for middle school or high school), and some remedial adult-level courses.

However, key areas were missing including elementary reading for grades K–2. These courses seemed to require audio and/or graphics, and consequently had to wait for system improvements.

There were also many areas not touched at all, including science, history, and so on. Other companies tried these, and CCC created a rigorous middle-school science course in 1991 (called Science Discovery), but science was never something that people expected from CCC.[12]

3.10.1   Courseware Choices and Usage

In the late 1970s, school districts usually had to choose a single vendor for CAI courseware. The vendor's systems were proprietary, and only courses provided by the vendor could run on a given system. Hence, there was a strong pressure on CCC to provide courses across a broad range, even if some courses were so specialized as to lack a large audience, or if the expertise and cost required to build a good course was high compared to the expected use. Courses like EX (Exploring Careers) or GED (GED Preparation) had this problem. Customers expressed an interest in such courses to which CCC responded, but the actual usage was low.

By the early 1990s, however, enough courses were available to establish some clear patterns of usage:

- Elementary math courses formed about 55–60% percent of usage, and elementary reading courses formed about 30% of usage. This pattern was observed even as new courses were created and new platforms developed.[13]
- Almost all installations continued to be focused on labs. With the CCC-17 allowing up to 128 terminals connected to the same system, labs with 32 terminals were common, allowing an entire class to use the system at the same time. With telephone lines, several schools might be connected to the same CCC-17. See Figure 64 for an example.
- Students in the elementary grades would go with their teacher to the lab and take back-to-back math and reading sessions at the same

---

[12]Suppes once commented that over the years, computerized courseware has seen a large number of science courses. They remain a favorite of high-tech innovators, but do not seem to have caught on to the degree one might hope.

[13]The last time for which the authors have seen data is 1992.

time. Since the lessons were generally individualized, each student was working rather independently.

- Often there was a *proctor* in the lab. This person was a paraprofessional who ran the lab, helped students and teachers, ran reports, and made trouble reports to CCC if appropriate.
- Labs became so organized that CCC generally even sold the tables along with the equipment. Since they were building, maintaining, and installing the hardware, a set of best practices evolved about how to run the CCC Instructional Lab.
- Over time, anecdotal evidence and some evaluations suggested that laboratory operations and logistics heavily affected the ultimate usage and results. CCC consultants periodically visited labs in order to keep things in shape. CCC field service representatives were dispatched from regional offices for hardware maintenance.

3.11 CCC's Departments by the End of the 1970s

After a decade in business, CCC had developed a corporate structure. Suppes never really liked structure and especially not "bureaucracy," but he recognized the need for it as the company grew. This recognition of business realities did not keep him from "managing by walking around," as the expression goes, and commandeering anyone for a task that he needed to have done.

Here are some comments about the departments.

- Executive: This comprised Pat Suppes, an attorney, personnel director (the precursor to HR), and several other administrators.
- Marketing: National and regional vice-presidents, support, product marketing, and sales representatives. A very important group was the CAI Consultants, who were generally former teachers, with the primary job of training and supporting the users. They could help teachers plan their use of the system, explain the structure of the curriculum, train people on system management, and importantly help sales reps to make their sales. With the CCC-17, a new and richer management system had come into existence, and teachers and proctors had to learn to use it to get the best results. Consultants often worked out of their homes near to the locations that they served. A large sale could involve locating and hiring new consultants within the district.
- Field Service: This was the hardware side of support. Field Service roughly paralleled Marketing in terms of the structure, with national and regional vice-presidents, and individual field service representatives. Like the consultants, they worked at home and would be

hired into cities where CCC had a concentration of business. They installed, updated, and fixed the hardware. Until the late 1980s everything was proprietary, and mostly built by CCC.

- Curriculum and Publications: Arguably the most important department in terms of the nature of the company, the Curriculum group designed and wrote the courseware. Publications wrote a large number of manuals, including courseware, management system, training, and hardware maintenance documents. Later, a Graphics group would be added.

- Software and Systems: Built all software (and most firmware), including software for device drivers, operating systems, terminals and special-purpose devices, and software for the management system, course drivers, and tools for curriculum development.

- Engineering: Designed the myriad devices that CCC was selling. By the late 1970s, everything was designed and built by CCC.

- Manufacturing: occupying a building on Del Medio Court in Mountain View, this group built all of the equipment from purchased components. It is difficult today to think of having a local group building, often by hand, small quantities of computers and terminals *in order to save money*, but this is exactly what they were doing.

Kathleen Adkins has a number of recollections about the company during this period. She joined CCC in 1969 and left in 1980. Her title was Vice President of Curriculum, but she remembers that the company tended to give out impressive titles to people. Interviewed in 2016, she remembers that the staff was mostly reporting directly to Suppes, and work was moved around according to who had the most time available.

She remembers hiring mostly new graduates for curriculum-authoring positions, and people learned on the job. Some worked out, some did not, but new courseware was often created very quickly when it was needed. The hardware and system software had a lot of bugs.

She vividly recalls spending time at customer sites and training people in the use of the courseware and the system itself. She was selected for this because of her ability to communicate with people. Often, the teachers and staff she worked with were very afraid of the computer. During the 1980s, CCC would greatly increase its focus on training and supporting customers.

Adkins overall impression of the company was that it was something of a hobby and not very well managed at the time. Suppes became aware of some of these issues, as discussed below.

After leaving Adkins had a career in professional development and training and felt that the experience at CCC had been very good for her.

3.12 CCC's Self-Appraisal After Ten Years in Business

In 1977–78, CCC did an extensive self-appraisal, in part to clarify its position and also to secure loans for expansion.[14]

CCC estimated the elementary-middle school market at about 7,000 terminals. Of this, 50% was provided by Hewlett-Packard (using courseware derived from Suppes's work at Stanford); CCC had 35%. Univac had one system in Chicago, and IBM had a small number of terminals. In the elementary market, CCC was the leader, with over 40% of the market. Control Data was starting to market the Plato system developed at the University of Illinois, but the prices were so high that CCC was not concerned.

Since introducing the A16 in 1974, CCC had done very well with bids. The new CCC-17 system, just introduced in 1977, was doing even better, and CCC was winning many bids.

CCC's market was mostly federally-funded for disadvantaged students. This included hearing-impaired and handicapped students. CCC felt very confident about this market, believing that the federal funds were secure and that customers agreed the product was effective. The annual continuation rate was 96% for federally-funded projects.

CCC now had a growing, professional sales staff on commission as well as several local distributors. In the early 1970s, company officers had been responsible for sales presentations. CCC recognized the need for funding to hire more sales people to cover territories that were not being adequately handled.

CCC's most successful product to date had been the A16. Sales of this system were limited by the courses available and also the number of terminals, restricted to 32. The CCC-17 could hold many new courses and could run up to 96 stations. While the production cost of the CCC-17 was about 30% higher than the A16 for a comparable configuration, the fact that a system could handle significantly more terminals made it more attractive to customers. CCC priced its systems to lead to a higher return on larger systems, with particular advantages in the cost of sales and support to larger configurations.

---

[14]This section draws upon unpublished memoranda possessed by Patrick Suppes and also conversations with staff.

There was great confidence in the CCC-17. Some CCC sales representatives were telling customers that the CCC-17 was so powerful that all future courses would run on it. This was certainly never company policy, but it reflected a sense of self-assurance in the ranks.

CCC was also now manufacturing terminals and supplying complete installations including tables and other supplies. In the courseware area, CCC had supplied an additional eight courses and significant updates to five established courses with the introduction of the CCC-17.

Overall, the company felt content with its product offerings and marketing strategies in 1978, projecting $5.3M of sales in 1978, $8.5M in 1979, and $12.7M in 1980.

While a number of issues and scenarios were discussed in available corporate documents, nothing was mentioned about the development of new chips by companies like Intel and Motorola, and the "microcomputers" that were beginning to be built.

CCC may have felt secure and felt that it understood the market, but this was an illusion.

4

University-Level Instruction at Stanford: 1971–1979

4.1 New Focus—Elementary to University Level

In 1970, the "Deaf Project" had started with funding from the Office of Education; see page 66. By 1971, the administrative framework for the project, connections to the affected schools, and courseware development was well established under the leadership of Jamesine Friend. When Friend left the project, Dexter Fletcher took over the leadership and directed the ongoing development, especially the evaluations of the efficacy of CAI used for hearing-impaired students.[1]

The Deaf Project was the largest effort Suppes attempted at Stanford using government funding for research into CAI. However, Suppes could see that government research in CAI was going to be reduced within the next few years. Based on the work that Stanford had done, he also believed that companies like CCC could now take over the delivery of basic skills instruction for K-12 students.[2]

To redirect the mission of the IMSSS laboratory, he decided to take on advanced courses for university instruction and to focus the research effort on difficult technical and economic issues. He would select areas that were quite forward-looking and unlikely to be resolved soon, rather than simple enhancements to techniques that were already established. He would avoid areas that were likely to be handled by the marketplace, such as inexpensive hardware and display terminals, and would seek to complement other groups rather than compete directly.

---

[1]Friend returned to manage the Radio Mathematics project a few years later; see 4.17. Fletcher went on to have a successful career working on educational and training issues for many government agencies.

[2]Suppes also allowed much later that he did not want a real or perceived conflict between his research at Stanford and the products at CCC. Eventually, he was to donate a large portion of his net worth to Stanford and other philanthropic enterprises.

4.2 CAI Developments Elsewhere

In the years between 1963 and 1971, the spread of CAI projects had been remarkably fast. The University of Wisconsin published the *Index to Computer Assisted Instruction*, third edition, in 1971 (see [62]). It listed over 300 pages of different programs—about 1200 programs altogether—using a template format that included name, author, description, length, etc. Most of the computer systems were mainframes such as IBM; the most popular languages were three versions of Coursewriter (see [18]); and the providers were mainly universities. Many of the programs appear to have contained short lessons (often less than one hour in duration), and ranging on a large number of topics. IMSSS listed its work along with the rest with each course having a single entry.

While many small projects were underway, there were also some large ones in addition to IMSSS. Here are some that Suppes followed and believed to be important.

4.2.1 CERL: The PLATO PROJECT

CERL (Computer-based Education Research Laboratory) at the University of Illinois—Champagne/Urbana had a large project to build a complete instructional system. CERL was led by engineering professor Donald Bitzer, who had invented the plasma display.[3] Like Suppes's IMSSS lab, it was largely sponsored by the National Science Foundation (NSF), but at a significantly higher level than IMSSS.

Bitzer's approach was very different from Suppes's. An engineer by training and inclination, he wanted to build a computer system, including distribution technology, displays, and authoring language, that would allow CAI to be developed and deployed. He saw himself as providing a system for creating and delivering CAI courses.

- The system was called PLATO (for Programmed Logic for Automatic Teaching Operations).
- The computer was originally an ILLIAC; a series of these machines was designed and built at the University of Illinois beginning in 1952. Eventually, Control Data Corporation sponsored the system, with President William Norris wanting to revolutionize education through PLATO.
- PLATO used specially-designed terminals with monochrome orange plasma displays. The "PLATO terminals" also had the ability to display images from microfiche cards, which were prepared for various courses.

---

[3]See Wikipedia "Plato (computer system)" [207] and "Donald Bitzer" [179].

- Bitzer innovated a communications distribution system that used leased video lines to multiplex data from many different terminals. This foreshadowed the Ethernet concept of a decade later, and was very nearly what cable television systems implemented to allow existing cable systems to carry Internet traffic nearly two decades later. Bitzer's motive was simply to reduce the cost of communications by using video lines supplied by the phone company.[4]
- Most importantly, PLATO programming and authoring was done in TUTOR, a specialized programming language built for instruction. It contained some general programming elements together with specific display, input, and "judging" functions.[5]

Using this system, a large number of interesting courses were written and used at a number of schools. PLATO wanted to encourage the writing of new courses.

PLATO was taken over by CDC and marketed for a number of years, but the costs of development were apparently huge and it was never profitable. One estimate was $300,000 per hour of instruction.

Courses are now marketed under the "PLATO" brand by Edmentum.[6]

In 1975, IMSSS received several PLATO terminals connected to CERL and the staff was able to evaluate them. The staff found that many things were quite easy to do with TUTOR, but if the author wanted to have more complex algorithms or programming, it became very difficult very quickly. Simple lessons with text, simple graphics, and standard question types could, however, be written with ease. A favorite program for users on the system was "Talk-O-Matic," which allowed multi-person chat sessions, similar to the "Talk" program written several years earlier at IMSSS.

The difference between PLATO and Suppes's approach could hardly be more profound.

1. At Stanford, Suppes wanted to use off-the-shelf hardware and systems software.

---

[4]Robert Smith remembers spending some time with Bitzer at his lab in 1972. He was enthusiastic and loved to explain about the technology and how various problems had been solved. He became very animated in talking about the phone company's efforts to charge him "data" rates on his use of video lines. He had a TV monitor there showing the "picture" created by the packets of data being sent. This story underscores the difficulties that pioneers at applying computers had with obtaining reasonable telephone data rates.

[5]See Wikipedia "TUTOR (programming language)" [230] for a history of this language.

[6]See Wikipedia "Plato (computer system)" [207] for some historical notes and https://www.edmentum.com/ for the corporate site of Edmentum.

2. He used standard programming languages, generally those designed for work in artificial intelligence, such as LISP and SAIL.

3. Authoring languages for expressing content were generally quite *ad-hoc* in character, in order to allow flexibility and to fit the content at hand.

4. Most importantly, Suppes's underlying goals dealt with the curriculum content and the psychology of learning, especially instructional optimization. The technology was always secondary to him.

4.2.2 MITRE's TICCIT Project

TICCIT (for Time-shared Interactive, Computer-Controlled Information Television) used high-quality commercial SONY NTSC television screens. The computer system was a Data General Nova, and it was claimed that over 100 simultaneous users could use the system. Courses teaching English and algebra were developed and tested as a part of the project, with more courses developed later. TICCIT was also funded by the National Science Foundation.

The TICCIT system was designed to not require "programming." Hence, it had limited kinds of interactional exchanges and course structure. Also, it tended not to enforce a certain path on students since browsing was strongly encouraged and students had the ability to determine their own paths through the content using a special keypad.

The TICCIT courseware did not do well in practice, however. One speculation on the reason for this was that students did not "receive sufficient feedback about their progress, and consequently made poor control decisions about what and when to study, practice, and test" ([78]). TICCIT did not have much historical influence.

See [167] and [78] for details and references about TICCIT.

4.2.3 Intelligent Tutoring Systems at Bolt, Beranek and Newman

By the early 1970s, Bolt, Beranek and Newman (BBN) was at the forefront of the advances in computer systems development. It had built the ground-breaking TENEX operating system, was operating the ARPANET, and had a number of important grants for artificial intelligence research, with a remarkable staff of people. Many of them moved to Xerox's Palo Alto Research Center by the mid-1970s. For a historical review of BBN's efforts in education over the years, see Wallace Feurzeig's writeup about BBN [37]. Much of this work was described as "intelligent tutors."

Two projects done in the early 1970s at BBN particularly impressed Suppes. They were the *Scholar* program built by Jaime Carbonelle and Allen Collins, and the *Sophie* program built by John Seely Brown, Richard Burton, and their colleagues.

Scholar: Dialogue about Geography

Scholar was a dialogue system for instructional use. In the dialogue, either the student or the program could ask questions. Feurzeig summarizes *Scholar* with the following:

> [Scholar] was implemented in LISP. Its knowledge base was organized as a semantic network (see Quillian [86]). The program's initial knowledge base contained geopolitical information about South America. For each country it stored such information as population, land area, capital, major cities, major rivers, major mountains, major religions. What could be taught by the approach was limited to a set of facts: "The area of Peru is approximately 400,000 square miles. The major cities in Brazil are Sao Paulo, Rio de Janeiro, Brasilia, ..." The natural-language semantics and syntax required for treating such information are highly constrained.[7]

A typical dialogue with Scholar follows. The student's inputs are surrounded by asterisks.

```
What is Chile?
*a country*
That's fine.
Select an alternative from the list:
    214,000; 800,300; 49,883; 63,690;
For the question: approximately what is the area of Chile?
*800,300*
Your answer is incorrect. The correct answer is 214,000.
The population in Chile is approx 850,000. True or False?
*true*
You are correct. (sic!)
*Tell me something about Peru.*
Wait a minute, I'm checking my files.
Let's proceed now.
Peru is a country.
It is in South America.
The population is approx 7,000,000 people.
The capital is Lima.
```

(See [37] p. 284)

Carbonelle came to Stanford and gave a demonstration to Suppes and his team. Suppes was so impressed that he offered Carbonelle a job

---

[7]See [21] and [22] for details about *Scholar*.

basically on the spot, hoping to create such dialogues as part of his courses. One issue that concerned him was that the use of a semantic net was appropriate for databases of geographical facts but would not be appropriate, or at least not a complete solution, for mathematics courses, where both proof-checking and symbolic-manipulation facilities would be required.

Sophie: Dialogue about Diagnosing Electronics Failures

John Seely Brown and Richard Burton worked on CAI issues, first at BBN and later at the Xerox Palo Alto Research Center. One of their first projects was *Sophie*, which taught electronic troubleshooting and problem-solving techniques to students. See [17] and [15].

Here is a description by Feurzeig:

> The electronic instrument used in Sophie is based on the Heathkit IP-28 power supply, a fairly sophisticated circuit with both current-limiting and voltage-limiting behavior. These two interrelated feedback loops make troubleshooting this circuit a nontrivial task. The following brief excerpt illustrates the kind of interaction made possible by Sophie. The student's inputs are preceded by two greater-than signs. Reviewer annotations are parenthesized. The student has asked Sophie to insert a fault in the circuit. Sophie randomly selects a fault and inserts it into the model of the circuit. ([37] p. 288)

```
The instrument has a fault and its present control settings
     are:
CC = 1.0 (Current Control - from 0.0 (Min Current) to 1.0)
CR = HIGH (Current Range Switch, HIGH = 1 Amp,
 LOW = 0.1 Amp)
LOAD = 20 (Load Resistance in Ohms)
VC = 1 (Voltage Control - from 0.0 (Min Voltage) to 1.0)
VR = HIGH (Voltage Range Switch, HIGH = 30, LOW = 10 Volts)
>>What is the output?
The output voltage is 11.7 volts.
>>What is it in a working instrument?
In a working circuit the output voltage is 19.9 volts.
>>What is the voltage between R8 and Q1?
The voltage at N1 is 47.6 volts.
>>What is the base emitter voltage of the voltage limiting
     transistor?
The base emitter voltage of Q5 is .037 millivolts.
 ...
```

Feurzeig notes that "Sophie sought to create a 'reactive' environment that fosters a student's learning while he tries out his ideas working on a complex electronics troubleshooting task (Brown, Burton, and Bell, 1975). Sophie supports a student in a close collaborative relationship with an 'expert' who helps the student explore, develop, and debug his own ideas."

Suppes liked this because it used a well-known circuit simulator named SPICE (see [225]) and a highly-tuned natural-language parser with vocabulary and grammatical constructions from the domain of electronic circuits.

4.3 Suppes's Research Agenda for the 1970s

Suppes decided to identify and focus on problems that would limit the application of computers to education in the future. In doing so, he would follow the general outline of the *Scientific American* article and work on tutorial and dialogue issues, but within areas that he and his collaborators could hope to deal with. See [117] and the previous discussion on page 32.

- *Evaluating "Natural" Student Proofs in Axiomatic Mathematics:* Suppes realized that it would not be possible to use proof-checkers beyond elementary logic without allowing students to express proofs in a natural way. This was partly a problem of understanding mathematical language and expression, but also involved creating underlying software that would check the proofs for correctness.
- *Dynamically-Generated Audio:* Suppes believed that hearing was critical to learning. It was also important to generate sounds dynamically out of words or phonemes in order to have a robust channel of communication about the content and work that the student was doing. Dynamically generated speech and speech recognition were psychologically critical to learning and interaction with the computer. This was not simply playing back sounds; it was also the dynamic generation of whole sentences from phonemes.
- *Cost-effective Audio:* Suppes also believed that there was not enough work underway on solving economic problems of audio delivery, especially compared to the work occurring with graphical display systems by the early 1970s.
- *Natural-language processing:* Understanding natural language was one of the biggest challenges that would be required for having dialogues with students. He felt that some progress was being made at BBN and other places, but he wanted his efforts to be focused on comprehensive courseware.
- *Economic issues:* Suppes realized that large government funding of CAI projects would likely wind down, and that commercialization would depend on making CAI more cost-effective. At CCC, he was concerned about this for the K-12 market, and he realized that

university-level efforts would have to prove cost-effective. He also was seeking out opportunities for using technology in education in undeveloped countries.

Suppes also believed that it was critical to have large numbers of actual students using and testing any innovations in for-credit courses. He was critical of research applications that looked good in demonstrations but didn't have the strength and resiliency to stand up to real student use. In order to have access to students, he decided to focus on university-level applications. These would offer substantial technical challenges while he and other faculty members would be able to develop and test their courses with Stanford students and eventually at other universities as well. Joe Van Campen's successful program for teaching Russian to Stanford students was the first university-level course taught by computer,[8] and he was anxious to try having all of the instructional delivery on the computer as the Van Campen's Russian course had done.

4.4   Logic

An elementary logic course was the very first example of a computer-based exercise at IMSSS in December of 1963 (see page 16), and the development of curriculum materials for teaching axiomatic mathematics remained a long-term interest.

4.4.1   Tutorials for Helping Students with Logic

Suppes had been interested in providing expert advice to students when they needed help with logic exercises. The courses had contained a number of hints, which the students could access with the "HINT" commands. These hints, however, were "canned" in the sense that every student would see the same hints. But the nature of creating a proof was that there were many different ways to solve the problem.

Adele Goldberg was a student in computer science at the University of Chicago. She met Suppes, and he invited her to come to Stanford. She took over the support and operation of the logic course, and also began working on a tutorial version of the logic proof checker.[9]

The key idea was to build a theorem prover component to the course. By typing "HELP," the student could ask for advice from the program about how to proceed with the proof that was underway. So, the the-

---

[8]See page 52.

[9]Goldberg's dissertation may be found at [46]. After IMSSS, Goldberg went to Xerox PARC where she worked on SmallTalk and the Alto computer system. She later became president of the Association for Computing Machinery. Suppes was quite proud of her success.

orem prover would have to begin where the student left off. At that time, the state of the art for theorem provers were provers based on the resolution principle.[10] Such provers could be powerful, but they did not work in such a way that one could readily extract help for the student.

Goldberg devised a heuristic theorem prover that would start with the proof in its current state and look for solutions in such a way that commands to the proof checker would start with the student's current proof and find a solution. This portion of the course was based on the logical theory of the abelian group for addition, which is decidable, although Goldberg's prover only dealt with a subset of that theory.[11] The program was built in LISP to run on the PDP-10 system.

At that point, logic was being taught to students at Walter Hays Elementary School in Palo Alto, and Goldberg was able to test out her version with the students. Figure 34 shows examples of a student using the HELP command to get hints. Note that the student asks for HELP twice. Each time, a different, context-dependent message is provided. Furthermore, the help is given in stages so that the student can say that he/she needs a more useful hint.

4.4.2 Models for Student Uses of the Logic Course (1970)

Two PhD theses dealt with statistical models using data from the logic course. Michael Kane studied the variability of student proofs using the 1970 version of the logic course.[12] Suppes summarized that Kane "concentrates on the diversity of student proofs. What is interesting is to find how much diversity there is even at the very elementary level of proofs in the logic course."[13] For example, Kane found that one student had a mean length of 20.5 steps on proofs for a selected set of theorems, while another student had a mean length of 8.6 steps on the same set of theorems. See [128] pp. 251–276.

James Moloney studied a model containing behavioral and structural variables used to measure student proofs. Behavioral variables included measurements such as "mean number of lines of a derivation" (variable B1). Structural variables included "the number of words in the statement of a problem" (S1). Regressions were used to compare such models to student performance. See [128] pp. 277–300.

---

[10]See Wikipedia "Resolution (logic)" [218] for details and citations.

[11]See Wikipedia "Presburger arithmetic" [209] for a discussion of Presburger's decision method for arithmetic with addition.

[12]Stanford students used the logic course in the summer of 1970 as a part of the instruction, together with standard lectures.

[13]See [128] p. xxxi.

```
*(START)
WHO ARE YOU (TYPE S OR T)?
*SS
PLEASE TYPE YOUR NUMBER.
*7S
LISA PREBLE
OK?
*YESS

1
DERIVE      (A = 0)->((A + B) = B)
P           (1)  (0 + B)= B

;*HELPS     TYPE THE ANTECEDENT OF THE
            CONDITIONAL YOU WANT TO DERIVE AS A
            WP.  DO YOU SEE HOW?
*NOS
            THE ANTECEDENT IS A=0.
            NOW DO YOU SEE?
*YESS


;*WPS       (2)        *A=0S

;*HELPS     DO YOU SEE HOW TO REPLACE 0 IN LINE 1
            BY A?
*NOS
            TRY TO APPLY THE CE RULE TO LINE 2.
            THEN REPLACE THE 0 IN LINE 1 BY A.


;*2CE1S     (3)        0 = A

;*1-3RE1S   (4)        (A + B)= B

;*2-4CPS    (5)  (A = 0)->((A + B) = B)

CORRECT...
```

FIGURE 34: Student Logic Proof with Tutorial

4.5 The EXCHECK Instructional System for Axiomatic Mathematics

4.5.1 Teaching the Stanford Logic Course On-line

Suppes had wanted to use computers entirely for teaching the logic course, Philosophy 57a. He had taught this course since the 1950s and had used his textbook in the course (see [113]). From 1969, the computer was to some extent integrated into the instruction, but there were still lectures and examinations.

Beginning in the spring quarter of 1972, all instruction was given on-line, using Teletype terminals in Casita Hall. The course was thereafter taught three quarters of the year.

At the beginning of the quarter, Suppes and the TAs would meet with the assembled students for a single meeting. The computer system was available much of each day, so students could work on their own schedules. There were no exams or other homework given, and students were graded by how far they were able to get in the course, so each student could set his or her own goal.

The logic course continued to be developed. By 1974, it used the EXCHECK courseware development system (see below) for axiomatic mathematics, and the curriculum had become more demanding.

4.5.2 "Natural" Proofs

It was obvious that if more complex axiomatics were to be attempted than elementary logic, Suppes would need a new concept of a proof checker. Even for the more advanced parts of the Stanford logic curriculum, the proofs were becoming too complex to express in ordinary mathematical language. This was certainly true for a set theory course.

As Suppes noted, "I want to be clear on the point that no one, or practically no one, has ever suggested that formal proofs characterized explicitly and completely in mathematical logic were ever meant to be a practical approach to the giving of proofs in any nontrivial mathematical domain" ([128] pp. 165).

The solution was to design a program that would emulate normal mathematical practice in terms of the level of detail required for a proof to be acceptable.

Set theory was a good place for this effort to begin. It is well known that set theory can be developed starting with first-order predicate logic (or some variant). Suppes wrote a set theory text in 1958 that was used as the basis for the course; see [114]. Suppes's text is an exposition of set theory using the Zermelo-Fraenkel axiomatization that is probably the most accepted by mathematicians. The proofs of the first theorems are relatively easy to render in first-order logic, but as things progress, the language used to teach the subject, as well as the language used by mathematicians themselves, becomes much richer and more informal.

The group still wanted to be able to "check" the proofs for correctness, and to allow the student to offer up any proof, not just a "canned" version. Ideally, the language would become as informal as possible, the system would still make a correct decision about whether or not the proof was valid.

4.5.3 Overall Design of EXCHECK—Requirements

The EXCHECK system was the general name for the overall program used for advanced logic, set theory, and other axiomatic mathematics. Some of the design goals for this new approach were as follows:

- EXCHECK should allow different mathematical languages and theories. There would be tools that would allow theory-specific vocabulary and syntax rules to be built into the system. The resulting language would obey formal rules but also be somewhat informal in character. The axioms, definitions, and theorems of the theory could also be input using this language.

- Theory-specific rules for displaying the steps of the proof in conventional mathematical language could be implemented and would allow proofs to be "pretty-printed" and summarized.

- Standard logical rules of inference would be included, but would be more forgiving and friendly than in any previous system. The implementation would take note of the many mathematically irrelevant user-interface details that students had complained about in the past.

- Theory-specific routines would be included that would allow inferences to be made based on known decision methods relevant to the theory in question.

- Theorem provers would be built tuned to the theory in question and used to implement rules like IMPLIES, which would invoke a resolution-theorem prover.

- The entire system would be built to have more attractive and user-friendly interfaces. The best display terminals that IMSSS had were used for these courses to allow custom character sets and visual displays of the proofs in progress.

- The system would also be built to use the new audio facilities that IMSSS was developing.

- The first version would be in use in 1974 and the audio facilities would be added in 1975. This schedule was almost met.

- A new authoring component was created with both old and new exercise types and new interfaces to the proof checking component. Old curriculum materials for logic were automatically translated, allowing the best parts of several different versions of the logic course to be assembled together.

- Significant new content was written for a new *Logic* course.

4.5.4 Implementation

The entire system was built in SAIL[14] and LISP. SAIL was used for all user interaction including parsing student input and displaying and summarizing proofs, and later for the audio processing. LISP was used for a resolution-based theorem prover[15] and also for the REDUCE symbolic manipulation system that was used in some theories.[16]

Context-free grammars were written for a new parser, and at the outset included languages for logic, set theory, and other courses later implemented.

Many of the commands used in previous logic courses were implemented but with generalizations and improvements. New commands were added as needed, and are described below.

See [128] pp. 81–119 for Lee Blaine's detailed discussion of the proof checking components of EXCHECK. This formed a part of his PhD dissertation. Others who worked on this include Jim McDonald, Lawrence Markosian (especially for the *Logic* course), and Robert Smith.

4.5.5 T: Tautology Command

A *tautology* in logic is a theorem that can be derived by using only the rules of sentential logic. Some examples are as follows:

- If A then A
- If A and B then A
- If John is a student and Mary is a student then Mary is a student.

The set of tautologies is mechanically decidable (within limits of time and space).[17]

At some point in a course in logic, the student is allowed to make a tautological argument in a single step by saying something like "and this is just a tautology." This is a simple but powerful way of reducing the amount of detail that the student has to deal with.

---

[14]SAIL was an ALGOL-like language used for artificial intelligence research.

[15]See Wikipedia "Resolution (logic)" [218]

[16]See http://reduce-algebra.com/documentation.htm.

[17]See Wikipedia "Propositional calculus" [211].

The T or Tautology rule was implemented in EXCHECK and included in all EXCHECK variants. It is more important in elementary first-order logic than in other theories.

4.5.6   BOOLE: Boolean Algebra Command

A good portion of elementary set theory deals with its Boolean algebra fragment. Here are some common theorems in this fragment that can be proven only by Boolean algebra.

- $A \subseteq A$
- $A \cup B = B \cup A$
- If $A \subseteq B$ and $B \subseteq C$ then $A \subseteq C$
- $A \cup (B \cap C) = (C \cap A) \cup (A \cap B)$

The set of statements provable using only Boolean algebra and sentential logic is also decidable, and was implemented.[18]

4.5.7   APPLY: Apply to a Situation

The concept of "applying" an axiom or a previously proven theorem is common in mathematical discourse. Unlike the T or BOOLE commands, it is not a straightforward algorithm and more of an informal way of speaking. The team built and deployed several versions before finding a satisfactory solution.

4.5.8   IMPLIES: A Result Follows "Directly"

Often in mathematical English, one speaks of a result "following directly" from a previous result, axiom, or definition. Depending on the level of the discourse, this can be an acceptable part of the proof. The assumption is that the listeners could fill in the details of that step by themselves.

For example, suppose we know that

$$A \subseteq B$$

Then, it follows directly from this and the definition of a subset that

$$(\forall x)(x \in A \rightarrow x \in B)$$

The IMPLIES command was the most important command used by students taking the EXCHECK version of the logic course.

4.5.9   ESTABLISH: Implies with Set Theory Rewrite Rules

The ESTABLISH command is similar to the command except that it builds some set theory knowledge into the command. The knowledge is primarily in the form of rewrite rules and commonly used principles that

---

[18]The proof is by W. V. Quine and is given in [87].

Informal Proof

Assume that $B \subset C$. We show that $C\neg \subseteq B$ by indirect proof. Assume $C \subseteq B$. Since $B \subset C$ then, by definition, $B \subseteq C$ and $B \neq C$ and $C \subseteq B$ then $B = C$. But this is a contradiction and, hence, the assumption that $C \subseteq B$ is false. QED.

First EXCHECK Proof of Th 2.4.5

```
Derive:  (∀ B,C)(B ⊂ C → C ¬⊆ B)

assume  (1)  B ⊂ C
assume  (2)  C ⊆ B
1 eliminate using definition proper subset
        (3)  B ⊆ C and B ≠ C
2, 3 establish
        (4)  B = C
2, 3, 4 contradiction
        (5)  C ¬⊆ B
1, 5 cp
        (6)  If B ⊂ C then C ¬⊆ B
6 ug    (7)  (∀ C,B)(B ⊂ C → C ¬⊆ B)
```

FIGURE 35: Set Theory Proof in Boolean Algebra

themselves are theorems. Use of the ESTABLISH command requires interaction with the user.

4.6 Sample EXCHECK Proofs in Set Theory

Ideally, proofs in EXCHECK should be as close to informal proofs as possible. The following examples demonstrate some classical results in elementary set theory and how the EXCHECK proofs appear.

Figure 35 shows a complete proof of the result that for all sets B and C, if $B \subset C$ then $C \not\subseteq B$.

Figure 36 shows a summary of a longer proof (originally 32 steps). The theorem states that every chain contained in a family of sets A is contained in a maximal chain in A. Note that the printout includes natural-language versions of statements such as "A is a family of sets."

4.7 Set Theory Curriculum

The course curriculum consisted of seven chapters and followed the text book of Suppes [114]; see Table 6. It was a treatment of the Zermelo-Fraenkel axioms (ZF), which is probably the most standard and accepted set theory formulation among mathematicians, especially when combined with the axiom of choice (ZFC). A reason for studying set theory axiomatically is its importance in all of mathematics, although in most mathematical discourse, set theory is treated informally.

```
Derive:  If A is a family of sets then
    every chain contained in A is contained in some maximal chain in A

Proof:
Abbreviate:  {B:  B is a chain and C ⊆ B and B ⊆ A}
      by:  C!Chains

Assume  (1)  A is a family of sets
    Assume  (2)  C is a chain and C ⊆ A
    By Zorn's lemma,
          (23)  C!Chains has a maximal element
    Let B be such that
          (24)  B is a maximal element of C!Chains
    Then    (25)  B is a chain and C ⊆ B and B ⊆ A
    So that (31)  B is a maximal chain in A
    Hence   (32)  C is contained in some maximal chain in A
```

FIGURE 36: Set Theory Proof Showing Summary Capability

TABLE 6: Chapters in *Axiomatic Set Theory*

	Chapter	Description	Theorems
1	Survey	Background of set theory and reasons for axiomatic development.	5
2	General Developments	Fundamental concepts such as inclusion, union and intersection, ordered pairs. Definitions and justifying theorems.	116
3	Theory of Relations and Functions	Binary relations, including standard definitions and theorems, well-ordering, theory of functions, and elementary operations.	216
4	Equipollence, Finite and Infinite Sets	Equipollence defined as the existence of a bijection function, Schroeder-Bernstein theorem, definition of finiteness, standard theorems.	87
5	Cardinal Numbers	Finite, infinite, and transfinite cardinals. [Students taking the course at Stanford for a "Pass" had to complete Chapter 5.]	61
6	Ordinal Numbers	This develops the ordinal number following von Neumann. Finite ordinals, infinite ordinals, and well-ordered sets.	101
7	The Axiom of Choice	The axiom and its equivalents, including choice functions, maximal principles, and applications such as the proof of the equivalence of Dedekind finite and finite.	33

In addition to proving theorems, there was also a substantial amount of content, including exposition, questions, and quizzes. The content was all presented on the terminal. Both visual and audio elements were a part of the presentation. The curriculum was written in a special language known as VOCAL (for Voice Oriented Curriculum Authoring Language).[19] See below for a discussion of the audio developments done for this course.

4.8 Student Experiences with the Set Theory Course

The experiences of the Stanford students taking this course were monitored very carefully. One reason was the number of experiments that were underway at the same time, including the new EXCHECK proof checker and decision methods, the audio presentation, and the various options available to the students. There was also concern that the course be taught properly in comparison to the standard lecture courses. See [128] pp. 3–80 especially.

4.8.1 Student Usage

Axiomatic Set Theory was taught exclusively on the computer at Stanford from 1974 until 1980, with the support of teaching assistants. This was an undergraduate course in set theory; Stanford also had advanced set theory courses intended for graduate students in mathematics and philosophy.

The number of students enrolled was similar overall in the 1974–1980 period to the numbers taught in previous years when the computer was not used. In previous years, the course was taught by a human instructor and was typically only available in one quarter, and there was a significant variance in the number of students enrolled compared to the computerized course.

Students were able to access the computer system at a wide variety of hours and could spend as much or as little time as desired or required. There were some check points throughout the quarter for student progress. A teaching assistant was available for about 10 scheduled hours per week. The flexibility of scheduling was highly prized by students taking the course.

4.8.2 Student Proof Behavior

Because of the ability to store and retrieve data about student usage, a large number of analyses were able to be run about the behavior of students using the EXCHECK system and in particular their use of the interactive theorem proving facilities. Table 7 lists some of the most

---

[19]See [50] and [128] pp. 791–816.

Table 7: Commands in the Set Theory Course (partial)

Command	Description	Frequency
THEOREM	A previously proven theorem is applied to steps in the current proof.	2,797
CP	Conditional proof: make an assumption in order to prove an implication.	1,518
DEFINITION	A previously stated definition is applied to the current proof.	1,496
ASSUME	Similar to CP.	1,178
VERIFY	Calls the theorem prover to prove a "trivial" step.	1,092
ESTABLISH	Calls a natural-deduction theorem prover to try a series of simple heuristics in an interaction with the student.	1,067
REPLACE	Replace an equivalent expression into a specific step.	879
HYPOTHESIS	Similar to CP and ASSUME.	808
IMPLIES	Uses the theorem prover to show that a current step implies a new step.	745
UG	Universal generalization—logical principal allowing generalization.	638

frequently used commands to the proof checker. [There were a total of 17,509 instances of using any command in this sample; a number of less-frequently used commands have not been included.]

Additional analysis includes the distribution of proofs done by each student, the distribution of the length of proofs, and transitional probabilities for sequences of commands in proofs.

4.9   Other Applications of the EXCHECK System

While most notably used for the set theory course, EXCHECK was used for several other courses. The largest and most important was Introduction to Logic; other courses included Social Decision Theory and an experimental course in Gödel's incompleteness theorem.

4.9.1 Introduction to Logic

The introductory course in logic was taught by computer every quarter from Spring 1972 until 1989.[20] Beginning in 1974, the EXCHECK system was used as the basis for the course delivery. There were teaching assistants for the course but no instructor, although Suppes was the instructor of record and monitored the operation.

The version of EXCHECK for logic contained many of the same commands as set theory, but configured for logic. EXCHECK had a declarative system of configuring the language, display, and the commands for each different theory and course.

Figures 37 and 38 display proofs by two different students of a theorem about conditional probability. Both proofs use the same three facts: the definition of conditional probability (used twice in both proofs); the symmetric property of set intersection (obtained using the BOOLE command in both cases); and law of division over addition.

The execution of the two proofs by the two students differs considerably, resulting in the differences in lengths. Student 509 uses the REPLACE command and several rules of sentential logic, while student 1427 uses the more powerful VERIFY and TEQ commands. Thus, student 1427 has created a proof that is not only shorter, but also highlights the essential elements in the proof.[21]

Logic Curriculum

There were 29 separate lessons in the course, plus additional lessons in Boolean algebra, qualitative probability theory, and social choice theory. The work in probability theory, in particular, required considerable effort on the part of the students. These additional lessons were optional and allowed the students to decide what grade they wanted and then do enough to earn that grade.

Enrollment

There were typically about 200 students enrolled per year throughout the three quarters, from 169 in 1972–73 to 249 in 1979–1980. Enrollment was limited and would likely have been more if the computing facilities had been available to support more students.

Evaluation by Students

By the 1970s, Stanford had a student evaluation process, and the logic course (Philosophy 57/157) was evaluated. In spring of 1980, 25 out of 97 students returned their forms. Ratings were generally positive with the highest scores for content and organization and the lowest for

---

[20] This was when the PDP-10 was decommissioned and sold for scrap.

[21] See [128] pp. 210–211.

```
assume      (1)   P(A) > 0
assume      (2)   P(B) > 0
1,2 fc      (3)   P(A) > 0 and P(B) > 0
Df. 2       (4)   P(A!B) = P(B^A)/P(B)
Th. 0.3
            (5)   If P(A) > 0 & P(B) > 0
                  then P(A) * [P(B^A)/P(A)]/P(B) = P(B^A)/P(B)
Df. 2       (6)   P(B!A) = P(A^B)/P(A)
6 boole
            (7)   P(A^B)/P(A) = P(B!A)
boole       (8)   A^B = B^A
7,8 replace
            (9)   P(B^A)/P(A) = P(B!A)
3,5 aa      (10)  P(A) * [P(B^A)/P(A)]/P(B) = P(B^A)/P(B)
Ax. 0.5
            (11)  P(A) * [P(B^A)/P(A)]/P(B) = [P(B^A)/P(A)]/P(B) * P(A)
10,11 replace
            (12)  [[P(B^A)/P(A)]/P(B)] * P(A) = P(B^A)/P(B)
12,9 replace
            (13)  [P(B!A)/P(B)] * P(A) = P(B^A)/P(B)
Ax. 0.5
            (14)  [P(B!A)/P(B)] * P(A) = P(A) * P(B!A)/P(B)
13,14 replace
            (15)  P(A) * P(B!A)/P(B) = P(B^A)/P(B)
15 boole
            (16)  P(B^A)/P(B) = P(A) * P(B!A)/P(B)
4 boole
            (17)  P(B^A)/P(B) = P(A!B)
16,17 replace
            (18)  P(A!B) = P(A) * P(B!A)/P(B)
3,18 cp
            (19)  If P(A) > 0 & P(B) > 0 then P(A!B) = P(A) * P(B!A)/P(B)
```

FIGURE 37: Proof of Theorem 7 by Student 509

```
hyp         (1)   P(A) > 0 and P(B) > 0
Df. 2       (2)   P(A!B) = P(B^A)/P(B)
1,2 verify Using:  Th. 0.3
            (3)   P(A!B) = P(A) * [P(B^A)/P(A)]/P(B)
boole       (4)   B^A = A^B
3,4 teq
            (5)   P(A!B) = P(A) * [P(A^B)/P(A)]/P(B)
5 verify Using:   Df. 2
            (6)   P(A!B) = P(A) * P(B!A)/P(B)
```

FIGURE 38: Proof of Theorem 7 by Student 1427

some of the methods of presentation. Students thought the assessment process was fair. By design, grades were assigned based on the amount of work completed, so students could set their own goals.

The students thought that the best feature of the course was the freedom to do the work whenever they pleased. Improvements suggested were largely technical: a better room, fewer computer failures (mostly hardware), and more terminals.

The teaching assistants were generally well thought of, but there were differences of opinions even about the same teaching assistant.

Analysis of Student Data

Because of the number of years the course was offered by computer and the relatively large number of students, there was a great deal of data to analyze. The analysis was similar to that done for the set theory course. Areas considered were time and number of proofs per student, command usage, length of proofs, and sequencing of commands. In the probability section, the use of the Boole command was important, since Boolean algebra underlies the notion of an event.

As was customary for all axiomatic mathematics courses Suppes worked on including the EXCHECK courses, an important feature is that there was no one "correct" answer to any proof exercise. There are different proofs with different properties that are still correct. The fact that such individual differences can be dealt with by the computer in this domain is a strength that Suppes always emphasized. In the case of EXCHECK, the differences were even more profound between different student proofs.

4.9.2 Social Decision Theory

The *Social Decision Course* taught the essence of the famous theorem of Kenneth Arrow on social decision theory.[22] Arrow considers the mathematics of aggregating the preferences of a number of individuals to form a "social decision" for the society as a whole; this is similar to a voting situation. Using a set of seemingly intuitive constraints on the process, Arrow shows that there is no solution that follows all of those constraints. This is a surprising result, and there have been many approaches taken to find a solution or to understand how this might effect voting and econometric situations.

In the 1970s there were two versions of a course on social decision theory that used EXCHECK. They were called SCT and SDT. The

---

[22]See Wikipedia "Kenneth Arrow" [190] for details about Arrow, and see "Social choice and individual values" [223] for details about his theorem.

SCT course taught an elegant version of this result by Sen. The first course, SDT, had stayed closer to Arrow's original formulation.[23]

The theorem itself is an exercise in the logic of relations and hence is easily representable in elementary set theory. The course used the extensive ability of EXCHECK to define the language of the proofs for a given theory to make them more natural.

4.9.3 Gödel's Incompleteness Theorems

Graduate student Wilfried Sieg developed a course on Gödel's incompleteness theorems to be used in Philosophy 167, a course on proof theory. Students Ingrid Lindstrom and Sten Lindstrom took over after Sieg's departure. The course used the standard facilities of other axiomatic courses including the VOCAL language and the EXCHECK proof checker. See [128] pp. 183–191.

The program was something of an experiment, in which it was discovered that the metamathematical character of the Gödel results were too complex to be formulated intuitively in the EXCHECK system.

Sieg, who is now a professor of philosophy at Carnegie-Mellon University, did not give up. He was able to obtain mechanical proofs within Zermelo-Fraenkel set theory by using a different method than the customary arithmetization of proof syntax. Sieg's work on teaching logic is also discussed on page 298.

4.10 Significance of the Work on Interactive Proof Checking

In [128] pp. 165–182, Suppes comments on the value and limitations of interactive proof-checking.

Suppes notes that the goal was to develop informal proofs that "were not, from the standpoint of the user, put into explicit logical form" (p. 165) but were nevertheless checked for correctness. He often mentioned the goal of "informal rigor" and noted that mathematicians in conversation with each other would outline their proofs by hitting on the high points only, calling some parts "trivial" and calling attention to other parts with something like "this is the key step." It was also common to state the general proof structure by referencing a general technique or comparing the proof to another known result.

The EXCHECK system fell far short of what is pedagogically needed for a serious treatment of normal mathematical discourse. He pointed out a number of ways in which he hoped future progress could be made.

[23]The course was developed by graduate student Benjamin Cohen; see [128] pp. 227–236. Sen's new proof of Arrow's theorem can be found in [123].

4.10.1 Pedagogical Aspects

Suppes notes that a number of mathematicians have criticized the preparation of students in writing rigorous proofs. He hoped that "over the next several decades we should be able to develop for elementary courses at the level of axiomatic set theory interactive theorem provers" that will fit each content domain area "so that the proofs have exactly the facilities required" ([128] p. 169).

Suppes did not believe in the "unity of science" or mathematics, and understood that different areas of mathematics would have different languages and different standards for informal mathematical expression. In [129] p. 121 he noted:

> My daughter Patricia has a PhD in neurophysiology, and to improve my understanding of what she does she gave me a subscription to what is supposed to be an expository journal.... After several efforts at reading this journal, I have reached the conclusion that the exposition is only for those in nearby disciplines.

A further challenge was to organize such interactive theorem provers to assist the students in thinking about how to approach the proof. "The good interactive theorem prover can contain hints and suggestions for the individual student" ([128] p. 170). Details about the student in question should be taken into account by the program in constructing hints.

4.10.2 Psychological Aspects

Suppes proposes that we think of proofs as a conversation, where a conversation has "the students providing all of the essential thinking but with the instructor playing the role of organizer" ([128] p. 171). He argues that the EXCHECK theorem prover already has some of these abilities while admitting that it is primitive.

The computer tutor should be helpful—but not too helpful—and should "[provide] a framework for thinking about the proof" (p. 171). The tutor will have to have a sense of which details are trivial, at this point in the student's learning process, while helping the student to appreciate the key points of the proof at hand.

Suppes claims that something like this conversation is happening in the EXCHECK system. But it is clear that a much greater degree of informality and insight into the situation of the student is going to be needed to have a true conversation rather than just a scripted interaction. Some examples of the kinds of questions a tutor might ask follow:[24]

---

[24]See [128] p. 176.

"Why not try beginning with the hypothesis of the theorem and see what you can do with it?"

"Do you see any previous theorem that would be really helpful in trying to prove this theorem?"

"Try a special case for the dimension two. It may be misleading but it should be suggestive."

Of course, prompting questions of this kind should not simply be stored with the theorem to be proven as "canned hints," but should be dynamically generated.

One suggestion is to characterize what we expect the student to remember about a particular proof. Suppes suggests that humans remember a kind of outline, associating proofs to concepts and to each other, but our memory doesn't have all of the messy details, which we will need to regenerate if we later need the proof.

> Thus, if somebody asks me to prove the Schroeder-Bernstein theorem, the first non-trivial theorem in the course in axiomatic set theory, I find I do not carry the details of the proof in my mind but I do have some general ideas of the function one constructs, mapping one set into the other to prove the theorem. ... There is a lot of routine work to a new proof but what is crucial is one or two key ideas. ([128] p. 177)

He proposes that a next step in developing interactive theorem provers for education is to develop a psychological theory of proofs. He notes that the place to start with this is in elementary courses, which require only a preliminary psychological theory.

4.10.3 Technological Aspects of Productivity

At this stage, Suppes held an underlying view that technology could improve the productivity of teaching courses that are not, in fact, in very high demand but nevertheless should continue to be taught for a number of reasons. The idea is that by putting such courses into a mechanically delivered format, they can be taught over a long period of time and to a geographically broad audience, with their developmental costs eventually amortized.

In particular, courses like set theory and social decision theory do not attract large audiences, but their mechanization could make them more feasible. Of particular interest in the case of axiomatic mathematics is that of learning how to prove theorems. By having the proofs developed on an interactive computer system, each student can in principal benefit from having interaction with an "expert."

4.11 Follow-up Work in Teaching Mathematical Proofs via the Computer

Since the 1970s, many mathematical tools with uses in education have appeared, as have some applications of computers to proving theorems. Some are mentioned below. There has, however, been little new work on teaching axiomatic mathematics using computers.

4.11.1 Mathematical Tools Used in Education

Mathematica[25] is a very powerful system that does symbolic manipulations, algebra, and calculus, and includes a LISP-like programming language. Another symbolic manipulation tool, Maxima,[26] derived from the Macsyma[27] system developed at MIT in the 1960s and 70s, is used in education.

4.11.2 New Proofs "Discovered" by Computer

There have also been mathematical proofs that have had a portion of the proof done by a computer program. The most famous example is the *four-color theorem*, which states that four is the largest number of "colors" that are needed to color a map on a sphere such that no two adjacent "countries" have the same color. The conjecture has a long history, which was finally solved in 1976.[28]

The theorem was proven by a combination of man-machine activities. In a series of steps over time, mathematicians showed that if there was a counterexample, it would have to appear in one of a finite list of maps, specifically 1,936 identified maps. The proof required over 1,000 hours of compute time on a supercomputer. The overall structure of the proof was a proof by cases, where mathematicians supplied the cases analytically and the computer "proved" each one of the cases.

The resulting proof has proven controversial. Many mathematicians were skeptical, and no one seems to find the proof satisfying. It seems to fail to provide any insight into the original problem.[29] Suppes believed that this proof was completely acceptable, noting that many hand-checked proofs are structured by a reduction to a finite number of cases, sometimes dozens. The number of cases is certainly large, necessitating a computerized approach, in order to get the result. As a practical matter, Suppes believed that the computer would be a more accurate checker than human checkers, and certainly faster and cheaper.

---

[25] See Wikipedia "Wolfram Mathematica" [232].
[26] See Wikipedia "Maxima (software)" [197].
[27] See Wikipedia "Macsyma" [196]
[28] See Wikipedia "Four color theorem" [183] for details and references.
[29] See the philosophical discussion in [159].

4.11.3 Recent Proof Checkers

There are some new proof checkers, one of which is Mizar.[30] Mizar is used by specialists and claims to have the largest stored collection of formal proofs. Mizar is not, however, based on the idea of informal, natural proofs, and would probably not be suitable for direct educational applications at the undergraduate level.

4.11.4 Proof Checkers and Current Mathematical Trends

Suppes had predicted that there would be more educational applications of interactive theorem proving similar to the EXCHECK courses. This has not proven to be the case.

Recently, Suppes reflected on the reasons for this.[31] Suppes came to believe that the discipline of mathematics might be seeing less value in the skill of proving theorems. He noted that proofs today of new results are often so complicated that only a few specialists can understand them.

In addition, the traditional role that proofs previously played in subjects like geometry have been minimized in current courses, with high-school courses and standards emphasizing more descriptive and computational topics rather than understanding the details of constructing proofs. Euclidean geometry, for example, has traditionally been taught by having students construct proofs directly from the axioms.

Perhaps more importantly, the recent explosion in online education has not included much work on what was referred to as "intelligent tutoring" in the 1970s. Courses created in most frameworks (such as those provided by Blackboard and Coursera) may contain a lot of video and graphics, some expositional text and questions, but are lacking any intelligent engine that would do something like check a student's steps in an argument. Suppes believed that these things are still coming but will take more time.

4.12 Research in Computer-Generated Speech

The use of speech in CAI, and the fundamental importance of audio in learning, were early interests of Suppes and Atkinson during the 1960s and were to remain important at CCC. Most of the earlier work had been directed by Atkinson for use in reading for the elementary grades.[32] In addition, Van Campen had used audio for the university-level Russian course.[33]

---

[30]See Wikipedia "Mizar system" [200] and http://mizar.uwb.edu.pl/.
[31]Private communication, 2014.
[32]See [3], [39], and [6]
[33]See [128] pp. 665–674.

Suppes's volume *University-level Computer-Assisted Instruction at Stanford: 1968–1980* [128] contains a large number of technical papers on audio developments as well as discussions about uses in the audio-based courses, on pp. 301–600. The exposition here focuses on usage by students.

The specific goals of the audio research in the 1970s follow.

1. Use audio in courses other than the obvious examples of reading and languages, and develop models for audio use as a mode of communication connected to visual communication.
2. Store a lot of audio inexpensively: At this time, PCM ("pulse-code modulation") was available but the storage requirements were about 64,000 bits per second, an excessive amount of bandwidth in the 1970s.[34]
3. Random-access playback: Analog tape-recording methods, such as those used at Stanford in the 1960s, were high quality but random access had never been very successful with tape.
4. Intelligibility to students: Students had to be able to understand the speech. In a reading or language course, in particular, intelligibility becomes difficult, and words without context can easily be confused. The entire range of phonemes and other speech features had to be handled.
5. Generation of dynamic speech: For many educational purposes, sentences needed to be generated "on the fly" from individual words and phrases. The system had to be able to make the generated sentence or paragraph flow naturally.
6. Demonstration of effectiveness: The system had to be embedded within actual courses that would stress the design and test how well it worked.
7. Economy: The system had to be economical enough to be used in practice, at least after some additional development.

The overall research plan to meet these goals was as follows:

1. Select a basic speech technology and algorithms and build it.
2. Build the software tools to allow the speech to be integrated into courseware.
3. Develop courses that would use speech in a sophisticated manner.
4. Test the quality and intelligibility of the speech.
5. Test student acceptance of the speech in the context of the courses.
6. Consider next steps.

The following sections detail the steps in the research plan.

---

[34]Sanders, private communication.

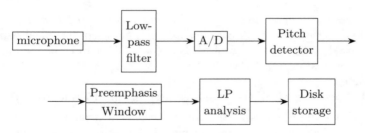

FIGURE 39: Basic Workflow of the MISS Machine

4.12.1 LPC Encoding and the MISS Machine

Gerard Benbassat came to Stanford from France to work on speech in the early 1970s. He was working on applications of linear-predictive encoding (LPC) to speech synthesis. After some successful tests, he and Sil Sanders designed and built the Microprogrammed Intoned Speech Synthesizer (MISS) machine. It used LPC as a method of encoding and "compressing" speech. The whole effort took about five years. See [128] Part II pp. 301–600 for an overall description of the MISS machine.

The MISS machine was capable of both playing back recorded sounds (sometimes these were lengthy and therefore called "long sounds") and also capable of assembling individual words and phrases into sentences that sounded reasonable. Prosodic adjustment was made by modifying the fundamental frequency contour of a sound, the duration, and the amplitude of the words. For example, a question might end with an increase of the pitch of the last word of a sentence.[35]

The basic workflow of processing and saving a sound for later playback by the MISS machine is shown in Figure 39 above.[36] In the process flow, the speech is spoken into a microphone, which applies a low-pass filter and then an analog-to-digital (A/D) converter. The resulting data is passed through a pitch detector and pre-emphasis window, and then the LP analysis is performed. This results in a set of parameters that takes much less space to store than the original speech. In practice, the sounds were recorded using PCM storage and then processed and saved for later. This process is described in more detail in [128] pp. 308–310.

On playback for the student, the sound is generated by the process flow shown in Figure 40 below.[37] The compressed sound files are first read into the "System memory." The data is then fed into the "humming

---

[35]*Prosody* refers to the adjustments that speakers make to words when they are built into a sentence. The adjustments include the pitch, speed, and contour of the words in the utterance. See Wikipedia "Prosody (linguistics)" [212].

[36]See [128] p. 309.

[37]See [128] p. 310.

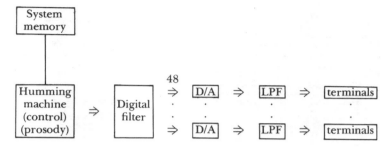

FIGURE 40: Hardware Diagram of the MISS Machine

machine" that modifies the prosody in real time, then fed into a digital filter, a digital-to-analog converter (D/A), a low-pass filter (LPF), and finally to the headphones associated with a student's terminal. There were 48 parallel outputs, allowing 48 students to use the MISS machine at the same time. See [128] pp. 310–325 for details.[38]

The sound files created during intake were stored on the TENEX system's hard disks and read as needed, together with the instructions for concatenation of the sounds. Some modifications had been made to the TENEX operating system on the PDP-10 in order to make this happen in real time so that the MISS machine could play the sounds in real time without pauses and synchronized to the display on the student's terminal.

The MISS machine could take command strings that would tell it how to modify a given word or phrase. These command strings were created from the sentence that was to be spoken, and sometimes were also hand-coded. A sample command string is:

```
[SILENCE 250][FILL 1.1 103 .75 .7 1024] EXPERIMENTATION
```

This command string speaks the word "experimentation" but modifies it as it goes. The SILENCE waits for 250 (ms); FILL specifies the contour parameters (1.1 and 103), the duration fraction (.75), the amplitude fraction (.7), and how to handle the end (1024). See [128] p. 326 for more details.

Figure 41 shows the "Lexical" contour if no prosody changes had occurred, and the "Artificial" contour after prosody features were applied based on the above command for speaking the word *experimentation*. The x-axis is time, and the y-axis is hertz (frequency).

---

[38] The "system memory" was actually the memory of the mainframe PDP-10/TENEX system that IMSSS was using for this project.

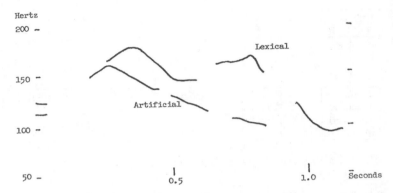

FIGURE 41: Lexical and Artificial F0 Contours for the Word *experimentation*

4.12.2 Courses Using MISS

Audio generated by the MISS machine was used in three courses in axiomatic mathematics (*Introduction to Logic, Set Theory,* and *Proof Theory*); *Armenian,* which used both English and Armenian; *Old Church Slavonic,* which used only English audio; and *Arabic,* which was only concerned with Arabic verbs.

To support these courses, the MISS machine contained a number of lexicons with words and phrases for each course. It could access these lexicons via a hash table, which then allowed the retrieval of the associated sound coefficients from which the sound could be recreated and modified. By the end of the project, there were about 19,000 English words, 13,000 logic words and phrases, 1,000 morphemes, and 10,000 Armenian words stored in the lexicons.

4.12.3 Software Tools for Audio Processing and Courseware Authoring

The MISS machine required extensive software tools. Some of them processed the sounds and constructed the lexicons into files on the TENEX system. Some of them parsed English strings to create MISS commands and were used in the creation of the curriculum. Similar tools were later written in C at CCC for use with the audio development there in the 1980s.

The curriculum for the MISS machine courses were written in the VOCAL language (Voice Oriented Curriculum Author Language) [50] designed by Robert Smith and implemented by John Prebus, with contributions from several authors. VOCAL contained commands in the following categories:

- "Normal" authoring language commands such as multiple choice, fill in the blank, and branching and browsing for a lesson-style course.

- Commands to invoke the interactive theorem provers used in the axiomatic mathematics courses.

- Screen display commands that controlled the display modes and positioning. The terminals used only had text and text effects including moving text dynamically, but multiple fonts and character sets were supported.

- Audio commands. These included synchronizing display on the screen with the audio, and commands that allowed the student to replay, slow down, or toggle the use of the audio.

When the author requested a sentence to be spoken, the sentence was parsed by a program that inserted the prosodic commands. The course author could also manipulate these strings to some extent to improve the speech.

The style of the curriculum written with VOCAL was an attempt to use two channels of communication at the same time, one on the screen, the other spoken. Often this meant that the audio would explain, comment on, or point to an important feature of the content on the screen.

An additional feature of the set theory course allowed dynamically-created student proofs to be read and explained in a manner that further summarized the proof from what was on the screen. To do this, the generator inserted the prosodic markings into parts of the proof by an algorithm developed by the course programmers. The normal parsing of text was therefore not used since the algorithm generated the prosodic commands.

Versions of VOCAL were used at Stanford into the 1990s for courseware authoring.

4.12.4   Quality and Intelligibility of the MISS Speech

MISS was not expected to sound "natural" and in fact was rather robotic.[39] It was, however, required that it be intelligible. Sanders tested intelligibility by presenting the same sounds to four different groups of 12 first-graders from a local school (48 in total). Each group was presented with the same sounds (letters and words) using four different speech technologies, as follows:

- MISS: the MISS machine from Stanford

---

[39]The team members sometimes compared it to the computer in the movie *Colossus: The Forbin Project*; see [26].

- MIT: synthesis algorithms as developed by John Allen and Dennis Klatt of MIT[40]
- Votrax: a machine for generating text-to-speech that was considered state-of-the-art for a commercial product in the 1970s[41]
- Control: the original PCM sounds presented on an analog tape machine

The analysis also dealt in detail with problematic sounds such as initial consonants (for example, "clock" versus "flock") and final consonant sounds ("let" versus "leg").

The results of the intelligibility tests of both letters and words showed that the control group was the best of the systems. They did, however, show that

> ...some form of computer-generated speech is adequate for use in computer-assisted instruction in initial reading. The scores of the LPC [i.e., the MISS machine] and the MIT systems, which were generally above 90% correct on both the letter and word experiments, are strong evidence of the adequacy of these systems. The scores of the Votrax, generally between 80% and 90%, are somewhat less impressive. ... At the time of this study, such systems [as LPC and MIT] are still too expensive.... ([128] p. 396)

4.12.5 Student Acceptance of the Audio

Student acceptance of the audio was tested by allowing students to set their own preferences about how audio was used in the *Logic Course*. These preferences were generally stated at the beginning of each computer session. The hypothesis was that individual students would have different preferences, but the percentages and reasons were initially unknown. Students were given a questionnaire at the end of the course in which they could state the reason for their preferences. See [128] pp. 399–430.

There were two audio modes: prosody mode, in which the sentences were made by concatenating sounds with prosodic manipulations, and "long sound" mode, in which longer phrases and sentences were used wherever possible. Students were able to select whether they wanted audio or display only, and if they wanted audio, which audio mode they wanted.

Logic was taught for many years at Stanford using the computer, so there were opportunities to change the experiments and to collect a lot of data.

---

[40]See [2] and [60].
[41]See Wikipedia "Votrax" [231].

Figure 42 shows the percentage (on the y-axis) of student logins using audio for each lesson (on the x-axis), averaged over all quarters of the experiment. The graph shows that students seem to trail off in their interest in using audio. The content, however, is structured in such a way that this might be expected.

- There were fewer lessons covered toward the end of the course.
- The course structure "has a large amount of discursive material early in the course but leans toward derivations in the later lessons" ([128] pp. 405–407).

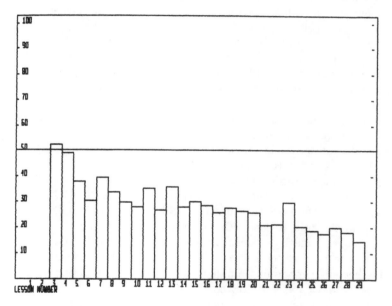

FIGURE 42: Percentage of Student Logins to Audio by Lesson

In the questionnaire given at the end, students were asked the reasons for their preference in presentation mode. Clearly, there was no universal preference, and some students preferred audio, others not.

Here is a summary of the conclusions:

1. Most students eventually selected a single presentation mode after a period of time experimenting.
2. A few students preferred prosody mode over long sounds.
3. A long period of "forced exposure" to audio seemed to increase the probability that students would select audio when they had "free choice."

4. Lighter headphones seemed to increase the use of audio by the students.

5. The most significant result is that, given a choice, students would form their own individual preferences. This suggests that such choices should be built into courses to accommodate individual differences in preference.

4.12.6   Conclusions: Looking Back at the Audio Research

A striking feature of the research is the great technical efforts that had to be made in order to make acceptable audio available in computerized courseware. The MISS machine was as large as a small refrigerator, and used the main disk storage of the TENEX system to store its sound parameter files and metadata.

Using LPC for speech storage was useful for two reasons: storage space was expensive, and LPC did a good job of saving space; and LPC allowed prosodic manipulations so that sentences could be constructed dynamically.

Of course, the MISS machine was a research project, and it was itself too expensive to be used for cost-effective instructional delivery. The NSF did fund a second machine called the MiniMISS machine in the late 1970s as a step towards commercialization.

Within a few years, however, Sil Sanders and Carolyn Gramlich were able to create similar but far less expensive systems at CCC. Two related devices, the DSS and later the CSS, were commercially very successful in the mid to late '80s in delivering speech as a part of CAI in reading and math courses. In the early '90s, the LPC-based systems gave way to far cheaper audio cards and compression schemes that have today become very common indeed, extending to cell phones and every manner of device at very low costs. See Chapter 5.

The research on computer generation of dynamic speech with prosodic features was relevant to conversation and dialogue in the instructional process. The techniques of speech synthesis have led to speech that is not only intelligent and natural, but even pleasant to listen to. See Wikipedia "Speech synthesis" [224] for an overview of the history and current state of speech synthesis.

While many of the technical issues about speech have been completely superseded, there remain some questions that have not been fully resolved. One of these is how speech should be employed in an on-line course to enhance learning.

Courses that present obvious opportunities for using speech include language learning, language arts, and reading. These have flourished, although much of the speech today is "canned" speech, possibly with video, and lacking dynamic qualities. The Rosetta Stone language learning courses are an example of high-quality courses employing speech.[42]

Cell phones including the Apple iPhone now use dynamically generated speech for a personal assistant named "Siri."[43] Siri was originally developed at SRI International with funding from DARPA.

The Stanford courses using the MISS machine did include language courses for Old Church Slavonic and Armenian. However, the main courses using the MISS machine's innovations taught logic and set theory to Stanford students, which were not "obvious" applications of audio.

Yet important questions were raised, questions which largely remain. These courses developed a model of having audio be a second channel of communication, with the audio providing a summary or emphasis to content on the screen during the lecture portions. To assess and explain student proofs, course authors created review procedures that summarized the proof, with dynamically generated audio that read through the important parts of a proof by way of emphasis and explication.

This is a technique that could be used universally in all online instructional materials in any subject, opening audio to a broad array of uses, most of which are apparently not being pursued today in current online projects. There are surely many video lectures with audio as a ubiquitous feature of modern computerized courseware, but few examples of dynamically generated audio explicating a student's work.

Finally, the audio research introduced the idea that different modalities and combinations of media in learning might appeal to different students. While a majority of students in the *Logic* course preferred display only, it was far from unanimous, with many students believing that audio helped them learn. While it is more expensive to create such student-driven options in a course, it may well be worthwhile and should be pursued.

4.13   Research in Natural-Language Processing

Motivation for research in natural-language processing came from a number of perspectives. Suppes was interested in the logical issues concerning meaning, and psychological issues concerning dialogue and communication, and also wanted to build practical instructional systems that would engage students in conversation. Natural language fit right into the other main research areas of the 1970s work at IMSSS.

---

[42]See http://www.rosettastone.com/.
[43]See Wikipedia "Siri" [222] for details.

4.13.1 Probabilistic Context-free Grammars and Set-theoretical Semantics

Suppes believed that the use of context-free grammars (CFGs) was an appropriate formalism for describing the syntax of natural languages. CFGs were practical for computing purposes and also could express a reasonable amount of syntactic information. In addition, by affixing probabilities to the rules, one could model observed behavior and learning of the language over time. Suppes investigated issues concerned with associating set-theoretical operations to context-free grammars in order to provide a semantics for the rules. Finally, he was interested in using such techniques in CAI. See [124] for a discussion of probabilistic grammars, [125] for the semantics of context-free languages, and [127] for a theory of the congruence of meaning.

4.13.2 Syntax of Reading Textbooks

Working with Suppes, Betsy Macken Gammon examined the language in two basal reading series (Ginn and Scott Foresman). This included over 7,000 utterances. She wrote several probabilistic grammars to cover portions of this corpus and developed some statistical models testing the goodness of fit.

4.13.3 Syntax and Semantics of Children's Language

Also working with Suppes, Robert Smith curated a corpus of conversations of a 32-month old girl known as "Erica." The corpus comprised more than 9,000 child utterances. The conversations were coded into computer files and corrected. The purpose of this project was to study children's language as a preparation to building interactive dialogues into programs. See [101] for Smith's PhD thesis.

Smith wrote a set of programs for analyzing such psycholinguistic corpora, including building frequency lists, concordances, and parsing with various syntactic and semantic options. Critical steps were parsing the sentences using a probabilistic CFG, generating frequency distributions, and most importantly generating the meaning as a set-theoretical statement by using semantic rules associated with the CFG rules. There were about 120 rules in the grammar.

The programs were used for the next several years with other similar projects.

4.13.4 Language of Elementary Mathematics Textbooks

Nancy Smith and Freeman Rawson undertook to build the foundation of a question-answering system using the accumulated techniques. They analyzed the language of elementary mathematics from Suppes's *Sets and Numbers* textbook series. Smith built the syntactic portion of the study, and Rawson built the semantics. See [100] and [91].

Rawson and Robert Smith felt that the set-theoretical approach required huge structures of sets in order to actually work, and hence questioned the elegant set-theoretic model proposed by Suppes. Instead, they proposed using encoding methods and multi-processing techniques to process the surface structure syntax in a way that allowed reasonable computations of the semantics. This is described in [102]. They envisioned a semantic engine that would contain both a symbolic reduction system and a database of mathematical facts.

4.13.5 Probabilistic Models of Language Acquisition by a Child

The culmination of these efforts in natural-language study involved the language of a child learning French in collaboration with Madeleine Leveille of the Laboratoire de Psychologie Expérimentale et Comparée associé au Centre Nation de la Recherche Scientifique in Paris, France. Robert Smith of Stanford worked with Leveille, all under the direction of Patrick Suppes. See [155] for details of the first portion of the study, and [149] for the work concerning developmental models. This research was funded by the Office of Naval Research.

Leveille had 33 conversations with a French child "Philippe" starting when he was 25 months old and ending when he was 40 months old. This constituted more utterances (about 15,000) than previous efforts. More importantly, the 33 conversations spread out over a longer period of time, allowing great changes to occur in Philippe's speech.

The team wrote a grammar with 350 context-free rules. The probabilistic fits and semantic studies were conducted similarly to the earlier Erica corpus. Given the longitudinal nature of the data, it was decided that in the second half of the study, the team would focus on the developmental aspects of the syntax of Philippe's language.

The basic idea was that the grammar would contain rules to parse the language at any stage of the 33 conversations. However, as time progressed and Philippe's use of language became more sophisticated, the probabilities associated with the CFG rules would likewise change.

Suppes suggested that this was an opportunity to examine two competing ideas for how children learn: by stages, in which things would tend to "jump" rather quickly from one state to another, or by increments, in which a smoother change would appear throughout the longitudinal data. Both stage and incremental models were therefore examined.

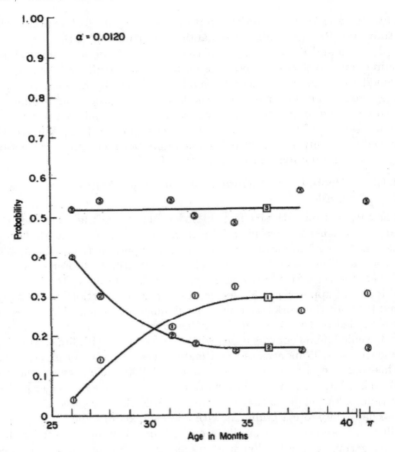

FIGURE 43: Incremental Model for Rules in the Highest Group

Figure 43 shows the incremental model for one of about 40 rule classes. The abscissa shows Philippe's age (in months), and the ordinate shows the probability. For each rule-subgroup of the rule class in the grammar, the encircled numbers show the observed data points. The curves, labeled with corresponding numbers in square boxes, show the theoretical curves predicted by the incremental model. The asymptotic value of the parameters is shown on the far right.

The conclusion was that systematic developmental trends for the use of individual grammatical rules could easily be identified by the incremental model, which might therefore also give a first-approximation probabilistic model.

4.14 Language Instruction: Old Church Slavonic, Armenian, French, and German

4.14.1 Old Church Slavonic

Professor Joseph Van Campen worked for some years on Russian CAI. The first experiment—and one of the most successful experiments in CAI in the opinion of Patrick Suppes—was done in the 1960s; see 2.10 for details.

Van Campen was interested in the idea that teaching low-volume courses via computer would ultimately improve the productivity of a faculty member, after the costs of development were amortized. Suppes was also interested in this concept; see [154] and [128] pp. 665–674 for details.

Van Campen chose *Old Church Slavonic* (OCS) as his test case. This course typically has very small enrollments, but it is a necessary course for graduate students in Russian as a matter of the general knowledge of such students. OCS became the canonical example for this idea of productivity.

In the spring of the 1972–73 academic year, Van Campen offered OCS on the computer. Five graduate students took the course, which was taught on IMLAC display terminals outfitted with Cyrillic keyboards and programmed to display Cyrillic as well as Roman character sets. Audio used the new MISS sounds, which reduced the logistical complexities of offering the course. The course consisted of 24 lessons. There was some classroom activity as well as the use of the CAI lab.

All students passed, with grades of one A$^-$, three B$^+$s, and one B$^-$.

On the final exam, CAI students did as well as previous non-CAI delivery on understanding forms in context. CAI students did not do very well on the parts of the exam relating to generating OCS or handling forms out of context. This kind of analysis was not included in the course and surely should have been.

This represented a marked change from the spectacular results of the CAI Russian course in previous years.

Van Campen concluded that the course needed a lot of work. The number of CAI lessons should be increased, and more attention paid to the skills that had presented some problems.

In terms of productivity, the instructor time was reduced from 30 hours to 8. Van Campen felt that he could reduce this more by increasing the number of lessons, and that "within these limits, the CAI course in OCS can be considered as successful as the traditionally taught one" ([128] p. 673).

It should be noted that the suggested changes were never made and the OCS course was not taught again using CAI.

4.14.2 Russian Literacy Course

With the technical and pedagogical assistance of Van Campen, Richard Schupbach wrote a CAI course in the History of the Russian Language. See [128] pp. 657–664. This is probably the most "inappropriate" course Suppes's team ever attempted to computerize; Schupbach was very critical of the limitations of the technology and extremely thoughtful in his appraisal of the difficulties. It is therefore an interesting "data point," as Suppes would say. The history of the Russian language requires examples of Russian, Old Russian, and Old Church Slavonic and discussions of their similarities and differences. The course describes the kinds of changes that languages undergo through time in general, and in Russian in particular. It is a curriculum of concepts and ideas more than of systematic drill.

After programming 11 lessons—slowly and painfully, Schupbach recounts—the course was taught using CAI for the first time in the spring quarter of 1973 with 11 lessons available. All 20 planned lessons were available by the winter quarter of 1974.

The Model 35 Teletypes with Cyrillic characters and keyboards were brought back for the course. They were clunky and noisy, and in some ways this was more objectionable than it had been with Russian drills. For one reason, the speed was so slow (10 characters per second) that Schupbach found he could only display six lines of text before he inserted a question, in order to keep the student's attention, and discursive text was an important element of the course. This required that the content be divided somewhat unnaturally. Discussion of the specific evolutionary changes in Old Russian seemed acceptable, but some more general material did not work well.

Schupbach noted that the available history itself has some "factual gaps," and he felt that in a normal classroom "these factors give rise to only minor problems; however, in developing material for CAI, they can be of crucial importance" ([128] p. 659). Professors can smooth things over that become glaring on the stark paper of the Teletype.

Schupbach wondered how carefully the students were reading the material and thinking about it. He observed that "the visual stimulus of the Teletype printout is answered not by a thought, but by a digital response."

The answer processing capabilities of the existing software were very weak, forcing him to rephrase questions so that the students would have to answer unambiguously.

Schupbach thoughtfully allows that "The use of the comparatively slow hardware, while limiting the programming of certain material, requires a clarity and brevity of exposition and a degree of involvement of the student that are not likely to be achieved where their existence is not made imperative by circumstance" ([128] p. 661). This has been a common view by people in many media of expression (including novels, film, etc.) where people find that the constraints of the medium force them to do what they otherwise could not do. But it is a questionable benefit.

How did the students perform? Schupbach said that they performed surprising well, indeed as well as the non-CAI students had performed. This indicates that the approach was not a detriment. The students liked it, and he felt that the CAI version was in many ways more effective than a standard classroom presentation. However, he did not "envision the programming of the entire course and the effective elimination of the instructor" ([128] p. 661).

Update: in 2016, Schupbach recounted his technical frustrations with developing the course. He now realizes that almost all of his objections have been addressed for decades. He did not, however, attempt to computerize other courses personally. He thinks that this particular course would be better taught if a significant portion—but not all—were computerized. He also believes that faculty are generally not interested in reducing their instructional workloads out of a concern that such a practice would reduce the number of faculty positions.

Suppes appreciated both Van Campen's approach and Schupbach's. He loved Van Campen's attitude of resourceful problem-solving and willingness to move on. He also thought that Schupbach's outlook and concerns were very valuable, especially in the longer run, for improving CAI.

4.14.3 Armenian

A team led by Joseph Van Campen and Lawrence Markosian, including Hasmig Seropian and Dikran Karagueuzian, developed a course in Armenian beginning in 1977. The teaching of the Armenian language was considered particularly adaptable to CAI delivery for several reasons. For one thing, the Armenian population in the United States of about three-quarters of a million was very widely distributed throughout the country, with some centers including Fresno, CA, and New York, so organizing local efforts would be very difficult. On the other hand, Armenians in America and throughout the world are keenly interested in their heritage and want the language and culture to be taught, but there is a shortage of qualified instructors. This made it an ideal candidate for Suppes's "productivity" model for CAI development.[44]

---

[44]One indicator of the intense interest in the teaching of the Armenian language is the fact that this project was funded by grants to Stanford from wealthy Armenians.

The course largely used technology being developed at IMSSS. These new innovations resolved a good many of the technical issues that Schupbach had experienced when he developed his course on the history of the Russian language a few years earlier, such as the speed of delivery and the noise of the teletypes; see above.

- Van Campen used his drill-generation technology to assist in creating the course.
- Markosian used the VOCAL language, which he had pioneered in the *Logic* course, for the curriculum and control of the audio and display.
- Audio was generated by the new MISS machine.
- The 38-character Armenian alphabet was programmed using the IM-LAC terminals, and a special keyboard was used for the course.

The design of the drills largely followed Van Campen's experience in creating of the Russian course. Special attention was paid in the course design to a feature of Armenian where two characters are combined together to create a sound in a way that other languages would only use one. Such characters are called "secondary characters."

The *Armenian* course was offered for credit at Stanford through the Special Languages Program. Four Stanford undergraduates finished the course, and their usage data was collected and analyzed. The secondary characters accounted for a large number of observed student errors, especially when the correct answer was phonetically equivalent to the incorrect one.

4.14.4 Grading Grammar Instruction

Improving the analysis of student responses was, and remains, a significant problem for CAI. Many systems end up with hard-coded responses rather than having any general solutions. When the subject being taught is the grammar of a natural language, this is particularly difficult.

David Levine's PhD dissertation created an analysis and grading program for German grammar.[45] Levine says:

> Grading is based on built-in grammatical knowledge and general algorithms, augmented by a structural description of the expected response. ... In addition, the analyzer attempts to infer the mislearned rules underlying observed wrong answers. ([128] p. 675)

---

[45]David Levine is a truly exceptional computer programmer and teacher. In his years at IMSSS, he wrote many programs and trained and mentored many people in his art. He later became a software engineer with a number of companies in the Cambridge, MA area.

The program makes the assumption that the student's response is something near to the desired response. This is not unreasonable in this context, which focuses on instructional system development. The analysis is divided into two phases, the matching algorithm and the diagnosis of the student's response. The matching algorithm uses the "expected response" to provide general guidance to the system. The diagnostic phase has the responsibility of checking various grammatical rules. See [128] pp. 675–684 for details.

4.14.5 Other Language Projects

Projects in French, Chinese, and Arabic were also carried out at IMSSS during this period; see [128].

4.15 Other Courses

4.15.1 BIP: Basic Instructional Program

IMSSS undertook a programming course in BASIC, called BIP (Basic Instructional Program). The project was performed by Avron Barr, Marian Beard, Keith Wescourt, and Laura Gould.[46] IMSSS had previously done programming courses in BASIC and especially AID, which were successfully used with many students. Those courses were traditional CAI courses for the most part, but they included programming assignments that used interpreters running on the PDP-10.

The BIP course included a BASIC interpreter specially built to be a part of the instructional system, implemented in SAIL. It had student-oriented but general-purpose error messages and diagnostics. The curriculum included instructional material about the BASIC language and programming in general, in addition to over 100 programming problems of varying difficulty.

The most distinct feature of this course was a "Curriculum Information Network" (CIN). The CIN had nearly 100 identified programming skills. A given programming exercise was annotated with the programming skills that the exercise focused on or supported.[47]

As a student passed through the curriculum, the BIP system updated a profile about that student, in terms of the programming skills and how well the student had performed with that skill. This enabled the BIP system to select the next programming exercise using the CIN, basing the selection not only on a programming exercise's general level of difficulty and placement within the curriculum, but also how well the student had mastered the skills so far.

---

[46]The project was funded by the Office of Naval Research; Patrick Suppes was not primarily involved.

[47]See [163], [10], and [154]

The BIP course represented a new kind of instructional optimization and student individualization for IMSSS. The 1968 version of the elementary math course had used strands to track the progress through a series of concept classes in a given concept area, such as addition. The strands approach worked very well when the structure of each strand was clear and the relationships between strands (say, between the addition and multiplication strands) was also well articulated. In the case of BIP, the authors argued that the set of skills was sufficiently multidimensional with many interactions that a different curriculum model and instructional strategy was indicated.

The BIP course was used with over 300 undergraduate students at DeAnza College, the University of San Francisco, and Stanford University. Similar ideas were used for CCC courses in the 1980s.

Programming Experiments with Children

In 1973–75, Steve Weyer and Alex Cannara conducted some experiments with teaching children computer programming and observing their work. See [165] for the initial experiment, and [20] for the final results. The latter is Cannara's PhD dissertation, for which Suppes was the advisor. Two very different languages were used: SIMPER, an artificial machine-language designed for teaching by Lorton and Slimick (see [66]); and LOGO, a language for teaching children invented by Wallace Feurzeig, Seymour Papert, and Cynthia Solomon at BBN and later at MIT (see [38]).

LOGO is a variant of LISP with syntax similar to BASIC, including line numbers. LOGO programming focused on "turtle geometry" in which graphics were created by moving a physical or virtual "turtle" on a plane. In addition, LOGO is strongly associated with the pedagogical ideas of Seymour Papert, which are marked by the belief that children should explore and learn things on their own paths, supported by capable but flexible tutors, in order to learn how to think. While the LOGO language has largely ceased to be used, Papert's ideas are still very common if not prevalent among educators who believe that computers should be used as media for creation and experimentation rather than for didactic instructional delivery.

In this experiment, about thirty students aged 10 to 15 were recruited from nearby schools and came to Stanford to use the PDP-10 system with both display terminals and Teletypes. Graduate students and programmers acted as tutors at a ratio of about one tutor to five students.

Curriculum content was given to the students on paper containing sample exercises and ideas, many of which were graphical, but also some numerical and string exercises. There was no formal instruction in either language or in programming techniques. Students were encouraged to experiment, to learn from each other, and to vary from the sample exercises if they liked.

The tutors and authors made observations, which were used for the written reports.

It should be noted that the underlying ideas behind this project were not congruent to Suppes's customary research interests. However, Suppes recognized that there were many ways to use computers, and he wanted to support this experiment and his graduate students. He did believe that a combination of methods would find practical and effective results.

4.15.2 Music Course

Starting in 1972, Paul Lorton, Jr., Rosemary Killiam, and Wolfgang Kuhn developed a course in music. Software was written on the PDP-10 computer and the student interaction used a Model 33 Teletype. The music itself was created using a Thomas solid state organ. The organ was interfaced to the PDP-10 by having 8-bit character streams from the computer translated into commands for the organ. The organ had 64 notes that it could play. Lorton wrote the software, and Lorton and Kuhn wrote the curriculum. See [128] pp. 877–893.

The curriculum was divided into "strands," which had become familiar from other courses at IMSSS. As of 1975, the strands included intervals, triads, melody, rhythm, chords, and modulation. Other strands were created for research purposes.

Nineteen students were recruited from students enrolled in undergraduate music theory courses at Stanford. Data was collected by focusing on interval and triad perception.

This project began when Prof. Wolfgang Kuhn of the Music Department walked into the lab and asked if anyone was interested in developing a course in music. He was fortunate enough to talk to Paul Lorton, Jr., a graduate student who had worked on a variety of projects. As usual, Lorton was interested, and it moved forward.[48]

4.16   Visitors to the Lab, including Doug Hofstadter and Koko the Gorilla

Many visitors came to the IMSSS lab and participated in the stimulating atmosphere, just like Wolfgang Kuhn as reported above. Some of

---

[48] As busy as Lorton was with many projects, it took him some time to finish writing up his own dissertation. Adele Goldberg, always the manager, once threatened that she would write it up for him. Lorton is now a professor of information systems and technology at the University of San Francisco.

them joined projects underway and others did their own work, enjoying the state-of-the-art computers and the California sun. One of these was Doug Hofstadter, who had finished his PhD in physics in about 1974 and came back to Stanford where his parents lived. He was invited to spend time at IMSSS.

During his stay, Hofstadter revisited an old idea that he had about Gödel's incompleteness theorem; he felt he had a new way of looking at the result that might make a short paper.

Gradually, this took form as a much larger book. Hofstadter saw an exhibition of M. C. Escher's graphic art and thought he would add something about that to the evolving work. Chapter after chapter rolled off of the "IMLAC room" lineprinter while the programmers waited for their listings, which were paying for the facility. Hofstadter would gladly regale people with selected, dramatized readings and cheerfully receive their comments.

In the end, Hofstadter's Pulitzer-prize-winning book *Gödel, Escher, Bach: An Eternal Golden Braid* was an unexpected product of the IMSSS environment.[49]

Another occasional visitor was Koko the gorilla and her caregiver Penny Patterson. They were exploring language acquisition by gorillas using sign language.[50] Patterson's work with Koko is now well known and has changed our ideas about animal's abilities. See [160].

4.17 Interactive Radio Mathematics

The focus of the 1970s work was on university-level instruction. The Nicaragua Radio Mathematics project at IMSSS stands out as different from any of the other work of the '70s (or any time period), and yet it is an important historical precursor of significant global distance education projects still in existence today.

The basic idea of this project was that elementary mathematics lessons were delivered over the radio to students in developing countries. Tutors would lead the students in interacting with each other and their teacher in answering questions. Usage data and test scores were sent back to Stanford for analysis. There was no computer component in the delivery of the lessons, but the term "interactive" was used because of the design of the lessons and the way in which students would respond.

This simple idea using an old technology turned out to be very effective and is still in use. A recent report, "Education for All 2000–

---

[49]See Wikipedia "Douglas Hofstadter" [180] for details of his book and career.

[50]Robert Smith remembers that one day he entered Ventura Hall and Koko gently grabbed his face and kissed him on the mouth. Those were the '70s.

2015: Achievements and Challenges" by Scientific United Nations Educational, UNESCO Publishing [32] points out the continued influence and even resurgence in Interactive Radio Instruction (IRI):

> Older technology remains cost-effective. Radio programming is an enduring and successful example of technology use, in particular for children in isolated or underserved settings. Since the 1970s, interactive radio instruction has been used to enrich teaching processes by introducing interactive learning activities. Over the past decade, a resurgence of interactive radio instruction has helped counteract poor resources, inadequate teacher training and low levels of learner achievement. A review of 15 projects since the early 2000s shows they improve learning outcomes in a range of developing countries, in particular for early grade pupils in fragile states. ([32] p. 211)

4.17.1   Background and Future of the Radio Math Project

Suppes's History of Interest In Global Education

Suppes had a long history of interest in serving the global population of students through technology. Examples include the demonstration he presented at the 1961 ACCRA Conference on Mathematics in Africa[51] and his direction of a curriculum development effort in Ghana from 1962–65.[52] Suppes was a member of the African Education Program Mathematics Steering Committee (see [34]) and the author of a 1969 IMSSS proposal (at the request of AID) for a radio Entebbe project[53] to present the Entebbe math materials by radio to African students.

Suppes, Dean Jamison, and Stuart Wells had also published a survey of the effectiveness of nontraditional media in education in radio; see [54].

However, strangely, Barbara Searle remembers that Suppes did not initiate this project; he was not eager to do it when the funding agency proposed it to him; and he had doubts about its success. He simply remembered that "We worked on computers, but then USAID asked if we could use radio, because it was cheaper."[54] Suppes believed that, while radio was cheaper, it had none of the interactive features that IMSSS

---

[51] see [73]

[52] Arthur Singer reports in his memoir "Easy to Forget, and So Hard to Remember" that he became involved in math education in Africa in 1962: "I arrived in Accra, Ghana and was met by Pat Suppes, who also became a life-long friend. Pat was trying out an elementary math curriculum, which he had developed for kids in East Palo Alto, in Ghanaian schools. We attended some classes and observed the teachers and students cope with Pat's innovative curriculum. . . Pat revealed it was his fortieth birthday. . . . The streets of Accra were filled with music and dancing. . . [We] high-lifed the night away." ([99] p. 16)

[53] Unpublished [121].

[54] Private communications from Barbara Searle and Patrick Suppes, 2014.

was so interested in developing for CAI. Suppes remembered that he had a number of discussions about using computers and satellites, but the AID program directors were very persistent.[55]

Finally, Suppes did accept the funding in 1973 and set up an exceptionally strong project team to whom he turned over the major responsibility to ensure success of the project from 1974 to 1979. The Stanford staff included: based at IMSSS—Barbara Searle (Director, Radio Mathematics Program) and Dean Jamison, and based in Nicaragua—Jamesine Friend (Project Director in Nicaragua), Thomas Tilson, and Klaus Galda.[56] There were as many as 35 additional local staff including maintenance, security, clerical, artists, and training/curriculum developers.

The curriculum that they developed was in fact "interactive" in a way that the early history of radio in education had not been. The students needed to react to the material during the broadcast, as will be discussed in the next section.

When research for this current book showed the overwhelming ongoing success of this style of radio education since that time, Suppes was surprised (but pleased) as he had not followed up himself and was unaware of the significant role that he played as the founder of what is now called "Interactive Radio Instruction (IRI)."[57]

Potential of Radio and the Ongoing Success Stories

IRI has featured prominently in the history of technology to serve this global need.

How does it compare to CAI? The focus in CAI is on use of computers for content delivery where available technology often strongly influences the design. Educational products (particularly in the commercial marketplace) that are based on the current hardware, pedagogical theories, and commercial viability can change relatively quickly, so there have been many shifts in the array of available products. In the current day, educational professionals continue to debate the potential for computers in education, the number and variety of students who can benefit, and how to best develop programs.

Meanwhile, IRI projects have brought to reality the potential of radio to serve staggering numbers of the most needy students globally

---

[55]Private communication, 2014.

[56]The Stanford crew, including Friend, Tilson, and Galda moved their families and belongings with only "home leaves" to visit stateside.

[57]As a side-effect of this 2014 conversation on Radio Math with Suppes and others, Anne Trumbore—who was working at EPGY around that time teaching and updating the Writing Course—heard about the history of Radio Math. She was so fascinated that she interviewed Suppes and wrote an article; see [161].

who have few other acceptable methods of education, under stringent curriculum design controls, monitoring, and learning evaluation, but have done so with little notice in the usual literature. IRI is astounding against the backdrop of CAI because of the very stability of its non-computer-based technology paired with its well-planned project design. These have led to an extraordinary longevity and documented success for this technology, albeit without significant popular recognition.

The Radio Mathematics Project (1974–79) in Nicaragua conducted by Suppes's team laid the foundations of modern IRI.[58] References in the literature show that the self-described successors to this original program are still serving millions of students daily in the global areas of greatest need with cost-effective, results-verified lessons with projects in over 50 countries over the past 30 years; see [51]. This includes one of the largest and newest USAID projects begun in India in 2003, which "has been reaching out to 42 million students across 300,000 schools in eight partner states" ([79]). The demonstrated successful learning from these radio-based projects is noteworthy with hundreds of articles in the literature, dozens of projects, and millions of students served where the Nicaragua Radio Mathematics program is credited as the original model. For example:

> IRI was first developed in the 1970s in Nicaragua by Stanford University, funded by the United States Agency for International Development (USAID). Evaluation data gathered between 1975 and 2000 demonstrated that IRI had improved learning outcomes in conventional classrooms when compared with control classrooms not using IRI (Tilson, et al, 1991; Leigh, 1995; Corrales, 1995; Bosch, 1997; Dock and Helwig, 1999). In addition, IRI was repeatedly found to narrow achievement gaps between boys and girls, as well as between urban and rural students (Tilson et al, 1991; Hartenberger et al, 1996; Bosch, 2001). Programs during this time period often had relatively well-funded evaluation components, often taught a single subject, and focused almost entirely on improving quality. ([51] p. 35)

There is a rich history of research and evaluation for each of these projects as the proposals for funding (such as USAID) have required careful detail, well-planned curriculum development to incorporate local factors, and consistent performance of follow-up studies and learning measurement.

---

[58]Three books published in 1976 [97], 1978 [153], and 1980 [44] form the main documentation for this project.

4.17.2   History and Evaluation of the Nicaragua Radio Math Project (1974–79)

Congressional Interest in Educational Issues for the "Poor Majority" in Developing Countries

Congress expressed its desire to tackle the problem of improving education for less developed countries in the 1973 amendment to the Foreign Assistance Act which directed the Agency for International Development (AID) to focus its program on the "poor majority" in the least developed countries. As a result, AID approached Suppes, resulting in a signed contract with IMSSS on 7/1/1973 with the following objectives:

- Develop and test a cost-effective prototype system of radio mathematics instruction for elementary grades in a developing country that could, with minor adaptations and translation, be used in many developing countries.
- Develop a methodology for (a) producing radio-instructional materials based on the rapid and specific reporting of previous student responses to the materials developers and (b) using feedback on achievement and rates of learning to provide for administrative quality control.
- Begin a program of research on major variables affecting learning through radio.
- Help build capabilities in an appropriate institution of a developing country to continue or even expand the project with minimal further assistance from external experts.

Selection of Nicaragua

Nicaragua was chosen "because it had no existing radio instruction program, the students are taught in their native language, and the government was willing to support the project with local staff and facilities" ([107]). Also the Nicaraguan Ministry of Education had recently rewritten the mathematics curriculum, which appeared adequate for the purposes and closely resembled that of other developing countries so that the radio math program developed could be easily disseminated to other regions.[59]

On April 1, 1974, AID and the Ministry of Public Education (MPE) in Nicaragua signed the formal agreement specifying cooperation and assistance from MPE but implementation and final responsibility with IMSSS for the Nicaragua Radio Mathematics Project.

---

[59]See the 1980 volume [44] for a discussion of the criteria, details of site visits to 12 potential countries, and the final decision.

Designing the Radio Math Curriculum

The basic idea was to use standardized, approved curriculum that students could listen to with their teachers in the classroom across large geographic areas and on a very large scale. This equalized the experience of children with varying qualities of local teachers and materials available. For example, teachers were typically graduates of the primary school with five years of post-primary education, class sizes ranged from 15–60, school was 3 to 4 hours per day, and 30% of the urban and 50% of the rural students were in first grade. In this program, the radio lesson would be the students' only math instruction.

Friend described their approach by saying "Appropriate techniques were developed to engage young children actively in the learning process. Lessons are planned as a 'conversation' between the children and the radio; scripts are written as half of a dialogue, with pauses carefully timed so that students can contribute their half" ([43]).

They developed the curriculum materials in two phases with testing in the field and improvements during each. The major lesson learned was the need for interactivity to keep the students' attention and reinforce the learning, which was finally achieved by increasing to 40–50 "activities" in a 20 minute lesson. These activities included: asking questions to which students would give oral response, teaching songs (especially about math), recitation (e.g. counting, days of week), physical activity such as holding up fingers (see Figure 44) and pointing, and written answers on worksheet or blackboard (see Figure 45).

Note that the primary authors (Friend and Searle) had been extensively involved in the development of the courseware discussed in section 2.15 so this effort built on the earlier lessons learned on curriculum development plus the unique needs of this project.[60]

Searle describes their work in the following:

Especially early in the game, but ultimately all through lesson development, for all four grades, the first broadcast of a lesson was watched (and some written material may have been collected). If the observer saw that a significant number of children in the classroom didn't respond as expected, the material was retaught soon after, with a revised instructional strategy that the developers expected would work better. This procedure was inspired by the way we used data in the development of the CAI Math Strands program. Note that we did *not* rewrite lessons—we compensated for shortfalls downstream. This was very important because the point of the model was to demonstrate that curriculum development and delivery, as well as classroom instruction,

---

[60]There was also a series of pilot radio lessons developed and tested in California as preparation for the Nicaragua pilot lessons [97].

was *very* low cost. (The strategy of downstream correction was one of those things which ultimately came from Pat, though not directly, because all of us from Stanford—Jamey, Tom, Klaus and myself—had by that time been thoroughly indoctrinated in the Suppes approach to curriculum development and Jamey quickly figured out how to apply the principles in new situations.)[61]

The radio scripts and other materials were developed with local curriculum specialists, script writers, artists, teacher training experts, and actors as many of the scripts called for two people talking to each other (although this was found to be less effective for the student's learning then having the radio personality talk directly to the student). Figure 46 shows a local artist working on drawings.

The curriculum developed by this comprehensive method proved to be very effective. Searle has recently noted that "The teachers learned a great deal from the radio programs. My own view was that many of them would be much more effective teachers, even if [when] the radio programs went away."[62]

Implementation of the Radio Math Lessons

Searle and Suppes described the lessons:

> A daily lesson consists of a 20-minute radio presentation followed by approximately 20 minutes of teacher directed activities, (instructions are provided in a project-developed teachers' guide). No textbooks are used and printed material is limited to a one-page worksheet for each child. Teachers are asked to supply simple materials, such as bottle caps and sticks and the project occasionally provides other supplementary materials such as rulers printed on cardboard. The focus of our research is how best to use these limited resources–the radio, a worksheet, a teachers' guide, some simple materials–to teach mathematics.[63]

The worksheets and tests were entered on punch cards to a computer which produced a magnetic tape to send back to Stanford for correction and then stored for program evaluation as well as analysis used in improving the program.

To give a sense of a typical broadcast which "have been characterized as a cross between Sesame Street and programmed instruction" ([153]

---

[61]Private communication on 8/8/2016 where Searle also added: "Another point ... is the distinction between facts and concepts. It is always easier to give examples using fact acquisition $(5 + 10 = 15)$ but remember we taught algorithms (even the long division algorithm, with no supporting textual material!), carrying and borrowing, and other even more conceptual material. Jamey was a genius!

[62]Private communication from Barbara Searle, 8 September 2016.

[63]In fact, even the cost of the workbooks proved too much and students later wrote their answers on the blackboard and only used paper once a week to take a test. See [152].

FIGURE 44: Elementary School Students in Managua Respond to a Lesson

photo by Tom Tilson

FIGURE 45: Instructor Fills Out Answers from Radio Math Students

p. 3) with songs, jokes, riddles, games, and stories:

> The day's lesson was broadcast to all participating classrooms, and students participated as a group. In each classroom, the teacher turned on the radio, music began, and a nationally-known singer introduced the program with a song. (This song became a hit, and some objected that it made the study of math too popular.) Immediately, students were asked questions and expected to respond. The questions were posed in multiple forms to increase learning; for instance, an abstract question, "What is 5 plus 10?" was followed by the same question in concrete terms, "Juan earned five centavos yesterday, and ten centavos today. How much did he earn altogether?" Students were also asked to respond physically tapping their knees a certain number of times, or holding up a number of fingers. Because many of the interactions were verbal or physical, students could learn from each other's responses ... ([161] p. 27)

Lesson #171 won the coveted Japan Prize for International Educational Program for 1977, which had 166 radio and television submissions from 92 international broadcasting organizations. The Nicaragua MPE used the $2,000 prize to expand the program.

Here is a sample joke from that lesson; see [153] p. 25.

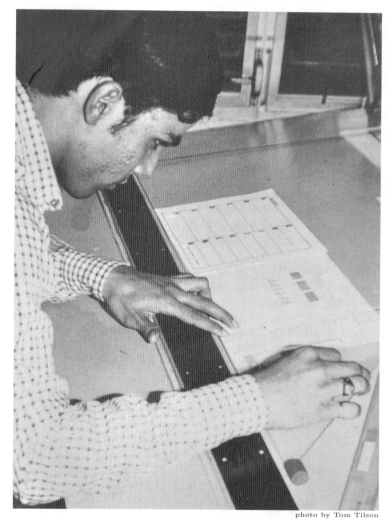

FIGURE 46: Artist Creates a Worksheet for Radio Math

```
VOICE:  The mother and child are talking.
CHILD:  Mommy, Mommy.  Give me a cordoba.
MOTHER: Another? But. . . what have you done with the one
    I gave you this morning?
CHILD:  I gave it to an old man.
MOTHER: I like it, son, that you are charitable.  Then take
    another cordoba.  ... But let's see, tell me, you won't
    give this cordoba to the old man, will you?
CHILD:  Of course, Mommy, because he is the one who sells
    candies.
```

Lessons Learned and Evaluation of Program Effectiveness

Searle, Friend, and Suppes reported the following general observations from the first year of the program: "children are most attentive to radio lessons when they are responding actively; mathematical activities are more engaging than stories for 1st grade children; children listen to instructions and in most cases, repetition is unnecessary; children can learn new topics from the radio lessons; and teachers are able to incorporate radio lessons into their daily routine" ([107] pp. 2–32). All the teachers participating in the first year, 1975, asked to continue.

There were several comprehensive evaluations done; see [97], [153] and [44] for details. However, this program provided a unique opportunity to run another important experiment comparing classrooms with no additional materials as the control group with two experimental groups: one with radio lessons and the other with textbooks. Over half the classrooms involved had three or fewer textbooks used only by the teachers. 88 classrooms with over 3,000 students participated. The 3 groups scored similarly on a 28 item pre-test. Teachers for the experimental groups were given a three-hour training, but no other contact was made during the year. The posttest results showed significant positive results for both experimental groups. "Availability of textbooks increased student posttest scores by about 3.5 items correct, approximately .33 of a standard deviation. Availability of the radio instructional program increased student posttest scores 14.9 items, about 1.5 standard deviations" ([55]).

As indicated above, all of the AID-funded projects throughout the history of IRI have a unique history of well-executed, impressive, and high-achieving program evaluations such as this!

Comments on Educational Practices

Several of the more recent articles draw parallels and/or attribute modern educational practices to lessons learned from Radio Math in Nicaragua.

Ho and Thukral note that "Most of the principles of interactive instruction identified by the original Nicaragua project have proved durable, appropriate and relevant. Where change has taken place, it has been additive" ([51] p. 4).

Trumbore gives Suppes credit for his even earlier work in establishing interactive learning, saying that "at the time that NRMP was designed, the idea that active learning promoted deeper learning was still in its infancy. In fact, Suppes published some of the first papers testing this hypothesis," (see [143]). Her examples of current interactive student responses are: "educational computer games, instructional videos with embedded quizzes, polling, and even the use of clickers in a live classroom" ([161] p. 27).

She also finds an interesting modern parallel in the shift from instructors focused on "content delivery" to being "learning facilitators" in today's "flipped classrooms."

4.17.3 Suppes's Contributions to Radio Math Project

The IRI projects that followed frequently gave credit to Suppes's Nicaragua project as the original interactive use of radio to teach mathematics and other subjects. He had a creative and dedicated team working on this project locally and at Stanford to make it a success. However, certain features highlight Suppes's own unique contribution including:

- The emphasis on music as part of the program, which was extremely important to Suppes in a number of his curriculums over the years.
- The use of the existing Nicaraguan curriculum as the foundation for others. It was another of his common themes to utilize and improve previous work in order to both be cost effective and capitalize on experience.
- The extensive evaluation performed at every step of the project— again learning from experience and demonstrating the value of the project.
- The high level of interactivity (as discussed in the preceding section).

4.17.4 Politics Cause End of Radio Math in Nicaragua in 1978

The political atmosphere in Nicaragua was changing with increasing disturbances and civil unrest in 1978.[64] The Ministry was also having

---

[64]Barbara Searle said, "I liked to tell people that we did the first (and probably only) controlled experiment on the effect of civil war on learning in schools. During the last year, about half our control classes were in areas where schools were closed for weeks at a time. There was no significant difference in the amount students learned in control schools, whether closed or not, which I suspect was true because the kids in the control schools were learning hardly anything anyway."

difficulty finding the funding internally to expand the program nationally, causing USAID and Stanford to withdraw their financial support since they wanted the government to cover a significant portion of the costs.

In July 1978, Galda, who had a sense of humor, wrote in the letter accompanying his expense report, "I'm still busy dodging bombs down here. Things are getting worse by the day and it looks like a revolution may be around the corner. Keep sending money anyhow." Then in September when Tilson filed for reimbursement of the required medical exams for his family returning home, the letter back to him from IMSSS said "We have heard from Klaus and he and our offices there are still intact. Some buildings were destroyed less than a mile away, and there were bullet holes through the air conditioning equipment on our building, but that was 'all' so far. He is probably getting fairly eager to return!"

However, 1978 was also a year of expansion and stability of the curriculum itself even with the US staff leaving. In addition, there were increased dissemination activities by this same staff attending international conferences and conducting program exploration in other countries.

4.17.5 Continued AID Contract through July 1981

IMSSS had a follow-on contract with AID from 1979–1981 which Searle described as "a level of dissemination[65] beyond that customary in development projects.[66] We are encouraged and excited by the acceptance of project materials that has resulted ... we are just now reaping the benefits of the travel and publishing that AID has supported over the past two years."[67] This time period covered a number of projects, including:

- *General Translation:* Preparing four of the lessons in French, Spanish, and English for use in other areas. Arabic was originally proposed but not felt to be in sufficient demand. Friend[68] was hired as a consultant to oversee the translators, actors, and production consultants.

---

[65]Note that a three-volume book series containing articles on The Radio Mathematics Project and edited by Searle, Friend, and Suppes was published in 1976, 1978, and 1980. There was also a funded International Conference on the Use of Radio as an Instructional Tool in Primary Schools hosted by the Stanford team in Managua, Nicaragua in September 1976 with 14 participants from 11 developing countries to share experiences and methodologies.

[66]History has shown this to be a huge understatement!

[67]Private communication to AID, December 1980.

[68]Friend had by this time left Stanford and was working at Xerox.

- *Thailand:* Designing a replication of the Nicaragua Radio Math Program in Thailand, providing technical assistance to a World Bank education project which began broadcasting second-grade lessons in May 1980 with expansion plans. Galda was a genius at learning languages and was learning Thai.
- *Columbia:* Working with the Human Ecology Research Foundation of Cali, Columbia to play the first- and second-grade math lessons on cassette recorders to 20 schools beginning in November 1980.
- *Kenya:* Subcontracting to the Academy for Educational Development for a radio language arts program.
- *Other Countries:* Beginning work, talking to, or visiting a number of countries including: Guatemala, Costa Rica, India, Nepal, the Philippines, Peru, Paraguay, Indonesia, Papua New Guinea, Dominican Republic, Botswana, Swaziland, and Brazil.

The AID extension for IMSSS after 1981 was not funded, but Searle reports now that "Radio Math had a very long and diversified life after I left and went to the World Bank. (Not in Nicaragua, where the revolutionaries threw AID out.) AID financed replications in several countries but also branched out into other subjects. As I recall, much of the work was managed by the Academy for Educational Development here in Washington."[69]

IRI has continued successfully up to today because it provides highly cost-effective education (see [54]) to the most needy students globally with proven results. This was a different project for Suppes and his team, but it ended by the '80s; and their sole focus returned to CAI where the cost vs. benefits analysis was not nearly as straightforward a win.

4.18 The Cost-Benefits of CAI Research ca. 1979

In 1979, Dean Jamison gave an economic assessment of Patrick Suppes's work in education. This section uses his facts and ideas, as well as some updates. See [56].

4.18.1 Funding from Government Sources

Jamison claimed that between 1963 and 1979, Suppes and his team spent approximately $25 million on developing CAI at Stanford University. During the same period, the U.S. Office of Education spent a total of $161 million on about 500 CAI projects. NSF had spent over $10 million on PLATO and TICCIT,[70] and several million on Suppes's

---

[69] Private communication from Barbara Searle, 1 July 2016.

[70] Some other sources put this at up to $30 million; see [78]

work. Assessing this reduction in funding, Jamison states:

> By 1972 the Office of Education had virtually ceased supporting CAI and by 1977 the National Science Foundation, too, had drastically reduced its commitments. Realizing the potential of CAI proved far more difficult than recognizing it; neither the funding agencies nor, by and large, had the developers pursued CAI's potential to its operational realization. ([56] p. 190)

Jamison goes on to point out that Suppes had, in 1967, founded Computer Curriculum Corporation, which by that time had more than 90 employees and close to 5,000 student terminals in operation. He estimated that CCC's terminals probably reached 2% to 3% of the compensatory population. Suppes's group at Stanford had included about 200 people at its height (including graduate students), and by 1979 was down to about 35, which was diminishing.

Jamison argues that CAI of the type being offered at CCC for elementary education was in fact cost-effective in at least the sense that the cost is less than the amount typically allocated by compensatory funds, namely Title I.

So, the conclusion was that further development of CAI would have to proceed via private companies rather than with government or foundation support.

But the question remains: what did the government get for its money, in aggregate less than $200 million? See Chapter 8 for Suppes's observations on the relationship between funded university research and commercial deployment.

4.18.2 Productivity in University Education

Suppes developed an argument justifying expenditures for university-level courses, even those that support only a small number of students; see [154]. Basically, the argument is that the teacher-to-student ratio of a course like *Old Church Slavonic* is so low that it does not justify having faculty teach such a course, but instead the course should be taught by computer. Writing in 1979, Jamison finds the argument "somewhat strange." At that time, the costs of operating IMSSS clearly were not justified by the number of Stanford students reached with the courses, and when the supporting NSF funding went away, the courses started to disappear from computer delivery.

Suppes's argument may however be correct, it just has to be considered in a different technical light than was available in 1979. Dick Schupbach, one of the developers of Stanford's Slavic language courses, commented that the big thing that he and Joe Van Campen needed to expand the use of their courses was "transportability" (see page 55).

There was simply no way in 1979 to share Stanford's courses with other universities.

Efforts at transportability would be made during the 1980s at Stanford by Suppes's group, leading to Internet delivery; (see Chapter 7).

5

Mainstream Development at CCC 1981–1985

5.1 Introduction

By 1981, the main sources of funding at Stanford had disappeared. The National Science Foundation continued some work on transportability, which is described later. Suppes's primary focus in computer applications became CCC, where he devoted an increasing amount of time and energy. The late '70s had seen the new development of minicomputers and "microcomputers" (or "personal computers"), which became key opportunities. Suppes also hoped that he might prepare the company for sale, as the company later learned.

The completion of many projects at Stanford led to many people leaving the IMSSS laboratory. Some, like Ron Roberts, remained at the university to lead networking efforts in the coming decades. Some accepted jobs at CCC, including Sil Sanders and Carolyn Gramlich, who had led the audio effort at IMSSS in the mid-1970s, Betsy Macken, who became Vice President of curriculum and publications, and Mario Zanotti, whose title was later Vice President of Research and Evaluation.

5.2 Audio Developments

5.2.1 Audio Hardware

At IMSSS, Sanders had developed the MISS machine for computer-generated audio under NSF support. Working with Gerard Benbassat and Carolyn Gramlich, the MISS machine was able to generate highly-intelligible speech in real time, including dynamic speech with prosodic features. See page 120.

CCC had achieved success with the CCC-17 system and the lower cost per student "terminal." A terminal was sold with the terminal hardware for about $700, plus annual licenses to use all of the courses on the host computer for about $1,300. This added up to around $2,000. There was also the initial cost of the CCC-17 hardware and system software, plus annual software and hardware support fees.

Audio was, in Suppes's opinion then and always, absolutely critical in communication and learning. Regardless of the marketing issues, Suppes always wanted to focus on proper ways of using audio, believing that this would further enhance learning.

While every curriculum could benefit from audio, certain courses seemed to require it. Reading (as done by Atkinson and team at IMSSS), foreign languages (Russian as done by Van Campen at IMSSS), and of course ESL were considered critical applications for audio.

Sanders led a team of three engineers plus a designer to create something similar to the MiniMISS machine out of more modern components, and at an affordable price. Thus was born the Digital Speech System, or DSS.

The DSS was designed to take commands through a serial port. The CCC-17 used a serial connection "daisy-chaining" from the CCC-17 to the MiniAce terminal concentrator, then to the DSS. The character stream from the CCC-17 contained DSS commands along with the multiplexed characters to and from the terminals. Thus, the controlling program in the CCC-17 would send characters to be displayed on the terminal intermixed with DSS commands, with up to eight terminals and headphones connected to a DSS. Sanders brought this to the market by about 1982.

5.2.2 Audio Courses

The curriculum team developed two more courses to use the new audio capabilities: ARP and ESL (primarily for adults). There was also a major effort for Dial-A-Drill, as described below.

ARP

The ARP (Audio Reading Program) was developed under the direction of Susan Awbrey, who had the reputation for generating a lot of curriculum that was spot-on very quickly. The ARP course was for grades 1 and 2, and focused primarily on skills such as word identification. ARP came out in 1982 and was clearly an important addition to the CCC-17, but sales were not as good as had been hoped according to Sanders, due he believed to the limited courseware using audio and the still-high cost of the audio hardware.

ESL

The ESL (English as a Second Language) course was more ambitious than ARP. Kim Sheehan (formerly Merriam), an ESL teacher, joined CCC in 1980. Professor Joe Van Campen of Stanford University, who had developed the very successful Russian course at IMSSS in the 1960s, also joined and brought his expertise in developing sentence generation programs to the Project.[1] Vice President of Curriculum Betsy Macken supervised the development of the course structure and details of motion, and Diane MacNicholl, the most experienced programmer of motion drivers, built the software, which was a challenge.

The course was huge. It had eight strands, over 70,000 exercises, and over 13,500 sounds including recorded words, phrases, and whole sentences. The course used "source languages," which were audio in the language that the student already spoke. The available source languages were Spanish, Italian, Japanese, Mandarin Chinese, Arabic, and Hmong. It took until about 1984 to complete the course.

In addition to being a lot of work, the course was not a commercial success. Looking back on this, Kim Sheehan has some candid explanations, as follows:

- While a lot of research was done in preparation for this course, there was not enough research into the trends within the ESL community itself. For example, CCC had prepared a large set of exercises that they thought appropriate for the course, but these did not necessarily match what ESL teachers wanted to see. Sheehan did what she could to inject some reality into the product.
- Van Campen's sentence generation programs had done well for Russian but did not do as well for ESL. While the coding programs could control when and how frequently vocabulary items and sentence structure elements were introduced, they failed to produce reasonable or appropriate exercises in many cases, and a full-time staff member was hired to do the filtering, often finding really strange sentences.
- The course motion in practice seemed to operate too slowly, requiring considerable adjustment after initial trials. Tools CCC would develop in a few years would have revealed this in the QA process, but that was too late for ESL.
- The use of "source languages" was controversial. In the absence of any kind of graphics or animation, however, source language was essential to give the student the necessary support to learn English in an independent learning environment.

---

[1] See page 52.

- Deploying the course was difficult, requiring audio equipment, special wiring, and larger hard drives to hold all of the course content.

- Perhaps most importantly, ESL was out of the range of the customers who normally used CCC. CCC had some success with adult populations, for example in remediation programs and in federal prisons, but the marketing effort for ESL was not successful. Suppes had great ideas about marketing the system in China, but nothing really happened. Sales reps made some efforts, but basically fell back on the main bread-and-butter courses such as math and reading.

Kim Sheehan went on to work on the Readers Workshop course, became Director of Curriculum Development, and worked until 1999 in various roles at CCC. She now works at the College of San Mateo in the Language Arts Department.

5.3   Dial-A-Drill™ Revisited

Dial-A-Drill had been an early product of CCC in 1969, see page 76. It was considered an innovation in 1969, one that was ahead of its time and too expensive. It was not until the 1980s that a majority of residential customers had Touch-Tone phones, see Wikipedia "Push-button telephone" [215] for a history.

Suppes was still convinced that Dial-A-Drill was a good idea. The DSS Speech System provided the audio, and the CCC-17 could provide the curriculum content and programming. All that was needed was a way to connect to the telephone system.

5.3.1   TAU: Telephone Access Unit

Enter the TAU, for Telephone Access Unit. The TAU was built to fit into the same "daisy chain" along with the CCC-17, the DSS, and the terminal concentrator. Each TAU could support up to eight telephone lines.

The TAU contained hardware that would "read" Touch-Tone codes sent by the student's telephone and convert them to ANSI character codes. So the "1" key would become the ANSI "1" character. In contexts where an alphabetic character was required, a pair of Touch-Tone keys would be decoded to the text character. Thus, "1" "2" meant the first alphabetic character on the 2 key, which is "A."

The TAU could also dial out to the student's phone allowing the system to initiate the phone call. Later in 1984 on the Microhost, a scheduling program even allowed a teacher to schedule phone calls to the student's home at specified times, on individual days or repeatedly. It would also call back students who had not answered, and record whether or not students took their lessons. The ability of the support person at the school to monitor Dial-A-Drill students also increased student participation.

5.3.2 Dial-A-Drill Courseware

In the 1969 Dial-A-Drill project in New York, math had been the only course implemented. See page 76.

For the CCC-17, there were three courses:

- DIAL-A-DRILL MENTAL ARITHMETIC: This course provided practice in mental calculations and also estimation and problem-solving, including content for grades 1 through 8. This followed the emerging concept that more emphasis should be placed on mental calculations and estimation in the light of increasing use of calculators and computers. The content and programming was adapted from the existing MK course for the CCC-17.
- DIAL-A-DRILL READING. This course used printed handbooks that were distributed to students, who read the material and then answered questions using the telephone. The course was for students in grades 1 to 4. Existing content from the "Reading for Comprehension" (RC) course was used, together with newly written passages for the handbooks.
- DIAL-A-DRILL SPELLING. This course gave drills in spelling. It presented the word in a sentence, then repeated the word and asked the student to spell it. Care was taken to select words that would be easy to understand using the speech technology, and sentences that would help disambiguate the word from similar sounding words. Standard spelling lists were used for this course aimed at grades 2 through 8.
- If more than one course was being used, they would be wrapped into a single short session, generally ten minutes long.
- Users found the math and spelling to be surprisingly engaging, but the reading was somewhat difficult to follow due to the use of workbooks. CCC staff and their children reported enjoying the course during QA testing.

5.3.3 Dial-A-Drill Marketing to the Home

Suppes had been interested in marketing to the home, especially for gifted students. Touch-Tone phones were now in a majority of homes, especially in higher socio-economic families.

Nancy Smith[2] was asked to be product/project manager for Dial-A-Drill based on her recent project management experience at Bell

---

[2]Suppes was her PhD advisor at Stanford 1970–1974 then her employer at CCC 1982–1996 and later at EPGY 2007–2013.

FIGURE 47: Dial-A-Drill Brochure with Cartoon Telephone

Laboratories. For the first time at CCC, Gantt charts started to appear with timelines and action items. Smith researched the issues with publishing and technology for the home market, and suddenly realized how unprepared CCC was to deal with a very different world.

To approach the home market, CCC developed an advertising brochure that included cartoons. Figure 47 shows the cartoon character created for the Touch-Tone phone, and Figure 48 displays a cartoon of a student happily using Dial-A-Drill. The brochure also included educational details such as a sample of the reports mailed to students shown in Figure 49.

The use of cartoons was highly controversial within CCC. Detractors objected that the cartoons undermined CCC's reputation for quality instruction. Defenders noted that the cartoons were attractive and the content of the advertising was accurate and educationally solid. Heated discussions on this topic took place at all levels of the company. It is noteworthy that when Dial-A-Drill collateral materials were developed for the school market, the cartoons were missing.

From Smith's perspective, she was dealing with a staid, academically-oriented company that had an almost deliberately dull image. From the

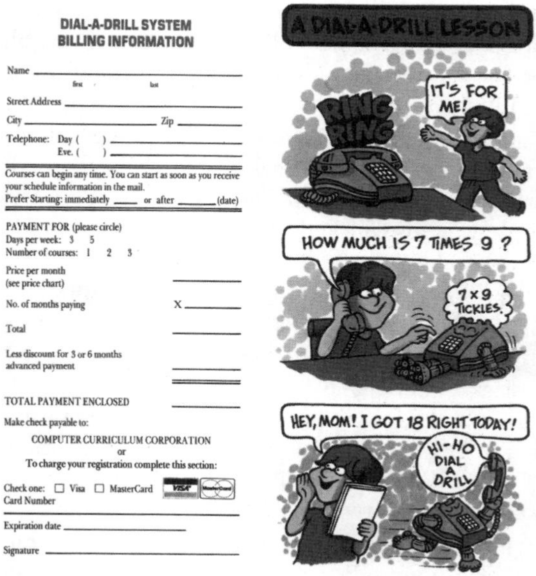

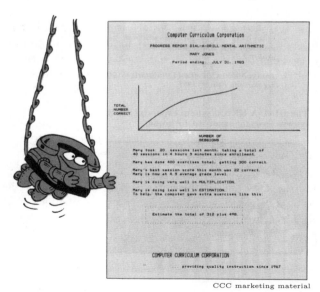

CCC marketing material

FIGURE 48: Dial-A-Drill Order Page

CCC marketing material

FIGURE 49: Dial-A-Drill Sample Student Reports

people she talked to and the things she read, she saw a very different home marketplace than the school market as of 1983. She lacked the experience or the authority to do much at that time to change CCC's image, either internally or in the marketplace.

She scheduled the launch, developed marketing collaterals, and set up a press conference, which was reasonably well attended and resulted in positive articles such as in *InfoWorld* [67] and the *Christian Science Monitor* [25]. It was also picked up on the AP wire and a number of radio interviews.

Ironically, the *InfoWorld* editor took a very different stance than his/her reporter that shocked CCC. *InfoWorld* published an editorial one week after the earlier positive article calling Dial-A-Drill a "high-tech hickory stick" ([52]). The lengthy editorial said that Dial-A-Drill flew "in the face of all educational innovations in the past 15 years" and raised "Ghosts of Big Brother," and "we must ensure that the benefits of this 'high-tech hickory stick' do not come at the expense of more innovative educational software."

InfoWorld missed the point of Dial-A-Drill almost completely. This was 1983, and most homes did not have still-expensive microcomputers. They did, however, have Touch-Tone phones. The Dial-A-Drill course-ware did not address all issues, but it did provide practice on needed skills, especially estimation.

CCC was also missing a point. Things were changing in educational computing, and many people wanted to go beyond drill and practice in how they used computers. The fact that CCC was so worried about its "image" that they were concerned about using cartoons suggests that the company did not understand the home market.

In a decade, CCC was using cartoons in many ways, and even modified its logo to have cartoon elements. In just a few years, CCC was to decide to select a new terminal with color graphics and to aggressively change the look and feel of the courseware, see page 203.[3]

As for Dial-A-Drill for home users, there were some customers who used it and liked it, but it was not a successful product. The cost of telephones again proved a major issue. Suppes concluded that he had to build a market for it in the schools instead of counting on the home market.

---

[3]Suppes remembered Smith's product-management skills and stance on marketing Dial-A-Drill, and she was asked to lead the search for a graphics programming team and a viable graphics terminal.

5.3.4 The Chicago and Detroit Public Schools Dial-A-Drill Implementations

Suppes made Dial-A-Drill a priority for the sales team. Mary Wallace, later to become Vice President of Sales, took the message seriously and sold extensive Dial-A-Drill systems to both Detroit Public Schools and Chicago Public Schools. There was some interest at other districts. However, since CCC had a number of other projects underway, no one but Suppes and Sanders was very worried about Dial-A-Drill.

In late 1984, Wallace convinced a Chicago school principal to implement a Dial-A-Drill project as a school-to-home project. The elementary school was located in the middle of a housing project on Chicago's south side and served over 1200 children. There was some concern that the project apartments would not have the required Touch-tone telephones, but a survey showed that all homes with telephones had Touch-tone instruments although in some cases families turned out to be sharing phones which complicated the scheduling.

When the purchase order came in, just before Christmas, the Software Department had to finish the programming for the scheduling component. Members of all departments, including Software, Field Service, and the Sales Consultants converged on the school to ensure correct installation and operation. Mark Ogborn of Software flew out to train the other CCC staffers and supervise the installation. The principal and school educational staff spent many nights addressing issues that students were having. This installation received positive local press and the school principal was later recognized as the "Chicago Principal of the Year." Just one software update was needed.[4]

The Dial-A-Drill system was used at Williams Elementary School in Chicago for as long as the hardware was operational. They loved the product, arguing that it increased involvement between teachers and parents. When new products came out that did not support Dial-A-Drill, the Chicago authorities were dismayed.

The Chicago and Detroit implementations were similar in that they served eligible students after school, but different in that Chicago served only those students at Williams Elementary School, while Detroit served students across the entire district. The Chicago project provided instruction for over 700 students five days a week. The Detroit implementation served over 200 students.

---

[4] Personal communication from Betty Menacher,

5.4 Microcomputers In Education: The SMC-70 Decision

By 1981, "personal computers" and "microcomputers" were becoming very popular in education, at least as a concept if not a reality. The story is well known, but we review a portion here because of its relevance to CCC.

The Apple II had been introduced in 1977, along with rivals from Tandy (the TRS-80) and Commodore (PET). The introduction of $5\frac{1}{4}$ inch floppy disks and the VisiCalc spreadsheet program (a forerunner of Lotus-1-2-3 and Excel) made the Apple II a major product by the end of the 1970s.[5]

Digital Research pioneered the CP/M operating system for the Intel 8080 processor; a number of manufacturers built CP/M-based computers, and CP/M became a standard for business-oriented personal computing.

Viewing this, IBM decided to build a personal computer and decided to use available parts and software rather than building their own. They selected the new Intel 8086 chips and licensed the software, named MS-DOS, from a very nimble Microsoft Corporation that managed to get a non-exclusive contract with IBM. MS-DOS was essentially a clone, conceptually, of the work done at Digital Research to build a version of CP/M for the 8086. The future success of both Intel and Microsoft ended up deriving from this decision of IBM.[6] The IBM PC, running PC-DOS (as it was originally called), was shipped in 1981 and became an immediate hit for IBM. Since Microsoft had only licensed the software (saving IBM some money), they were able to license MS-DOS to other manufacturers.

In 1981, CCC could only know how this had started, not where it would end. In any event, in December, 1981, a team started evaluating the options. This included Suppes, Sanders, marketing vice-presidents Dave Voorhees and Dave Munson, and Robert Smith.[7]

On a casual yet fateful day after Christmas 1981, the group gathered to discuss three options for a microcomputer-based product:

- Apple II
- IBM PC

---

[5]The Apple II gave way to the Apple IIe in 1983 and in the late 1980s, the Apple II-GS. Apple released its first Macintosh in 1984, but no Macintosh was powerful enough or inexpensive enough to be used by CCC until 1990. See page 220.

[6]See Wikipedia "MS-DOS" [201].

[7]Robert Smith had been brought from Rutgers University where he was teaching computer science to replace Rainer Schulz as the Vice President of Software and Systems; Schulz had joined an AI startup located in Palo Alto.

- Sony SMC-70

It had been decided that an exact port of the CCC courseware would be done for the microcomputer project. The machine would use floppy disks to hold the program and student data, and would have a new version of the CCC courseware management system. But which computer?

The Apple II had already gathered the mind-share of educators, but it was the opinion of Smith and Sanders that it was not powerful enough to allow the CCC courseware to be ported. The IBM PC was still new and had an industrial look to it.

The Sony SMC-70 was a CP/M machine with 64KB of memory, making it a technology that was about to be doomed by the PC. But the review team was far more impressed by the Sony's style, color, and graphics, which were all first-rate as a product built by Sony in its heyday. So, they chose the SONY SMC-70.

This decision was later regretted as the years passed and the MS-DOS operating system succeeded.

The development of the courseware and software to run on the SMC-70 was greatly influenced by another project that had been underway for two years, the development of the Microhost system. This multi-user system was intended to replace the CCC-17.

5.5 The Microhost Instructional System: Software Development Plan

5.5.1 The First Plan for the Microhost

In about 1980, Rainer Schultz of Software and Ken Chin of Engineering had begun the development of the Microhost. This was to be a replacement for the CCC-17 and would be basically a faster and more powerful version of all the earlier systems that CCC had built. The original design called for three Zilog Z8000 computational processors, separate IO processors, up to four 1MB memory boards, and multiplexed terminal ports to connect up to 128 terminals. It was intended to support up to 128 students with any combination of courses, and allow the creation of more courses that were very similar in structure and computational requirements to the current ones. By using standard components, the system would be more cost-effective and maintainable than previous hardware.

Schultz had also planned to program the operating system and all course drivers in assembly language, in very much the style that had made the CCC-17 capable of supporting a large number of students.

5.5.2 The Revised Plan for the Microhost

Upon becoming Schultz's replacement, Smith reassessed the design and proposed instead using a port of the UNIX operating system (written in C) and making all software development for the courseware in C; Sanders supported this.

Smith and Sanders were trying to be more forward-looking.[8] They saw the previous systems as being appropriate for the 1970s, but believed that more complex programming, informed by research in artificial intelligence, would be appropriate for the next decade. As an assistant professor of computer science at Rutgers, Smith had interactions with the researchers at nearby Bell Labs where UNIX was developed, and had studied UNIX architecture while his wife Nancy Smith had been at Bell Labs on the UNIX production team.

Smith also saw that he had *two* development projects at the same time: the SMC-70 and the Microhost. Marketing wanted the SMC-70 in late 1982, and the Microhost would be released no later than early 1984. Since the Microhost hardware was still under development, the SMC-70 became the immediate priority, but a unified development plan was needed.

CCC saw its product as an instructional system that would contain a variety of courses and a management system. The natural assumption was that all courses would run (the same way!) on all platforms. This could not be true, of course, although CCC came close by designing for the "lowest common denominator." This meant that a development plan that would allow most of the existing courses to simply run on either the SMC-70 or the Microhost was needed. A side effect of this plan was failing to take advantage of the SMC-70s capabilities as one of the best color/graphics microcomputers of its generation.

Making allies of Ken Chin of Engineering and Betsy Macken of Curriculum, Smith and Sanders proposed an overall plan for simultaneous development of the SMC-70 and Microhost, as follows:

- Since the Microhost would run UNIX™, a UNIX engineer was hired. He left soon, and was replaced by Howard Botwinick and Mark Schulz, who carried the UNIX port and modifications through to completion. The company bought a Zilog computer running UNIX, under the assumption that Zilog chips would be used for the Microhost itself. They later changed to the Motorola chip sets, which turned out to be a great idea.

---

[8]Smith now notes that he and Sanders could argue very vigorously but always seemed to come to the same conclusion on any important issue. Smith has not asked Sanders what he thinks about this observation.

- C would be used for the courseware interpreters, drivers, and management system. The C code would, from the outset, be written using conditional compilation allowing it to run on CP/M and the Microhost. Most existing courses would use the same code base.
- Development of drivers for motion had always been a concern. The motion was similar from one course to another, but the details varied. Macken had an idea for a "general driver," which Smith embraced. The general driver was implemented and used for several courses, eventually becoming more of a documentation language than an actual tool.
- A number of tools were developed on the company's DecSystem 20s to support this project, including an interpreter for the Sony SMC-70 and new compilers for the "general driver." Smith and Sanders felt that internal tool development had been insufficient at CCC, and tried in a number of ways to enhance this.
- A new management system based on menus and better interaction was built to replace the awkward commands used on the CCC-17. The management system was important because it allowed proctors and teachers to control and monitor instruction.

5.6   SMC-70 Product Release and Reception

The overall development plan had placed the SMC-70 ahead of the Microhost, which required more hardware and firmware development. The SMC-70 with courses was shipped in late 1982. More courses followed into 1983. Figure 50 shows a list of the courses and some of their features.

The CCC courses ran the same on the SMC-70, as the initial plan specified. While the Sony SMC-70 was one of the best graphics computers in its price range, very little was done with these graphic capabilities. CCC made some modest use of color in the various text fields. They also put "splash Screens" on the beginning of the courses, which were drawn by artists. But the combination of the desire to have "platform compatibility" and not have to rewrite the courseware kept the use of graphics to a minimum.

There was also a clear interest in marketing the SMC-70 as a *microcomputer* that could do more than run the CCC courses. CCC marketed programming languages and other tools available for the SMC-70. Since it ran the CP/M operating system, the SMC-70 supported an array of business-oriented software, although not much educational software outside of CCC's offerings.

2 CCC COURSEWARE

The courses are comprehensive, covering major objectives in the subject area usually for several grade years. Each course has an accompanying teacher handbook, some courses a student text.

MATHEMATICS	READING
MATH SKILLS, GRADES 1-7	BASIC READING
PROBLEM SOLVING, GRADES 3-6	READING, GRADES 3-6
ENRICHMENT MODULES	READING FOR COMPREHENSION
INTRODUCTION TO ALGEBRA	CRITICAL READING SKILLS 1
	CRITICAL READING SKILLS 2
LANGUAGE ARTS	ADULT READING SKILLS
LANGUAGE ARTS STRANDS,	OTHER
GRADES 3-6	SURVIVAL SKILLS
FUNDAMENTALS OF ENGLISH	GED CURRICULUM
ADULT LANGUAGE SKILLS 1	CCC GAMES
ADULT LANGUAGE SKILLS 2	
NEW: COMPUTER LITERACY ELEMENTARY	NEW: COMPUTER LITERACY SECONDARY

Many courses have SPECIAL FEATURES appropriate to the subject. Reading and language arts courses have an answer processing system that recognizes variations of the correct answer; Problem Solving includes a calculator mode, and Computer Literacy includes three special programming environments.

All courses include a BUILT-IN MANAGEMENT SYSTEM that individualizes the course for each student, keeps track of student progress and produces printed reports. Diagnostic reports show each student's current placement in the course and show gains over time. A program to copy disks for backup is included.

Some courses are organized by STRANDS. This means that the course is divided into skill areas or strands and the adjustment of level takes place within each strand. The teacher can also enroll the student in selected strands for focused work in particular skill areas.

Other courses are organized by topics into MODULES and LESSONS, and give each student appropriate additional practice and tutorial help in needed topics.

As the student responds to exercises, the computer evaluates the student's performance. The computer automatically adjusts the level of difficulty of the exercises.

The courses not only take account of differences between students but also each student's varying abilities. Students work at their own pace— with privacy and success!

3 INDIVIDUALIZATION IN CCC'S COURSES

By using CCC's courses, the teacher gains the assistance of the computer to improve students' skills. The courses diagnose each student's understanding of a concept and present practice exercises suited to each student's skill level.

4 RESEARCH AND RESULTS

CCC's instruction works! Years of research and evaluation of CCC's courses show the positive results of using CCC's computer-assisted instruction (CAI) lessons to supplement classwork. The courses help raise student achievement levels and improve learning attitudes.

CCC marketing material

FIGURE 50: Sony SMC-70 Description

During this time period, Sony was known for its quality technology products, its modern and sleek designs, and its small components, such as the original Sony Walkman and hand-held TVs. With the SMC-70, Sony had also developed the 3.5-inch hard-sided diskette; media so small it could be slipped into one's shirt pocket. But CCC courseware, with one course holding up to seven years of academic material and exercises, required much more storage than the Sony 3.5-inch diskette would allow. CCC used 8-inch floppy disks (one 8-inch floppy disk per course, with each disk storing up to 50 student histories). CCC courseware also required an external 8-inch floppy disk drive (a large piece of equipment), to be attached to the SMC-70.

During Sony's 1982 "Introduction to the SMC-70," CCC was invited to New York City to join Sony and other software vendors in presenting programs that were already using the SMC-70 microcomputer. Although there was some interest in an education solution, many attendees chuckled at the CCC system set-up because of the large and clumsy-looking 8-inch floppy disk drive (comments such as "anchor," "relic," "old-technology," "too big and heavy.") When interested enough to listen to the explanation of why such a large disk and drive were necessary, there was some degree of understanding, although the CCC consultant most vividly remembers the "scoffing."[9]

Suppes recalled that CCC sold more SMC-70s than any of Sony's other dealerships. Despite this dubious record, the SMC-70 was not much of a success in the marketplace. It had superb graphics, but the CP/M operating system limited it to 64KB of main memory. The SMC-70 had some additional memory for graphics, but it was difficult to program and non-standard.

One marketing purpose of the SMC-70 was to say, "see, CCC has a microcomputer product, CCC is Modern," and it certainly could be used for that. The courses ran very well and looked better than any other CCC product to date, including the upcoming Microhost.

In the early-80s, Suppes was actively looking for new marketing opportunities and submitted proposals to many RFPs, including new ones that required microcomputers for the bids. The closest to success of these proposals was to the Department of Defense Dependent Schools for overseas training of children of the military using the standard CCC courses on the SMC-70. The proposal was ranked first in content but lost out to Atari Corporation, which was first in cost.

Around this time, a serious product issue was exposed by the SMC-70, a lesson that CCC learned once again. Since there was no networking, each machine would have only the student records for the students using that machine. CCC had built a new and superior management system for the SMC-70, only to miss the point that there was not very much to manage. If you had a number of SMC-70s and a class of students, the proctor would have to make sure that a given student used the same machine each day. There were plans to have the student records shared among a cluster of machines, but this feature was never implemented.

Most SMC-70s that CCC sold were deployed in small clusters and for special purposes. This satisfied some customers and found entries to some districts, but the cost of sales was high compared to the company's expectations.

Nevertheless, the experience allowed CCC to make a good objection to the Apples and TRS-80s that customers would be buying. While the Apple might look good and be fun to use, there was no convenient way to manage a class of students on it. CCC marketing pointed this out with great success to those who were primarily interested in measuring educational gains.

A former engineer remembers a day that he was at a school using the Microhost system, in about 1985. The school had a lab with 32 terminals that was in constant use with classes coming in every 30 minutes

---

[9]Personal communication from Betty Menacher.

or so. There was a darkened room across the hall. The proctor pointed this room out and said, "That is our Apple lab. We don't use it very much because there is no basic skills software that we can get reports out of." While true at the time, it must be said that this assertion proved to be increasingly illusory as time went on.

Another lesson only learned years after the SMC-70 experience was that CCC had picked the wrong microcomputer! In a few years, the IBM PC and its MS-DOS "clones" had become a huge factor in business and also education. Companies like ETSC in San Diego (later Jostens Learning and now Compass Learning) were providing courseware similar to CCC's on networked PCs, and were becoming a serious marketing threat. CCC had missed a clear opportunity to get into MS-DOS systems at the very outset.

5.7   The Microhost Completion and Reception

Now with UNIX as its operating system, C as its programming language, and equipped with industry-standard components, the Microhost was ready to go. Figure 51 shows the first marketing collateral about the system.

- Once again, the "complete" set of courses was promised, together with a management system.

- UNIX was highlighted as being "famous." UNIX capabilities like email, file transfer, word processing, and general-purpose computing were mentioned. While a number of customers actually did take advantage of UNIX capabilities directly when CCC added tools for courseware evaluation (see page 175), most schools were not ready for UNIX.[10]

- The new management system was much easier to use and had more capabilities for manipulating a large number of student records.

The official "birthday" for the Microhost was April 15, 1984. This was *just in time*. One of CCC's issues was how to keep sales going with the CCC-17 while they completed and then started selling the Microhost. There had been a number of cases in the industry where products were "pre-announced" in such a way that existing products were no longer of interest to customers while new products were not ready yet. This is sometimes called "the Osborne effect" after an early Silicon Valley firm called Osborne Computer.[11] CCC was wary of this problem.

---

[10] The IPS team also created a UNIX course to help with the user training both in-house and for customers.

[11] See Wikipedia "Osborne Computer Corporation" [204].

CCC marketing material

FIGURE 51: Microhost Promotional Piece

However, CCC also needed to manufacture "just enough" CCC-17 systems in order to be able to meet demands without making too many. CCC ended up with just one extra machine.

In the last few months of 1983 and up to 1984, CCC had a difficult time getting the Microhost ready to ship. Nancy Smith recalls:

> I was pregnant with our daughter Karen, and Bob [Smith] was busy day and night with the Microhost. I left work myself early at 5pm one day in the beginning of April 1984, but he spent another few hours of last-minute work, not showing up until 5am to go to the hospital while telling me that I had chosen a very bad time to have the baby—clearly the Microhost was his baby!

5.7.1 Later Additions to the Microhost

Associated developments over the next few years included the following:

- The Dial-A-Drill product was once again reborn, this time with a new scheduling system for schools. See the earlier discussion in 5.3.4.
- A new terminal, the SLS11, was designed and marketed. It was similar to the DEC VT100/ANSI terminals, but contained special features for multiplexing a number of terminals together. Since each terminal now had its own logic, the MiniAce box was no longer needed.

- A new speech system called the CSS was built about 1985. The CSS used a similar physical design to the Microhost, and was basically a repackaging and less expensive design from the DSS.
- The IPS product was introduced with the Microhost, developed using UNIX tools, and begun in 1984 just as the Microhost hit production. IPS stood for "Individualized Prescriptive Strategy," and predicted the future results in a course for each individual student as a function of that student's previous results. This was the most innovative research done by CCC since its founding in 1967. See section 5.8.

5.7.2   Search for Alternative Markets

Nancy Smith had come onboard at CCC in 1982 with the specific job of exploring other opportunities for the company whether it was new products or new markets that would complement the existing courseware offerings to schools. Smith and her team pursued several approaches:

- RFPs: Many proposals written in response to RFPs for government and private sector training of various sorts (including the military and adult education)[12] were mostly unsuccessful.
- Retail Outlets: Smith[13] scouted locations in the Bay Area and priced the potential service, which didn't appear feasible. Of course, SCORE set up exactly such a center 10 years later in Palo Alto in 1992 (licensing the curriculum from CCC) and adding the concept of a tutor which would later be used by EPGY as well. SCORE expanded to 165 centers before closing down in 2009.[14] So this was probably an idea before its time.
- Dial-A-Drill for the Home Market: Smith set up a small pilot using only Dial-A-Drill (DAD) offered to local parents for a fee, see page 160.
- UNIX Tools: Smith believed in the general utility and power of computing tools even for less experienced users.[15] So she didn't want to take a powerful new UNIX machine like the Microhost and present it only as a turn-key system where students, teachers, and administrators had no access to the computer itself. Providing access, making the tools usable by educational personnel, and supporting their usage would be a big and expensive undertaking, but the addition that

---

[12]See page 169 for one of the closest to successful of these.

[13]References to "Smith" in this section refer to Nancy Smith.

[14]See Wikipedia "Score! Educational Centers" [220].

[15]An earlier job was at SUMEX supporting and finding ways to get AI researchers in medicine to develop and share computer tools nationally in the early 1970s using the ARPANET.

she wanted could be turned into a new product by offering access to the UNIX system at an add-on price. Suppes, as he so often did, found an RFP for Smith to win that would provide the funding for development of the tools package.

This latter offering evolved further over the next year to turn into IPS.

5.8 Individualized Prescriptive Strategy (IPS)

5.8.1 What is IPS?

IPS was designed to work in schools in conjunction with the major basic skills courses to:

- Set a gain-in-grade-placement goal for each student.

- Predict on a regular basis how long it would take the student to reach this goal.

- Recommend specific intervention early when the prediction was that the student would not make the agreed-upon goal.[16]

The concept of learning trajectories, which was the foundation of IPS, was conceived by Suppes and Mario Zanotti much earlier and developed into a "quick" prototype in the UNIX awk programming language by Nancy Smith in 1985 for IPS.[17] UNIX shell scripts ran the programs automatically on the local Microhost installed in the school district and returned the results nightly over dialup lines to corporate headquarters, where further scripts ran to compile monthly usage and prescriptive reports to be sent to the district administrators and school personnel. Then utilizing the collected data from an entire year, plus the upload of student standardized test scores, annual evaluation reports were provided.

The first annual report for Fort Worth Parochial Schools was sent at the end of the 1985–1986 school year. The last IPS reports were produced for 1995–96 in the Philadelphia Parochial School District so the product had over a 10 year run in both large parochial and public school districts.

IPS was a typical case for Suppes of the right product at the right time with the convergence of fundamental research ideas looking for a home, new technology looking for productive uses, and the company looking to expand marketing opportunities.

---

[16]CCC in 1993 published an offer in Education Week to **guarantee** results based on IPS if the students followed the program's recommendations, see [31].

[17]Note that as with many prototypes, there was never another version done.

5.8.2 Background of Learning Research for IPS

Early research at IMSSS and CCC developed the theory of learning trajectories for CAI. The fundamental idea in lay terms was that most people strongly believe that time on task predicts the amount of learning, but there was no common formula that could be used for all subject material or all students to quantify that intuition. Each student will have an individual learning curve that does not match other students and is not necessarily linear for that student when you plot the time and progress through the course.

Determining the coefficients of this individual learning curve up to the current time will allow one to construct a "trajectory" of learning for that student which can predict the learning results for any given amount of time spent or conversely predict the time needed to reach any given learning target. Figure 52 shows a good example of four students with very different patterns in their learning trajectories. Figure 53[18] has the data for the highest achieving student (STUD#=931) with one line for each actual session showing the cumulative time after that session (TIME), the cumulative gain since IPM (GAIN SINCE IPM), and the level (AVG) in the course as well as the predicted value (EAVG) from the trajectory, how far off the prediction EAVG was from the actual AVG (DIFF), and other values such as the gain per hour (GAIN/HOUR), the cumulative total correct answers (TCORR), and the percentage correct (%).

A dotted line divides the actual sessions from the predicted sessions. Following the dotted line are the projected values of gain with more increments of time. Note that this student had already reached the goal of 1.1 gain by approximately 480 minutes, but if he/she had not already reached the goal then the values below the line would show the minutes to reach 1.10. This student was enrolled at 1.00 and after 10 sessions (about 100 minutes) had reached 1.97 which is therefore a gain of 0.00 since IPM. By the end of June, the gain was 1.3. Had the student spent 1,000 minutes, then the predicted gain would have been close to 2.0.

The formula for the trajectory is $AVG(t) = a + bt^k$ where $AVG(t)$ is student's average grade placement at time t, a is the student's starting grade placement after Initial Placement Motion (IPM), and b and k are the fit parameters estimated for each student.

---

[18]Pages included in IPS annual training materials for October 11–14, 1989, unpublished.

Learning Trajectories for Students 931, 933, 936, 938

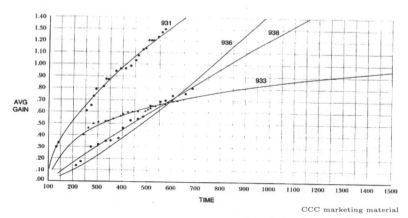

CCC marketing material

FIGURE 52: IPS Four Individual Learning Patterns

For more technical details, see [140], [139], [71],[19] [70],[20] [157], [156],[21] and [69].[22]

5.8.3 Putting It Together to Develop IPS!

The time was right: CCC had the fundamental research, the marketing drive, and the technology. At an early point in the discussions of packaging the new UNIX product,[23] Suppes and Smith realized that Smith could also use her UNIX programming experience to develop new educational tools sold to sites that would be specifically designed to enhance student learning; these could be included in the add-on package sold to specific sites. Suppes could have the implementation of learning trajectories for prediction that he'd wanted for a long time. Suppes and Zanotti (who was already on staff at CCC doing evaluations of school programs) designed the algorithm which Smith programmed as an implementation of their learning trajectories theory.

---

[19]CCC later described the evolution of the research in the following way: "[Earlier work] concentrated on mathematically **describing** student trajectories through the curriculum by fitting curves to a set of points that have already been observed. Here we focus on the somewhat different problem of **predicting** a future trajectory from past observations"

[20]Good discussion with sample trajectories.

[21]Tock gives a good explanation of the mathematical formula for computing trajectories.

[22]Very early use of trajectory analysis at IMSSS for home-based, gifted student learning.

[23]See page 174.

ROUP: CHRIST THE KING   REPORT DATE: 87-02-28

COURSE = MK

STUD#	TIME	GAIN SINCE IPM	AVG	EAVG	DIFF.	GAIN/HR	TCORR	%
931	0	0.00	1.00					
931	101	0.00	1.973					
931	111	0.20	2.17	2.16438	0.00562	0.37065	576	77
931	131	0.29	2.26	2.26372	0.00372	0.25359	699	77
931	141	0.33	2.30	2.30385	0.00385	0.22960	746	76
931	251	0.60	2.57	2.62548	0.05548	0.14544	1133	71
931	271	0.65	2.62	2.67291	0.05291	0.13928	1171	71
931	281	0.73	2.70	2.69589	0.00411	0.13656	1211	71
931	291	0.79	2.76	2.71844	0.04156	0.13403	1243	71
931	321	0.81	2.78	2.78374	0.00374	0.12741	1327	70
931	331	0.88	2.85	2.80482	0.04518	0.12547	1368	70
931	351	0.88	2.85	2.84603	0.00397	0.12191	1425	69
931	371	0.94	2.91	2.88613	0.02387	0.11871	1475	69
931	391	0.96	2.93	2.92521	0.00479	0.11581	1543	69
931	411	0.96	2.93	2.96337	0.03337	0.11318	1606	69
931	431	0.98	2.95	3.00068	0.05068	0.11076	1680	69
931	451	1.03	3.00	3.03723	0.03723	0.10853	1734	69
931	461	1.07	3.04	3.05523	0.01523	0.10748	1775	70
931	481	1.12	3.09	3.09072	0.00072	0.10549	1818	70
931	491	1.13	3.10	3.10822	0.00822	0.10455	1847	70
931	501	1.20	3.17	3.12557	0.04443	0.10364	1880	70
931	511	1.20	3.17	3.14277	0.02723	0.10276	1904	70
931	521	1.20	3.17	3.15982	0.01018	0.10191	1937	70
931	537	1.25	3.22	3.18682	0.03318	0.10060	1993	70
931	556	1.29	3.26	3.21844	0.04156	0.09913	2048	70
931	566	1.30	3.27	3.23490	0.03510	0.09838	2080	70
931	716	1.50		3.47000		0.08929		
931	892	1.75		3.72000		0.08187		
931	1082	2.00		3.97000		0.07600		
931	1286	2.25		4.22000		0.07120		
931	1504	2.50		4.47000		0.06718		

Target gain of 1.1 already reached.
b=.0209087
k=.654543
a=2.07
A.M.D. = .0244137
S.E.E. = .0306822
MAX D. = .0554841

FIGURE 53: IPS Data for Student 931

The plan was designed and implemented, then followed by a successful marketing launch. The product was installed in Fort Worth Parochial Schools by the start of school in September 1985, including the programs, underlying UNIX administrative packages, the new course in UNIX, and complete documentation.

With the large success at the original sites, Suppes then created the Evaluation Department led by Zanotti to oversee the production of the ongoing annual evaluation reports for the participating districts.

5.8.4   IPS: The Benefits

The IPS package had its marketing sizzle! IPS brought a variety of benefits to CCC and the schools:

- Allowed more revenue per site (for software license and support fees) with no additional equipment costs except the modem for dialup.

- Took advantage of a new marketing opportunity where public school districts could provide CAI for remediation of Chapter 1 students in parochial schools in compliance with the Supreme Court decision (*Aguilar v. Felton*, 1984)[24] through a setup such as CCC's IPS. The ruling disallowed the school districts from sending teachers into the parochial schools. A number of the IPS sites were parochial schools, but not all.[25]

- Included budget for adequate support (CCC consultant time) as a pre-requisite to IPS so that schools would have the support that they needed but weren't always willing to pay for.

- Offered computing power to schools that were becoming increasingly computer literate and able to take advantage.

- Provided a way to ensure smooth, efficient running of sites not only from a distance but in fact with no human resources required as the monitoring took place through automated software.

- Performed maintenance/troubleshooting of the new IPS software from corporate headquarters rather than adding product training for all of the Field Service personnel.

- Enabled central data collection using only a dialup line rather than expensive, difficult-to-maintain networking capability.

- Increased overall customer satisfaction (as perceived) due to the active monitoring and reporting.

- Increased overall student effectiveness (as measured) through teacher use of the reports to make student interventions.

---

[24]See Wikipedia "Aguilar v. Felton" [169].
[25]See a more detailed discussion on page 195.

- Developed a set of CCC consultants with special experience enhanced through annual corporate training sessions.

5.8.5   Installation and Implementation of IPS Onsite

The IPS school districts even hired a single point of contact—usually selected in consultation with CCC—who was familiar with UNIX (or willing to be trained) and given the title of Technical Support. Each district was also assigned to one of CCC's specially trained consultants for considerable help and monitoring.

This became a tight-knit, well-functioning group including among many others: Betty Menacher as Vice President of Consultant Services, Barbara Tingey from Marketing at corporate who led the annual training boot camps, Sandy Hestes, the lead consultant in Texas which was home to most of the IPS sites, and newcomers like Tom Runtagh who was the Tech Support in Philadelphia. John Sheehan, a student of Suppes also worked with Zanotti on a number of statistical evaluations for certain customers.[26] Garrett Lai later also worked with Sheehan and Zanotti on technical issues. Lai was a student of Sheehan at San Francisco State, to carry on a tradition that Suppes approved of.

There were many stories of both the issues (dealing with thefts, fires, and other calamities in poor districts) and the inspiration provided by the students and nuns at the parochial schools so happy with the program.[27]

No customer list remains, and no one remembers precisely, but there were at least a dozen large school districts with an average of two Microhosts each; Philadelphia was the largest installation with six machines. Each of these 20+ machines served 4–8 schools. Interestingly over half of the IPS sites were in Texas.

The Tech Support and the CCC consultant had to setup a regular turnkey Microhost for IPS by first using a key to turn off the machine, reboot in local mode, type in the root password at the console, and assign that machine its unique nodename. Then they needed to edit the .password and .profile files, create necessary directories and set file permissions, and then notify CCC to transfer the IPS files to the new machine. The next set of tasks were filling out (using vi) all the information needed in the newly received files to set up schools, classes, and students with all their information, including pretest scores and at

---

[26]Sheehan was also married to Kim Merriam, now known as Kim Sheehan.

[27]Tom Runtagh said in a phone interview in 2014 that in his entire life this was "one of the most effective investments" of his time. Tom is presently working in Adult Education and has had several former students come up to him to say how much they "really learned math" in the IPS program.

the end of the year add the posttest. The Tech Support also needed to be the system administrator and was taught to monitor disk space and other tasks.

Throughout the year, the Tech Support was charged with making sure the school district personnel and teachers actually used the monthly reports to make interventions for the students. Every effort was made to have this be a distinctive service with perks for the participants, including special recognition and training.

Each year an attractive notebook cover in a different color was designed and produced by the CCC publications department to be sent out to school and district-level personnel in September to store that year's monthly reports culminating in the end-of-year evaluation.[28] The reports were run at CCC Headquarters and mailed out.[29]

The district personnel loved having reports that allowed them to both compare the schools in their district and show off their shiny new system. The principals could similarly compare the performance (both gains and time on task) of the classes for each of their teachers. And finally, the teachers and proctors had more control over the effectiveness of the learning for each of their students than ever available before (or possibly since).

5.8.6   IPS Monthly Reports and Intervention Strategies

There were three reports sent out monthly, which are shown in the following examples from the Fort Worth schools. Figure 54 shows the report on how many students were in each time band with the average gain for the students in that band—for the current month on the left and cumulatively for the year on the right. Figure 55 shows the Learning Trajectory Distribution indicating for each student how much more time was needed to make the target gain. The reports shown in Figure 56 gave the average time, gain, and gain per hour for each course for each school. The first two reports showed the information per school and within that per course, while the third report summarized for the district.

The reports were used as part of the intervention strategy for each individual student. They would be used to identify the students not performing as expected. The guidelines for intervention included: as-

---

[28]Schools were often not allowed to make their own printouts so this was a necessary part of the program plus it ensured that each person up to the Superintendent of Schools actually received the reports.

[29]Don't ask Smith and her staff about the photocopying nightmare involved with 5 reports for each of several users at the district level plus the principal, proctor, and other designated personnel at each of over 100 schools that had to be sent out every month through US mail.

CAI Gains and Time Report by School
Chapter I CAI Project, Greenville Parochial Schools

GROUP: ALL SAINTS   CURRENT PERIOD: 89-01-31 TO 89-02-29

CURRENT PERIOD AVERAGES   SINCE IPM AVERAGES

			(S.D.)				(S.D.)
COURSE	#STUD	TIME	GAIN	GAIN/HR	#STUD	TIME	GAIN	GAIN/HR
ARP		1-50				1-500		
		51-100			24	501-1000	0.64	0.04
	2	101-150	0.04	0.02	1	1001-1500	0.70	0.04
	16	151-200	0.11	0.04	1	1501-2000	0.72	0.02
	8	201+	0.16	0.04		2001+		
Total	26	187	0.12	0.04	26	937	0.64	0.04
		(46)	(0.05)	(0.02)		(214)	(0.22)	(0.01)

FIGURE 54: IPS CAI Gains and Time

LEARNING TRAJECTORIES DISTRIBUTION
Chapter I CAI Project, Greenville Parochial Schools

GROUP: ALL SAINTS   REPORT DATE: 88-04-30

COURSE = ARP

	TIME		GAIN	ADDITIONAL MINUTES TO REACH TARGET									
	TO	TARGET	SINCE	TOP									
STUD#	DATE	GAIN	IPM	OUT	NOW	200	400	600	800	1000	1200	1400	>1400
732	1161	1.10	0.65							732			
737	1079	1.10	0.80				737						
738	1156	1.10	1.25		738								
739	1110	1.10	1.01			739							
740	1147	1.10	1.20		740								
754	996	1.10	1.21		754								
757	829	1.10	0.88			757							
758	809	1.10	0.70				758						
TOTAL = 8				0	3	1	1	2	0	1	0	0	0

FIGURE 55: IPS Learning Trajectories Distribution

Summary of CAI Gains and Time
Chapter I CAI Project, Greenville Parochial Schools

REPORT DATE: 88-02-29

	#STUDENT	TIME SINCE IPM		GAIN SINCE IPM		GAIN PER HR	
		MEAN	S.D.	MEAN	S.D.	MEAN	S.D.
Audio Reading							
ALL SAINTS	26	937	214	0.64	0.22	0.04	0.01
OUR LADY OF VICTORY	7	1005	128	0.90	0.17	0.06	0.02
OUR MOTHER OF MERCY	7	854	71	0.83	0.22	0.06	0.01
SAINT GEORGE'S	4	754	291	0.73	0.18	0.07	0.03
SAINT RITA'S	6	948	105	1.04	0.18	0.07	0.01
TOTAL	50	922	198	0.76	0.25	0.05	0.02
Basic Reading							
ALL SAINTS	1	432	0	0.25	0.00	0.03	0.00
TOTAL	1	432	0	0.25	0.00	0.03	0.00
Language Arts Strands							
ALL SAINTS	2	746	65	0.94	0.04	0.08	0.01
OUR LADY OF VICTORY	3	770	106	1.41	0.11	0.11	0.02
OUR MOTHER OF MERCY	3	654	61	0.98	0.02	0.09	0.01
SAINT GEORGE'S	1	834	0	1.40	0.00	0.10	0.00
SAINT RITA'S	2	821	20	1.36	0.09	0.10	0.00
TOTAL	11	749	96	1.20	0.22	0.10	0.02

Action: If CAI gains or time for a school seem low, check the CAI Gains and Time Report (R1) for that school. The time partitions on that report will show the time spent per course. Encourage sufficient CAI time at all sites. Make sure the school personnel are using the Learning Trajectories Distribution Report (R2) to identify students who are making slow progress.

FIGURE 56: IPS Summary of CAI Gains and Time

signing additional CAI time to the student, having the teacher give extra assignments to the student in areas of difficulty, watching the student take a session to spot the problem, using computer-generated worksheets in the problem skill areas, assigning the student sessions in just the problem strands in addition to their regular sessions, and working on student motivation with goal setting and rewards.

These are the same strategies recommended for CAI in general. The difference with IPS was: 1) the focus and extra resources devoted to ensuring the interventions happened and 2) the tools provided to easily identify the students falling behind the expectations for that student. Note that there would otherwise be no way to tell if a student already going quickly through the material should actually be going faster or if a slow-moving student was already doing the best that should be expected since the learning all happens at the individual's own pace.

5.8.7 Debrief on IPS Success

Menacher, who later became the Vice President of Educational Services, was a huge key to the success of IPS. When asked for her recollections of the product and its use in schools, she gave the following very insightful analysis of what worked and how it could have done better: IPS was a product with amazing capabilities for informing educators about student learning and alerting them when students' learning progress stalled. Those schools where IPS was most successful were those where:

- Local educational administrators (superintendents, academic supervisors, and principals) were involved in initiating and monitoring the IPS program on a regular and consistent basis; districts where one or two strong individuals were hired/assigned to the program: technology specialist (for UNIX duties) and instructional specialist (for implementing the IPS program in the schools and working with the teachers).

- A district/school teacher support team was created to:
  - Print regular learning trajectories for individual schools, teachers, and parents.
  - Schedule targeted students for more time on appropriate CCC CAI course(s), as needed.
  - Assist in providing teachers with reports that identified specific students for whom additional instructional intervention was warranted and/or grouping students with similar needs.
  - Provide academic services to students needing instruction, review, and/or remediation in reading or math.

IPS was not as successful as it could have been when it was not implemented as recommended for some of the following reasons:

- Not enough computer stations in school to accommodate extra student sessions when needed.
- Not enough time in the school day to add CAI sessions for students who needed more time (including no staff available to supervise before/after-school programs.)
- No support to teachers to run/evaluate appropriate IPS and related CAI reports (with restrictions on amount of printer paper and ink allowed to be purchased!).
- Teacher fear of technology (it was mid-1980s and computers were just entering schools).
- Teacher suspicion of courseware, questioning whether or not it was educationally sound.
- Teacher skepticism of school "aides" (or other non-educator staff) giving instructional recommendations.
- Teacher workload in regular educational environment and time-restraints in terms of providing appropriate instructional support (particularly for individual and small-group tutorial/teaching guidance per the IPS reports).

Note: In the educational world of 2014, schools are required (by Federal Law; NCLB) to implement a whole-school "response to intervention" model in each building. The RTI model requires that students be assessed on a regular basis, provided with needed intervention (including instruction, review, and remediation) in areas of academic weakness, and then re-assessed to determine whether the intervention was successful. Although the IPS product was designed to provide similar services to educators, IPS (as with several other CCC products) was a "product before its time."[30]

5.8.8 IPS Effectiveness Evaluations

Each district was provided with a final report for each year of the program called, for example, "Effectiveness of the CCC CAI Program Fort Worth Parochial Schools, Global Evaluation for 1987–88." These reports were extremely well received. The reports were based on "the important and simple concept of time needed for achievement" as discussed in [158]:

> Many educational researchers have observed and documented that when time spent on any task is held constant, achievement among

---

[30]Most of this section was written by Betty in a private communication in 2014.

individual students varies significantly (most recently, Gettinger, 1985 [45]), and that the relation TIME SPENT/TIME NEEDED provides the most relevant information on student achievement. ([24])

There were six different types of analysis done each year. The following are some sample tables and figures of each type from the Fort Worth 1987–88 school year which are fairly representative.[31]

Analysis 1—Effectiveness of CAI Measured in NCE Units

The results were in terms of NCEs rather than the percentile gains that were often used by competitors to show huge 3-digit percentile gains. Zanotti had samples that he would frequently produce to show visitors how misleading those analyses could be. The use of NCEs made for a fair comparison as described by Zanotti in the boilerplate of each of the annual reports:

> To assess the educational meaningfulness of NCE gains, we must re-call that, relative to the national norming population, students with 0 NCE gain have maintained their pretest achievement status at posttest. Thus a mean NCE gain significantly different from 0 reveals that a significant gain in achievement status in the observed student population has occurred from pretest to posttest. Typically, students with a pretest percentile ranking of 50 and 0 NCE gain have achieved about one year's grade-equivalent growth, and students with a percentile ranking below 50 and 0 NCE gain have achieved less than one year's grade-equivalent growth.
>
> This measure of growth should not be confused with the sample mean grade-equivalent gain calculated directly from the observed individual students' achievement test grade-equivalent scores, a meaningless statistic since the grade-equivalent scale is not an interval scale.[32]

Each report gave a description of the implementation at that site and the student population, which in the case of Fort Worth was Chapter 1 students so expected to actually have an NCE loss each year without intervention. See Figure 57 for a table showing the mean Time Spent and NCE Gain for each school in Math.

Analysis 2—Frequency Distribution of Pretest and Posttest Scores

Zanotti explained in the report that the scores were summarized globally by center (mean) of the distribution and the standard deviation,

---

[31]See [11] pp. 38–39 for a more critical viewpoint on the usefulness of these evaluation reports.

[32]This argues that the results are only to be taken at the group level rather than for any individual student or summary of individual students—for this CCC recommended looking at the AVG growth in the courses.

NCE Achievement Gains Per School in Math

School	# of Students	Time Spent		NCE Gain		t Value
		Mean	(S.D.)	Mean	(S.D.)	
AS	15	1015	(429)	15.8	(25.4)	2.33
MCM	13	767	(318)	12.3	(13.5)	3.17
OLV	13	881	(85)	10.2	(8.7)	4.06
SG	6	757	(113)	11.0	(16.5)	1.50
SR	14	882	(107)	12.5	(8.1)	5.55
TOTAL	61	877	(285)	12.7	(16.1)	6.08

FIGURE 57: IPS NCE Achievement Gains Per School in Math

but "these parameters provide an insufficient characterization in the case of distributions exhibiting the asymmetry of the pretest achievement score distribution"[33] which "may lead to biased statistical estimates that ... mask the distributional features relevant to achievement changes in the student population."

Figure 58 with the solid black line for pretest shows the very clear pattern of growth.

Analysis 3—Effectiveness of CAI Measured by Course Average Scores

This analysis differs from the others because it focuses on gains in the CCC courseware. Zanotti points out that standardized tests are taken on a single day where many uncontrollable accidental factors can occur for the student. They test on only a small set of sample exercises, and are known to be most accurate at the mid-range of students rather than the population in this Chapter 1 group.

CCC believed that given the organization of their courses "in evenly spaced levels of difficulty and indexed by a scale in grade-level units matching the school grade in hundredths of a grade year" which covered the entire typical content for that year, then the student's record in the course could/should actually be substituted for the fallible standardized tests, although they never succeeded at getting any district to do this!

The course AVG value is "a precise summary of a continuously updated set of information on the student's performance in the ongoing

---

[33]Note that the pretest score distribution is cut off at the middle of the chart because these were all students with low pretests in order to be admitted to the program.

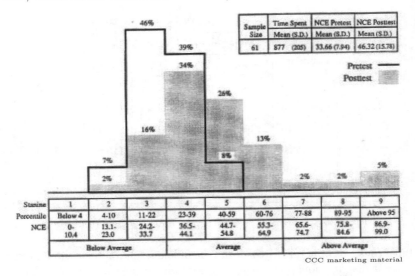

FIGURE 58: IPS Frequency Distribution of Scores in Math

daily learning activities." This analysis provides a summary of the AVG results as shown in Figure 59 for each grade with the mean time spent, originally enrolled mean grade level, mean grade level determined by IPM, mean gain since IPM, and mean final level at the end of the year.

AVG Achievement Gains Per Grade in MK

Grade	# of Students	Time Spent		Enrollment Level		End-of-IPM AVG		Gain Since IPM		End-of-Year AVG	
		Mean	(S.D.)	Mean	(S.D.)	Mean	(S.D.)	Mean	(S.D.)	Mean	(S.D.)
1	33	903	(217)	1.00	(0.00)	1.71	(0.31)	0.93	(0.28)	2.64	(0.34)
2	20	1277	(217)	1.58	(0.65)	2.14	(0.23)	0.95	(0.37)	3.09	(0.45)
3	2	1248	(281)	2.66	(0.40)	2.30	(0.08)	1.25	(0.22)	3.56	(0.30)
4	9	1010	(131)	2.59	(0.70)	2.90	(0.58)	1.40	(0.53)	4.30	(0.80)
5	12	990	(250)	2.83	(0.52)	3.27	(0.54)	1.47	(0.49)	4.74	(0.75)
6	11	932	(109)	4.18	(0.51)	3.93	(0.69)	1.00	(0.33)	4.93	(0.69)
7	5	753	(263)	4.96	(0.33)	4.37	(0.30)	0.94	(0.35)	5.30	(0.49)
TOTAL	110*	1010	(265)	2.26	(1.39)	2.63	(1.09)	1.11	(0.44)	3.74	(1.20

FIGURE 59: IPS Average Achievement Gains for Grade in MK

Analysis 4—Performance Variables

This section of the annual report discussed the inadequacy of any simple analysis and praised the complexities captured by the IPS learning trajectories for individual students. The student's learning rate as exemplified by the trajectory is of course not actually based on the amount

CAI Performance Variables in MK

Grade	# of Students	TIME/SES		TATT/SES		TATT/Hour		TCOR/TATT	
		Mean	(S.D.)	Mean	(S.D.)	Mean	(S.D.)	Mean	(S.D.)
1.0	12	9.91	(0.07)	39.90	(8.42)	241.67	(51.09)	0.61	(0.03)
1.5	22	9.92	(0.11)	31.26	(6.55)	189.13	(40.09)	0.63	(0.03)
2.0	33	9.91	(0.29)	32.26	(9.73)	195.63	(59.29)	0.65	(0.06)
2.5	10	9.69	(0.44)	36.79	(9.79)	228.08	(61.23)	0.70	(0.04)
3.0	9	9.60	(0.43)	29.99	(11.17)	187.68	(68.12)	0.69	(0.06)
3.5	7	9.48	(0.76)	31.20	(7.30)	198.98	(48.63)	0.70	(0.05)
4.0	11	9.90	(0.17)	32.87	(11.19)	199.11	(66.75)	0.71	(0.06)
4.5	6	9.10	(0.64)	26.13	(8.91)	170.83	(53.74)	0.72	(0.02)
TOTAL	110	9.82	(0.38)	32.86	(9.65)	201.08	(58.78)	0.66	(0.06)

FIGURE 60: IPS CAI Performance variables in MK

of time spent but rather on the learning activities taking place during that amount of time.

Figure 60 shows such performance variables as time spent and total number of exercises attempted (TATT) and correct (TCOR) in hours and/or sessions, plus the ratio of correct to attempted.[34]

Analysis 5—Individualized Prescriptive Strategy (IPS)

This analysis provided the district with planning information based on the formulas discussed and explained for the reader in the accompanying section of the report. It provided a good graphic representation. See Figure 61. The explanation for this figure follows.

Overall, the graph shows the relationship between "time on task" and gain in MCS. The time in minutes is shown on the Y-axis, and the gain in the MCS course is shown on the X-axis. In this case, if the students in Fort Worth spend the amount of time shown in the curve labeled T(Δ : MCS), then about 68% of the students would achieve the associated gain. If the students were to spend the amount of time shown in the higher T$*$(Δ : MCS) curve, then about 84% of the students would achieve the associated gain in the course. This emphasizes the fact that the relation of gain to time spent is predictable in the aggregate but also an individual issue with each student, which can also be predicted to some degree.

---

[34]The .66 value for TCOR/TATT here has achieved precisely what CCC recommended as a good value for learning (around 70%) because lower means the student is struggling and higher means the student already knew the content—remember that this value is averaged over the number of attempts for each concept or skill, which will start as incorrect exercises and end when the motion detects that the student has mastered the concept.

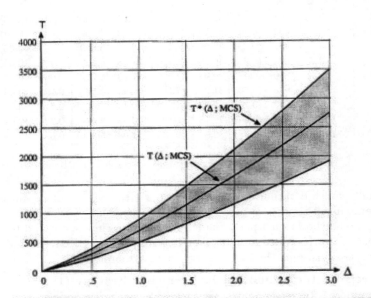

Figure 5. Relations Between Functional Gain and Time Needed for Math Concepts and Skills

Table 14
Relations Between Functional Gain and Time
Needed for Math Concepts and Skills

Δ	T(Δ;MCS)	T*(Δ;MCS)
1.00	700	900
1.25	925	1187
1.50	1162	1487
1.75	1409	1800
2.00	1665	2124
2.25	1929	2458
2.50	2200	2801
2.75	2479	3152
3.00	2764	3511

CCC marketing material

FIGURE 61: IPS Relation Between Functional Gain and Time in MCS

NCE Achievement Gains Per Year and Subject Area

	School Year	# of Students	Time Spent		NCE Gain	
			Mean	(S.D.)	Mean	(S.D.)
Mathematics	1985–86	75	769	(234)	8.4	(14.5)
	1986–87	89	557	(282)	16.0	(13.8)
	1987–88	61	877	(285)	12.7	(16.1)
Reading	1985–86	147	865	(269)	8.8	(13.8)
	1986–87	83	782	(380)	10.2	(14.4)
	1987–88	72	919	(243)	9.7	(10.6)
Language	1985–86	19	570	(240)	4.4	(8.7)
	1986–87	24	722	(182)	15.5	(15.5)
	1987–88	9	783	(130)	12.9	(11.6)
Combined	1985–86	241	812	(270)	8.3	(13.8)
	1986–87	196	763	(319)	13.5	(14.5)
	1987–88	142	892	(259)	11.2	(13.4)

FIGURE 62: IPS NCE Achievement Gains Per Year and Subject Area

Analysis 6—Replicability

Most of the districts had many years of success with the CCC CAI programs, as demonstrated in the Fort Worth Parochial Schools (see Figure 62 for a summary of their results between 1985 and 1988), although this was one of the smallest but also most successful programs.

5.8.9   The End of IPS

No new sites were added to IPS after the sale of CCC in 1990, and the existing contracts finally expired with the Philadelphia Parochial schools for the year 1995–96.

When asked for an analysis of what happened, Menacher responded:

Bottom line of why IPS ended and dropped from CCC product list? The time required from many levels of CCC employees to sell, implement, support, and monitor the IPS program was too much for the return to be profitable and sustainable. Also, too much time and commitment was required from CCC customers to implement IPS effectively. IPS required significant training and professional development (generally a full-time person for the district) and the product also required significant corporate support and time for problem-solving, frequent report analysis, and district end-of-year reporting.

In almost all cases, IPS was a program supplemental to the standard mainstream educational program and served only those students who met the requirements of Title 1. Regular education teachers with full class loads were frequently not willing/able to invest all the time necessary to understand and use IPS for just some of the students in their classrooms. Successful implementation of IPS involved additional (and flexible) time for student sessions and many extra sessions were difficult to add on to an already full school day. In some sites, additional student computer stations were needed to accommodate the additional session times indicated by reports. Although IPS report content and analysis became easier for classroom teachers to understand, their cooperation—in terms of time and academic intervention—was also required for IPS to be successful.

If IPS had ever become a mainstream classroom program, with all students able to benefit from the IPS report information, perhaps the product would still be alive![35]

Not only would the IPS product have required: a) more streamlining and automaticity to be easier to use and b) consideration of how to find a better fit in the classroom; but it would have also required porting to newer platforms. However, further development efforts of any sort were not made after the CCC sale.

5.9 Sales and Marketing

5.9.1 Organization and Operation of Marketing

The marketing organization had three main components: sales representatives, CAI consultants, and management/support/training. There were some traditional marketing people, most notably Barbara Tingey, Manager of Training for several decades, but in fact Suppes himself did most of the product marketing functions of setting the direction for: product development, pricing and terms, and how the products would be sold. This had been a strength in the early years, but the legacy of this policy created some growth issues in the 1990s, which were eventually resolved.[36]

In 1981, the sales team was divided into two regions: the Southwest, headquartered in Euless, Texas; and the West, in Palo Alto, CA. Each

---

[35]Private communication from Menacher on 16 August 2016.

[36]Ron Fortune provided much of the information in the section on sales and marketing, and Mary Wallace rewrote large sections of the text.

region had a vice president and a small team of salespeople and CAI consultants. In the early '80s, a decision was made to expand the sales team. David Munson, who had been the Vice President for the West, became the national Vice President of School Marketing. Ron Fortune was promoted to replace Munson and manage the West Region and a few sales reps in the Midwest and Southeast. By 1986, distinct sales teams in the Midwest and Southeast were established with Mary Wallace and Tom Foley as regional sales managers, respectively. The sales force doubled in this five-year period with a significant impact on sales. Dave Munson would remain in his position, until 1986 when Ron Fortune took over that role. There were also two distributors, Instructional Systems, Inc. in the Northeast and Southern Educational Media in the South, as discussed below.

Sales people had assigned territories and quotas, and were paid a small base salary plus commission. Suppes was fond of noting that a good sales rep could make more money than he did, and he was quite happy with that. Sales people were recruited for their knowledge and experience in the education market. Each sales representative and CAI consultant was required to attend two solid weeks (including the weekend) of product training led by Barbara Tingey. Internal communication took place mostly via phone on a weekly basis and a national sales training once a year in Palo Alto.

CCC did very little in the way of traditional marketing (trade shows, direct mail, etc.), so the sales cycle tended to be very long (18–24 months). CAI was a new concept, and the cost of implementation was high. Sales representatives had to make presentations and demonstrate software to multiple decision-makers at many levels. These often included curriculum committees, federal programs directors, superintendents, and board members.

In order to do a demo of the curriculum software in the '80s, a sales representative had to set up a Mini-Ace (p. 86) weighing 90 lbs. and four SLS terminals. Then they had to use a 1200 baud acoustic coupler to dial into one of CCC's remote sites in the Palo Alto, CA or Euless, TX offices. This was often a challenge as they had to make sure the demonstration site had an unrestricted phone line nearby that could be tied up for an hour or more.

As in all sales, providing a quality product and building a trusting relationship with the customer was key to CCC's success.

As time went on, districts became more formal, with RFPs and regulations about contacts with district people and the kinds of information that could be passed. Today, this process is very formal, with RFPs and rules about interactions designed to be fair to all vendors, but in the

1980s, things were still a matter of personal contact, especially in the South. During this period, the Southeast was the fastest growing region, followed by the Midwest. The Northeast, handled by a distributor, also continued to expand. (See below.)

5.9.2 Distributors

CCC had relationships with two distributors: Southern Educational Media (SEM), a small company in Louisiana that had the territory of Alabama, Mississippi and Louisiana, and a much larger organization, Instructional Systems Inc. (ISI) in New Jersey, whose territory included the New England states, New York, New Jersey, Delaware, Maryland and Washington, D.C. SEM successfully marketed the CCC products for a few years in the 1970s and early 1980s, mainly renting machines rather than selling them. As the older machines became obsolete and could no longer be rented, SEM suffered. In contrast, ISI was a key part of CCC's marketing organization.

ISI's most significant sales were in the states of New York and New Jersey. In New York, they worked with the Boards of Cooperative Educational Services (BOCES) to provide cost-effective instructional software to many small districts that could not afford to purchase their own central computer.[37] The BOCES ran regional facilities that many districts used and indeed often ended up being required to use for educational services. During this time, the BOCES ran regional computer labs, and many of them had chosen CCC as marketed by ISI. ISI and the BOCES were critically important to CCC. Special marketing and support arrangements were made for them, including providing BOCES staff with documentation and training to allow them to maintain the hardware.

Both of these distributor relationships created problems by the late 1980s. Suppes noted that it was very important to have distributor contracts written very carefully. The ISI relationship fell apart in the early 1990s. This resulted in a lawsuit after the purchase by Simon and Schuster. The lawsuit went all the way to the New Jersey Supreme Court, which ruled in favor of ISI in 1992. Simon and Schuster settled the suit by purchasing ISI. See [162] for details.

5.9.3 Sources of Funding

It was always important to identify sources of funding. School budgets tend to become fixed with items that are no longer needed still getting funding while new ideas find no place. CCC sales reps often had to

---

[37]See Wikipedia "Boards of Cooperative Educational Services" [174] for details about the BOCES.

help find new funds for potential customers as well as to work with customers who found a new funding source on their own.

The majority of sales were funded by the Elementary and Secondary Education Act Title 1, then Chapter 1, then Title 1 again under various re-authorizations. However, in many cases, these funds became tied up in staff and administration. Hence, a new funding source, e.g. *Felton v. Aguilar* (see below), would have to be found before a sale was possible. Two other large funding sources that the CCC sales team tapped into were the Job Training Partnership Act (JTPA) of 1982 and school desegregation funds through the 1980s. CCC also served many of the adult education programs nationwide, including GED programs in the public schools as well as state and federal prisons. Prisons were a surprisingly effective place since inmates tended to get absorbed in using the computer.[38] Often, when a school district purchased the CCC system, they were able to add 8–16 terminals in an adult education center.

5.9.4 Felton Decision

CCC was very good at noting trends and taking advantage of them. One such trend was brought about by the "Felton Decision."

Aguilar v. Felton was a 1985 court decision by the United States Supreme Court.[39] The decision forbade the use of public-school teachers in parochial schools. However, Title I funds were still available for the students attending parochial schools.[40]

When the initial decision came down, parochial schools were in an immediate panic to find ways to spend the Title I funds available to their students. CCC reacted by offering educational services using the Microhost system. The basic idea was that trailers would be installed on the school grounds in which the CCC terminals were kept. The students would go to the trailers for their lessons. Everything was handled in such a way that the schools were "hands off" from the instructional delivery, but students still benefited from Title I funding; so did CCC and other companies. Figure 63 displays the cover of a marketing brochure for CCC's "Felton solution."

The CCC system also accommodated multiple parochial schools in the same region by placing the main system at a central site and then clusters of terminals and sound systems at each school, sometimes housed in trailers. Figure 64 shows a drawing of a Microhost in

---

[38]This is before the Internet and issues of security.

[39]See Wikipedia "Aguilar v. Felton" [169] for details.

[40]This decision didn't make a lot of sense in practice and was overturned in *Agostini v. Felton* in 1997, see Wikipedia [168].

Look at this successful *Felton* solution

For parochial *and* public school Chapter I programs:
CCC's approved computer-assisted solution is ready to go

CCC marketing material

FIGURE 63: CCC Marketing Brochure for Felton Solution

use in Fort Worth, TX, servicing six schools, and hooked up to CCC Headquarters with IPS.[41]

Figure 65 shows a list of the benefits touted by CCC for parochial schools using the CCC-17 under the Felton decision. Note the seemingly odd "benefit" that the system could only be used for CCC courses! This was an aid in establishing the appropriateness under the rules used to implement the Felton decision. Surprisingly, in 1984, school districts sometimes believed that it was a benefit of CCC products that students and teachers could not run less educationally-oriented programs on the systems. By 1990, it was a benefit to have general-purpose machines in schools. Today, of course, many schools put many restrictions and filters on their Internet-based systems, given the wide variety of websites that are available. So the issue of finding the "proper" use of computers in schools remains.

During the time that the Felton decision was in place (until 1997), CCC sold a number of systems under this source of funding. The fact that the installations and training could be completed so quickly accounts for a good part of these sales since the schools needed a solu-

---

[41]Without IPS there was no communication between the local setup and corporate.

The Fort Worth Parochial School CAI Project

The MICROHOST computer sends individualized instruction to students at the parochial schools via phone lines. Individual performance data, used in a variety of progress reports, is sent back to the computer.

CCC marketing material

FIGURE 64: CCC Microhost for IPS in Fort Worth, TX, Servicing 6 Schools

tion. Also, there was an overall dip in CCC sales in this period (around 1985), so the unexpected Felton sales were very helpful. The sales team attributed this dip to a lack of industry-standard hardware and color graphics.

5.9.5 Reliance on Established Customers

Early adopters of CCC continued to use the CCC instructional learning system over decades and through the different hardware implementations. These early adopters were essential to CCC's continued growth by providing critical feedback regarding the instructional software and management systems. They also provided references for CCC to prospective customers, and were an ongoing source of revenue.

Some important visionaries were: Dr. Eugene Karol, Superintendent of Calvert County, MD Public Schools; Mr. Frank Fanning, Federal Programs Director for Fort Worth Public Schools; and Mr. Norm Rose, Federal Programs Director for Milwaukee Public Schools.

5.9.6 Competition

CCC belonged to a market called the "integrated learning systems" (ILS) marketplace. This was to distinguish it from software packages

How the CCC MICROHOST™ Instructional System helps meet the *Felton* requirements

- *No public school instruction or supervision is required.* Students receive individualized instruction at terminals in their own schools without requiring a teacher's assistance.

- *Access is limited.* Management software, stored in the system's central MICROHOST computer, eliminates unauthorized access to the courses. Only students enrolled in the system can take courses.

- *The system cannot be diverted to other uses.* Only CCC courseware runs on the system. A district can further limit access to only designated courses.

- *The system produces outstanding gains among both public and parochial Chapter I students.* Many districts using CCC systems have been recognized for achievement growth, including six projects that received "Exemplary Status" awards from the U.S. Department of Education. Since 1978, Milwaukee Public Schools has used a CCC system to serve twelve parochial schools, with excellent results.

- *The system is easy to implement.* Barely a month after the district's Board of Education and the Texas Education Agency approved the system, Fort Worth's six parochial school computer labs were operating smoothly and efficiently.

CCC marketing material

FIGURE 65: Benefits for Felton Decision Customers

that ran on microcomputers that lacked comprehensive courseware and management capabilities. Other companies in the ILS market included Prescription Learning Corporation, Wicat Systems, Inc., and PLATO[42] Prescription Learning was CCC's largest competitor in the K-8 market in the early '80s through 1989, when they merged with Jostens Learning Corporation.[43] Wicat was a strong competitor in the late '80s in K-8 market and was also acquired by Jostens Learning Corporation. PLATO was CCC's largest competitor in the high school and adult education market. The existence of these competitors actually helped to shape a perception of a product category that would meet certain needs. ILS companies emphasized their comprehensive courseware and management, product support and maintenance, and stability. CCC made a large point of results based on the research at Stanford. See [9] for some general discussion of ILS systems.

5.10   First Pass at Looking for a Buyer

In 1985, Suppes announced his desire to sell the company and began the process of looking for a "merger or acquisition" partner. He felt that the time was right within the computer industry to take computer-assisted instruction seriously, and especially felt that established textbook publishers would be keenly interested since computer delivery would be seen as the future. To support this effort, and to keep employees with the company, he instituted a broad-based stock option plan.

Representatives approached many potential acquirers. Interest by traditional publishers was tentative at best, which disappointed Suppes. The first serious acquirer to show interest was a for-profit company that arranged for high-school students to spend a year abroad. After some meetings and due-diligence, they lost interest because CCC's products were not running on the Apple and MS-DOS platforms; CCC also realized that this company had insufficient experience in technology to carry things forward.

The next to come forward was Prescription Learning of Springfield, IL, a multimedia diagnostic prescriptive program providing individualized instruction. They saw that CCC had a similar approach at some level, although Prescription Learning used tests to map out a program of instruction, while CCC was more interactive and adaptive at every stage. They withdrew without an explanation, but it seemed that the products were not very synergistic.

---

[42]See Wikipedia "Plato (computer system)" [207].
[43]See Wikipedia "Jostens" [188].

Jostens Corporation was, and remains, a large company supplying goods and services to schools. They are known for rings, caps and gowns, and yearbooks. They have a large salesforce, and they like to sell a large package of services to a district.[44] Jostens decided that they wanted to enter the educational computing market, and made an offer to buy CCC. This offer seemed very serious until the last minute when they dropped the purchase price considerably, Suppes later revealed.

Jostens seemed to want a company that was already using the MS-DOS platform. In short order, they purchased ESC of San Diego (formerly ETSC) and renamed themselves "Jostens Learning." They became the chief competitor to CCC in the early 1990s.

After about eighteen months of trying to sell the company, Suppes decided to try going public. The documents were prepared by Smith Barney and a meeting to sign was scheduled for a Monday morning, but a market crash in October 1987 canceled this approach as well. Suppes decided to go back to the drawing board and see how he could improve the prospects of a sale, especially to a publisher.

---

[44]See Wikipedia "Jostens" [188].

6

Color Graphics and an Acquisition for CCC 1985–1990

This chapter covers a critical period for CCC. Changes in computer technology enabled cost-effective graphics and audio, and industry-standard platforms became available that allowed CCC's courseware to run on hardware that people wanted for their general-purpose computing tools. The success of these efforts not only led to increased sales and market acceptance and a successful corporate acquisition, but actually also kept the company from going out of business.

6.1 After-shocks of *Not* Selling CCC

Suppes made an effort starting in 1985 to sell CCC. He thought that he was well situated but discovered that the potential buyers did not see the market the same way that he had. Here are some of the lessons learned:

- Color graphics were simply a necessity. While audio was showing some promise, increasingly sales representatives were reporting that they were being passed over because of the lack of color and graphics. It did not help that the Microhost system and terminals did not look very different from the CCC-17. (The Sony SMC-70 was by this time no longer being marketed by CCC, and its graphic capabilities were now out of date anyway.)

- Too many resources had been spent on courses that had little value to customers. This had been done in the belief that a large complement of courses was necessary to interest people in an "integrated solution." However, it was clear that courses like computer skills and keyboard skills were not getting much use. Also, customers often turned to other solutions for these needs and didn't mind having more than one brand of system by this time.

- The company had too many strange business deals, the accumulation of 20 years as a small private company run by a very entrepreneurial and imaginative (as well as generous) boss. Slowly these got undone, leaving a less complex story to tell potential acquisition partners.

6.2   The Plight of a High-tech Company

During the period of 1960 to 1990, many software companies faced ongoing challenges with the hardware platforms they supported. Often a company would be very successful for a time based on one implementation for one environment, but then fail to make a smooth transition to the next hardware/operating system environment.[1]

Most companies that transition successfully to a new hardware platform succeed by creating software that uses the new platform's capabilities in a pleasant way while retaining the benefits of the old implementation. For example, Microsoft was able to adapt its Word and Excel programs starting with Windows 1.0 and then continuing through all versions of Windows and Macintosh.

It is fair to say that CCC would have failed if it had not met the challenge of building graphics-based courses. Some of the requirements that needed to be balanced were:

- The right hardware/operating system had to be selected at the right price point. Ideally, the per-station cost with courseware charges would remain the same, about $2,000, with a similar profit. This limited the list price of the terminal hardware to about $1,000.
- The new courses had to support the windows/graphics/mouse interface in an intuitive and engaging manner. Indeed, they had to appear to be totally new and revolutionary.
- The courses had to have all of the features and educational advantages of the existing character-based software but immediately jump to higher quality presentation and user interface.
- The software and courseware had to be developed quickly and without too much expense. This suggested that the old curriculum and programs needed to be leveraged.
- The new terminal had to be something that would run other kinds of educational and productivity programs (even if in practice such use would be limited).

The decision to go for industry-standard hardware was not, however, without its difficulties. CCC had been manufacturing the hardware and

---

[1]Famous examples of products that failed to make a transition are WordPerfect [233] and Lotus 1-2-3 [193].

providing installation and maintenance services along with the course-ware. Manufacturing, installation, and maintenance supported profit centers within the company. By 1985, the hardware engineering and manufacturing capabilities had been wound down considerably with the completion of the Microhost, but there was still a large field service organization, and it made money. More than a few people questioned making the change to more industry-standard equipment.

In the past, some customers even saw reasons to prefer proprietary hardware. Since CCC's equipment was purpose-built, it was for a long time cheaper than any available hardware that would do the same thing. Since the CCC hardware basically only ran CCC applications and courses, there were customers who saw this as an advantage since it would not be possible to usurp the system for other purposes. See page 195 for a discussion of this attitude a few years earlier. However, most customers were beginning to want general-purpose systems.

The following sections work though the moves to graphics-based hardware, moving first to the Atari ST, then to MS-DOS/Windows systems, and finally to the Macintosh.

6.3 Graphics and the Atari ST

CCC had large courses with adaptive learning and a management system, so when prospective customers complained about the lack of graphics, CCC responded by saying that CCC had "power behind the screen." The truth was that the screen didn't look very interesting.

But educational software running on microcomputers such as the Apple II had become all of the rage in education, and some customers were expecting that video games and graphics would be the basis of anything that they would buy. Examples include the Reader Rabbit programs that taught reading and language arts starting in 1996[2] and the Oregon Trail originally from Minnesota Educational Computing Consortium in the 1970s.[3]

CCC, and many customers, saw that such programs were not the same as a full, rich curriculum covering a structured and comprehensive set of concepts and skills. But still the desire was everywhere to integrate color and graphics with CCC's courses.

In early 1985, a group met confidentially to look at overall requirements for a graphics terminal. Nancy Smith chaired the committee, and soon CCC hired Paul Resch, an experienced video game programmer and software engineer, to be the technical lead.

---

[2]See Wikipedia "Reader Rabbit" [217].
[3]See Wikipedia "The Oregon Trail (video game)" [203].

204 / Computers in Education

They agreed that the new "graphics terminal" should have the following features:

- Support color, graphics, and animations.
- Have a mouse and support a windows/icons/graphics look-and-feel as similar to the then-new Macintosh as possible.
- Allow implementation of all existing courseware as well as new and upgraded courses.
- Allow presentations with at least 24 lines and 80 columns of text; this would support compatibility with existing courseware, especially reading courses. Suppes insisted on this point, refusing to allow graphics to compromise educational quality.
- Allow connection to the Microhost system, which would store the content and also the student data with its management capabilities.
- Allow connection to the CSS for audio.
- Be inexpensive (about $1,000 list for each station) and fit into the overall pricing strategy that CCC used for about 15 years.

Some obvious candidates were tested for a number of features, including:

- The NAPLPS graphics protocol attracted some attention. CCC reviewed the protocol and brought in some NAPLPS equipment for review.[4]
- The Apple IIe had been the marketing favorite for years, but the team once again recognized that it was not capable of implementing CCC's courses.
- The early Macintosh (introduced in 1984) systems were surprisingly lacking in memory and compute power and were very expensive. The Macintosh was however the new paradigm for what customers wanted even though they couldn't afford them in quantity.
- IBM PCs and MS-DOS "clones" such as those made by Tandy came closer. The early graphics cards, however, could not handle 80 columns of text and more than a few colors at the same time and were expensive.
- Tests and calculations revealed that the team would not be able to use the Microhost for storage of the graphics-based curriculum because it was too slow at downloading through serial connections. So, the team decided to build a separate file server box.

---

[4]See Wikipedia "NAPLPS" [202]. The NAPLPS terminals were popular with early "videotext" systems because of their efficient use of bandwidth for creating vector graphics. The team decided that NAPLPS was an obsolete concept and would also be too expensive.

Two new machines not yet on the market were the Atari ST and the Commodore Amiga. The Amiga was a better machine in principle but was not ready yet, and Commodore did not respond to CCC's calls. Atari, in contrast, was more than happy to deal with CCC. The team met a number of times with Jack Tramiel and his key staff and got access to early machines for testing. The $1,000 list price point was nearly feasible, and CCC would have some margin as well.

Testing revealed the following:

1. The Atari ST used the GEM operating system developed by Digital Research; see Wikipedia "Graphical Environment Manager" [184]. GEM was very similar to the Mac OS and Windows 1.0.[5] The Atari had four colors in 640X480 mode. This allowed 80 columns and 24 lines of readable text. With dithering, CCC graphics artists found that they could create some reasonable color palettes and graphics. CCC software engineers determined that CCC's enhanced graphics courseware could run on the Atari.

2. Paul Resch was able to build a prototype tool (eventually called the Graphics Construction Set, or GCS) that allowed artists and authors to build screens and templates and connect them to events. The GCS was somewhat similar in function to Macromind Director.

3. Fast access to the graphics files was a problem until George Kauffman developed a design for a special-purpose computer with connectors that would connect to the Atari ST disk ports for read-only operation. This device was called the CCC Graphics Server. It also contained all of the static content of the new courses.

4. A team of authors including Kathleen Gilbert-MacMillan, Jeff Boenig, Karen Agulnick, and Steve Sodman started writing experimental lessons, with programmers like Jim Kienitz and Tom Hempel developing Atari code.

5. The plan was to develop several comprehensive graphics courses, while running the older courses on the Microhost. Eventually, the remaining courses were also converted to graphics. Since all of CCC's code base was written in C and the Atari ST was a "C machine," many pieces of code were easily converted with the use of some conditional compilation and new libraries. This same approach was used for porting for the next decade of new systems.

6. The management system could also be ported, with the menus being reworked for the "GUI."

---

[5]GEM was so similar to the Macintosh that Apple sued them in an early "look and feel" lawsuit.

This all was started or prototyped by early 1986. The next important decision would be which courses to convert/create.

Initially, CCC decided on the main math and reading courses. The MCS course ("Math Concepts and Skills") would derive much of its structure from the MK1-8 course, and the RW ("Reader's Workshop") course would derive from the existing RCR course ("Reading for Comprehension, Revised"). A third graphics-based course, Writer's Express, was developed concurrently but was delayed a year in order to perfect it. The key math and reading courses (MCS and RW) were shipped in August of 1987.

The basic approach was to convert some material and to add new material.

1. Jim Kienitz wrote an interpretive language called SCI that fit along with the GCS. In modern terms, the GCS handled layout and was like HTML, while the SCI was like Javascript. The scripts were separated. SCI was extended several times to become very powerful. One of the best extensions was created by Richard Walker, who put a complete math interpreter and "event handler" into the SCI, written in such a way that curriculum authors could readily use it.

2. The programming team wrote translators that would convert a large part of the existing content to SCI. Most of the reading course was converted automatically, and about half of the math course was converted automatically with reasonable success.

3. Lessons were added with new graphics. In about 25% of the cases, the new graphics were "substantive" (provided useful information to the student), and in about 75% they were merely "decorative." CCC hired several more graphics illustrators in 1986–88.

Much of the work was done in 1986, with the plan being for shipment of the first systems in the fall of 1987. This made for an awkward set of marketing meetings, when the CCC marketing and sales teams asked for a meeting with the product development groups. The sales team loudly and vigorously complained about the lack of color and graphics and told the development managers that they could not sell the current product's look-and-feel anymore. The development managers were frustrated but simply had to say, "We understand your message, tell us more about what you are hearing."

6.4 The Reception of the Atari Graphics Platform

Figure 66 shows an early marketing collateral for the graphics platform including the Atari ST.

FIGURE 66: Atari ST with Microhost Promotion Piece

The reception was excellent and exceeded CCC's hopes, for a number of reasons.

1. The Atari had better color and graphic capabilities than either the Apple IIe or the IBM PC systems prior to VGA given the 80X24 character grid. The Apple Macintosh computer line did not have a color system until 1987.[6]

2. The windows/icons/mouse interface of GEM made the system surprisingly like a Macintosh.

3. The $1,000 price point for a system with 1MB of memory was not only attractive, but it fit CCC's general pricing approach.[7]

4. Customers who had already purchased a Microhost (marketed since 1984) could buy the Atari ST stations and Graphics Servers and upgrade their Microhost. They could also use the Microhost with some existing terminals at the same time that they used the Atari terminals. This helped solve one of CCC's biggest problems: how to provide continuity of existing equipment while also providing the "latest and greatest."

5. In 1988, audio was added to the main graphics courses. This resulted in a great increase in the sale of the audio CSS units.

6.5 Industry-Standard Hardware

By 1988, the Atari ST was a success. CCC was shipping more Atari STs than any other distributor in the world except one in Europe according to Sam Tramiel, the president of Atari.[8] The Atari ST built quite a cult following, and remained a tremendous bargain. The entire platform was attracting more interest than anything CCC had sold before.[68]

Nevertheless, it was clear that more "compatible" platforms were going to be the future of the educational software industry, including CCC. Competitors like Jostens Learning and Wasatch were using MS-DOS PCs, and customers were asking more about Apple products and MS-DOS systems.

Obviously, any new platforms would have to support the entire set of courses now running on the Atari STs combined with the Microhost, so a number of requirements needed to be taken into account. These included the following:

---

[6]See Wikipedia "Macintosh II" [194].

[7]The first model was the 520ST with 512KB of main memory in 1985, followed by the 1040ST with 1MB of main memory. CCC decided to bypass the 520ST and go directly for the 1040ST.

[8]Private communication.

1. Networking: in order to support the full range of courses and also the management system's ability to have large groups of students, the "student work stations" would have to be networked together. Local area networks were beginning to supplant stand-alone PCs and Apples, but the costs were still high.

2. Support text and graphics: CCC needed to be able to run the same courses with at least the quality of the Atari ST. Criteria included text in 80 rows by 24 columns, more than four colors, and display speeds supporting simple animations.

3. Audio: CCC was using their own CSS units to supply the audio, in conjunction with the Microhost. This would no longer be a marketable platform, so the stations had to have built-in audio capability.

4. Industry-standard hardware: all hardware in the package would now have to be industry-standard if possible. A temporary exception was made for the audio card.

5. Simplify the platform: during the early 1980s, CCC systems had become very physically cluttered. The Atari platform had: a Microhost, graphics servers, CSS audio units, printers, and a host of wires and cables. It needed to be simpler. The decision was made to have only a file server, networking cables, stations, and a printer.

In addition to customers' opinions, CCC had been looking to be acquired by a larger company since 1985. A stumbling block was always the fact that the courses did not run on MS-DOS and Apple computers. CCC had refined answers to this objection since the late 1970s, mainly that industry-standard equipment was not cost-effective for the application. These explanations were, however, falling increasingly flat with both customers and acquirers who demanded Apple or MS-DOS solutions.

As they had done a few years earlier, CCC staff reviewed the possible systems and did some experiments, with the following results.

1. Apple Computer: CCC had discussions with Apple, and they recommended their new Apple IIGS, which had superior graphics; they gave CCC some for experiments.

   (a) Experiments with the Apple IIGS proved that the machine would not support the courseware in any way remotely similar to the Atari ST.

   (b) Apple "evangelists" allowed that they had no plans for a less expensive Macintosh aimed at the school market.

2. IBM, Tandy, and Zenith: CCC met with three of the largest MS-DOS equipment manufacturers.

   (a) IBM was offering VGA hardware with a mouse that CCC felt would work.

   (b) IBM had token-ring networking hardware while the Tandy and Zenith used Ethernet. Performance tests performed by CCC's QA group indicated that everything would work.

   (c) After meeting with Novell, CCC selected the Novell networking software.

   (d) CCC still needed to resolve details about the audio and software.

   (e) IBM, Tandy, and Zenith all had pricing programs for education.

6.6 MS-DOS Platform

CCC decided it was time to move forward with MS-DOS hardware, specifically from IBM very importantly but also from Tandy, which still had a large presence in schools. CCC also worked with Zenith.

CCC still needed to determine the graphics software and audio hardware.

6.6.1 GEM Operating System for Graphics on MS-DOS Systems

The Atari ST had established a "Mac-like" interface with graphics, windows, and the mouse for input, and the CCC courses had been adapted to it. CCC wanted something similar for the new PCs, so the software department investigated how to handle these capabilities. They had no interest in building their own operating system!

At this point (1987), Microsoft Windows was still very immature. CCC looked at Windows 2.0, but the pricing, memory requirements, feature set, and stability all ruled it out.

The Atari ST used the GEM operating system add-on, built by Digital Research (DRI). This also ran on top of MS-DOS (or DRI's own version of MS-DOS) and was similar enough to the Atari version to be plausible. There were, however, memory problems since CCC only wanted to require 1MB of memory. After some meetings with DRI in Monterey, CCC discovered a way to use the essential core of GEM and make it fit into available memory.[9] CCC licensed GEM and used it until 1993, when Windows 3.1 became the standard.

---

[9]The MS-DOS operating system was designed for 640KB of main memory. Many software vendors battled this problem until the 1990s.

How does 1MB of memory per student compare to previous and future requirements? A few years earlier, with the CCC-17, each math student used 90 bytes of main memory (plus shared program modules). By 1989, with MS-DOS/GEM, each student had 1MB of memory. A few years later, with Windows 3.1, each student had 4MB of memory. By 2016, each student would have between 4GB and 16GB of memory using Windows 10.

6.6.2 Audio for the IBM/MS-DOS Platform

Audio remained a problem. The decision was to find a vendor with a card that would produce high-quality audio running on MS-DOS. Available cards were for gaming applications and did not produce good speech. Sanders ran many intelligibility tests on various solutions, and nothing accessible worked.

Initial searches in 1988–89 failed to find anything workable. Therefore, the IBM platform was released in 1989–90 without audio support or audio courses, with the understanding that support would come later.

Without audio, sales were not substantial. The Atari ST platform was less expensive, the IBM platform seemed incomplete, and the marketplace was conflicted.

This problem was solved when Sanders discovered a vendor named Antex with a card that sounded very good and could be purchased in quantity at a reasonable price. Sanders suggested some improvements to them, and CCC shipped a new release in 1990 incorporating this card for IBM and Tandy machines with all courses. Sales improved, and at this point, the overall price was competitive with the Microhost/Atari ST system because the audio cards were cheaper than the CSS audio system built by CCC.

One intellectual loss was dropping the prosody features of previous speech systems. The CSS system, like the MISS machine at Stanford, had been capable of concatenating speech together from individual words and phrases and using "cartoons" to alter prosodic features of the speech to make it sound natural. This allowed speech to be created dynamically and still sound natural.

The new audio card simply played static sounds that had been stored in files and did not offer any prosodic manipulation. Sanders and the audio team went back and recorded enough additional sounds so that the prosody was no longer required. "Long sounds," as they were called, were used entirely, with some words inserted dynamically but without prosodic manipulation. Today, excellent speech synthesis software is available, such as the "Siri" voice on Apple iPhones.[10]

One side benefit of using prosody to generate sounds dynamically had been that less disk space was required to store individual words using LPC. Now, the number of sounds increased, and the space required to store them increased, but this was no longer a problem because inexpensive hard disks were available with hundreds of megabytes of storage.

6.7 SOLO Platform

Beginning in 1989, CCC distributed its courses on CD-ROM instead of magnetic tape. The Software Department had one of the first machines from Sony for making one-off CDs ($30,000, instructions in Japanese), which saved the company from trips to a production house that had similar equipment.

This led to the introduction, in 1990, of a new product category, a stand-alone PC with a CD-ROM drive that would support all content. This was called the SOLO platform, as shown in Figure 67.

CCC was able to fit all current courses with all audio files onto the 640MB of the CD-ROM. The speed of the CD was adequate for all courses and even the audio features even though CD-ROM drives only operated at the speed needed for CD sound in 1990.

As a product, the introduction was timely, since many people were asking for machines deployed at the rear of the classroom that were independent. In practice, however, most such installations used networked PCs so that the student records were all stored on the server. SOLOs were frequently sold to small non-public schools and to adult education (ABE/GED) programs. Many of the same issues relating to student usage and record-keeping were seen with the SOLO as were experienced with the stand-alone Sony SMC-70. In some cases, SOLOs were used to get a district or school started with CCC as much as anything. CCC sales reps were given SOLO stations to use as demo equipment, which were much easier to transport and to use than the networked system equipment of former years.

As with the Sony SMC-70 product eight years earlier, the main market was for networked systems with centralized management capabilities rather than stand-alone stations. But the SOLO was an excellent way to "open the door" to larger networked systems.

---

[10]See Wikipedia "Siri" [222].

FIGURE 67: SOLO Platform with MS-DOS Hardware

6.8 MCS Math Course

6.8.1 Overall Description of MCS

This section gives a detailed description of the MCS course by 1989 (Math Concepts and Skills for grades K-8). This version of MCS was running on the Atari ST platform. A different version without graphics was still in operation on the Microhost platform with text-only terminals such as the SLS11. The course was released on the MS-DOS platform in nearly the same version at the end of 1989.

MCS was a culmination of math courses going back to the earliest courses at IMSSS over twenty years earlier, and also the early CCC systems such as the M8 and A16. The course motion also was grounded in early theory. Suppes noted: "The learning model that Zanotti and I have applied to the situation described is one that very much fits into the family of models developed by Estes, Bush, Mosteller, and the rest of us working in the 1950s" ([132] p. 5).

MCS had 16 content areas, or "strands," with 1,119 skills taught in grades K-8. Each skill had a number of different exercises associated with it. The content areas are shown in Table 8. These strands were divided into "computational" and "applications" strands. A typical computational exercise is shown in Figure 68, and an application exercise is shown in Figure 69.

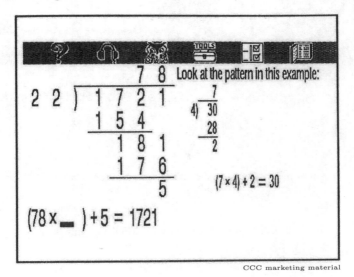

FIGURE 68: Computational Exercise in MCS

TABLE 8: Strands in Math Concepts and Skills

Strand name	Strand code	Grade levels
Addition	AD	1.00–8.90
Applications	AP	2.20–8.80
Decimals	DC	4.00–8.90
Division	DV	3.50–8.90
Equations	EQ	2.00–8.95
Fractions	FR	1.70–8.90
Geometry	GE	0.00–8.90
Measurement	ME	0.00–8.70
Multiplication	MU	2.60–8.90
Number Concepts	NC	1.00–8.90
Probability and Statistics	PR	7.00–8.90
Problem-Solving Strategies	PS	3.00–6.80
Science Applications	SA	3.30–7.40
Speed Games	SG	2.00–6.35
Subtraction	SU	1.60–8.90
Word Problems	WP	3.00–8.90

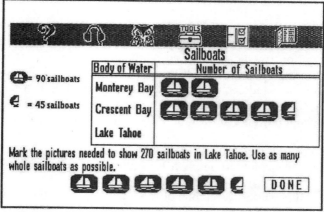

FIGURE 69: Application Exercise in MCS

The course started at grade K and went through grade 8. Not all strands had exercises at all grade levels, as seen by the grade-level ranges in Table 8. The content was calibrated so that the strands were "synchronized." In many cases, content would be introduced at one grade level and then used at a later grade level, either in the same or a different strand. For example, students should "master" addition of small numbers before attempting addition of larger numbers.

Records were kept of the student's work. This enabled detailed reports to be made, including IPS reports (see page 175). It was also used to determine the next content to be presented. Students who were doing well would move forward, and students who were not doing as well would be asked to repeat material. Through reports, teachers could monitor this progress.

The MCS "motion" system decided which exercises the student received next. The two important ingredients of this were: when a given skill had been "mastered," and when to switch to another strand. Both of these were calculated dynamically for each student. This was one of the most important points of individualization in the system, although there were others.

The content and motion rules were reorganized many times over the years. The reasons for this included new additions to standards used by the various states and districts, reports from users and CCC's consultant and sales staff, and also analysis done on actual student data. CCC requested data tapes from co-operating customers and analyzed the data both to determine effectiveness and to help identify places where the course and motion rules could be improved.

The standard recommendation for student session times in the previous math course (MK) was ten minutes per session. Although educators had the option to change automatic student session times within the management system, the default was set at ten minutes. Thorough data analysis of thousands of student MK histories resulted in a generic expectation that on average, students who took MK 10 minutes per day for 150 school days (1500 total minutes) could be expected to gain approximately 1.2 academic years. This could begin to close the academic achievement gap for students who were functioning below their grade placement level. More time on MK could result in greater academic gain.

When MCS was released, one of the unanticipated effects of the enhancements (graphics, animations, and student tools) was that it took students additional time to complete individual exercises, which decreased the number of items that could be completed during a session. The lesser number of items completed slowed overall progress and impacted the duration of time required to move through all the material. To accommodate this change, recommendations for student sessions times were increased from 10 to 15 minutes.

Recommendations for 15-minute student sessions in both reading and math created problems for many long-time CCC customers. Most schools had lab installations and students were scheduled for CAI sessions in tight 22–25 minute blocks, all day, every day. (Each student would take a ten-minute math session and a ten-minute reading session, with two-to-five minutes allocated for "travel," during which one group of students left the lab while the next group entered.) Schools had to figure out how to buy more computer stations, reschedule students, and/or prioritize services to allow only students in specific grade-levels or content areas to use CAI. The option of adding time to the school day was usually not possible because of the regular school day time constraints.

Nevertheless, negatives for using MCS in established school sites (restrictions on how many students could be served and scheduling issues) were far outweighed by the positives:

- Graphics allowed for development of needed instructional elements. Examples include enhancements to the measurement and geometry strands.
- Graphics and student tools made for an enriched curriculum and better learning environments for students.
- Students enjoyed the color, graphics, animations, and tools and were better engaged in the activities.
- Educators felt the system was "current" and modern.

6.8.2 Features of MCS to Individualize for Each Student

The most significant way in which the instruction was individualized was the mastery determination and motion through the curriculum as described above. Some of the additional ways in which the course individualized the instruction were as follows:

- *Student Settings:* Proctors and teachers could use the management system to adjust a number of parameters, including the length of a session in time, where the student was to start the course, and which strands were active.
- *Fixed Drill:* A group of students could be asked to do the same set of exercises in order to support classroom activities. This was called "fixed drill" and was a controversial feature. The reason it was included as a feature is that some teachers requested that they be able to give all students the same content at the same time in

order to support classroom instruction. It was controversial with CCC because most of the staff believed that the best results over time would be achieved by having students take the content that the motion algorithms computed. Moreover, CCC observed that, in practice, teachers did not make use of these kinds of features, in fact preferring to allow the computer to make the motion decisions. This controversy remains today, but with more emphasis on teacher control, which now comes under the heading of "blended learning." See [28] for some current thinking about these topics.

- *Initial Placement Motion:* When a student was first enrolled in the MCS course, the motion would typically attempt to find the optimal place for the student to begin. This generally happened in the first ten sessions, and was called Initial Placement Motion, or IPM. In using IPM with a class, a teacher would typically enroll all students to their grade level in school, and then allow IPM to move them around quickly. Then, the normal motion of the course would take over.

- *Multi-part Exercises:* Individual exercises often had a complex internal logic of interactions depending on the student's responses to the parts of that exercise. One example was the tutorials that could be activated to help students understand something that they seemed to be having difficulties with. Figure 70 shows one example.

- *Random Generation of Exercises:* Many types of exercises, especially computational exercises, contained random-generation algorithms that selected combinations of operands according to the exercise type. For example, if a skill was to add together three small numbers that have a sum smaller than ten, then combinations of numbers fulfilling this requirement were generated automatically. This was sometimes also done in such a way that the student did not see the same combination while doing the skill at hand.

6.8.3 Other Important Features of MCS

The MCS course also had a large number of features that played a role in the use and effectiveness of the course. These included the following:

- *Student Tools:* There was a set of tools available to the student, including a calculator, a tutor, a glossary, and a student report displaying recent progress.

- *Audio:* Audio instruction was available for much of the course, including tutorial messages. This could be turned on and off. Audio messages could be repeated at the request of the student.

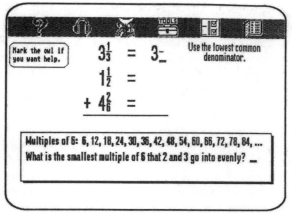

FIGURE 70: Example of a Tutorial in MCS

- *Mastery and Automaticity:* The design of the course was to lead from mastery to automaticity, which is where the student can perform the skill quickly and accurately without "thinking about it." Automaticity was encouraged by speed games, which asked the student to perform a basic skill quickly and repetitively, with positive reinforcement for good results. Skills were selected from those recently mastered.

- *Paper Worksheets:* The teacher could generate paper worksheets for individual students. The worksheets were randomly generated for each student, starting at the current position in each strand. Answers could be displayed at the bottom if desired. This proved to be a very important feature for teachers since they could give an activity to all students but have it individualized for each student. The results of the worksheet were not imported back into the MCS performance database. See Figure 71 for a sample.

```
This assignment is due Wednesday, May 20.
523 Ray Mendez                          Thu May 14 1992 16:46
Math Concepts and Skills Worksheet

(1)  9 + _ + 9 = 24        (2)  9 + _ + 8 = 22        (3)  _ + 9 + 9 = 26
(4)  _ + 7 + 9 = 24        (5)  _ + 9 + 8 = 24        (6)  5 + _ + 8 = 20
(7)  8 + 9 + _ = 26        (8)  9 + 8 + _ = 24        (9)  4 + _ + 9 = 21
(10) 5 + _ + 6 = 20        (11) 5 + 7 + _ = 20        (12) _ + 9 + 8 = 25
```

FIGURE 71: Example of MCS Worksheets

In the late 1980s, some objections were received to the name "worksheets." While the worksheets were individualized to each student and they were far more sophisticated than other products on the market, the problem was with the name. Customers requested the change to the name "practice sheets," which was accomplished within a few years.

6.8.4 Comparisons of MCS to Other CCC Courses

By 1989, there were several courses that had a "graphic" look similar to the one MCS had using the Atari ST. All courses had pretty much the same features, as appropriate, but MCS tended to be the first course to receive an enhancement. This was because MCS was by far the most popular and most used course on the system. One exception was the application of audio to the old MK math course, which received audio treatment rather late; audio sales picked up when audio came to MK.[11]

The strand structure and associated individualization scheme was not equally appropriate for all courses. The main reading courses such as RW had a similar structure and motion scheme, but it may not have been quite as effective since the underlying curriculum structure was not as precise. For example, in RW, the academic strands consisted primarily of practice of discrete skills (including letter and word identification, word and sentence comprehension, and reference skills). The only strand in which students were required to integrate these separate skills in order to make sense of written material was passage comprehension, and these passages were short and unrelated to the other skill strands. Other courses used a lesson structure in which the main content flow was linear, but with many small places where tutorials and review were inserted for students on an individualized basis.

6.9 Macintosh LC Deployment

Late in 1989, Apple Computer informed CCC that they were planning to introduce the Macintosh LC (for "low-cost color").[12] As late as 1988, Apple's policy had been to keep the price of Macintosh machines high, leaving areas like education to the Apple II product line.

Pressure from the MS-DOS, Windows, the Atari ST, and the Amiga forced Apple to reconsider this position. Apple released the Macintosh LC in early 1990.

The LC had 256 colors and 512X384 pixels of resolution. This was a larger color space than CCC had been accustomed to, but a smaller resolution, since VGA had 640X480 and CCC had recently refitted everything to VGA. Together with a monitor, the LC cost $2,000 list

---

[11]Private communication from Sil Sanders.
[12]See Wikipedia "Macintosh LC" [195] for details.

price. Most interestingly, the LC came with audio capability built in. Sanders judged it slightly inferior to the Antex card, but very workable.

Apple corporate was interested in working with CCC and was willing to give the CCC team equipment for development, but they were concerned about the "look and feel" of the product. They had seen older versions of the courseware and were unimpressed by its appearance.

In late 1989, CCC invited key Apple managers for a demonstration of the MS-DOS version, which used the GEM GUI environment and supported graphics and mouse input. Apple's "evangelists" explained that, of course, CCC was entitled to do whatever CCC wanted, but to obtain access to Apple's development and sales support, the product would have to be "Mac-like."

CCC's product managers took the visitors on a tour of the nicest looking portions of the courses, telling them how much better this would look on a Mac, without the restrictions of the IBM hardware and GEM software. CCC promised that all graphics would be redrawn for 256 colors, a promise that was kept by 70 graphics illustrators hired the next year. Apple's team pronounced that CCC was already "Mac-like" and they would give CCC full support, which they surely did.

Development was begun in late 1989. The LC version was announced in January of 1991 for release the summer of 1991. CCC was able to have its entire system ready by the launch of the hardware in the marketplace. This was considered a top marketing priority because it was believed that there was a huge pent-up demand for Apple-based solutions in the schools, and not being there at hardware launch was unthinkable. While Apple had been very demanding early-on, they proved to be excellent and helpful development and marketing partners.

Problems included the following:

1. The audio programming was developed on sample machines provided by Apple that were larger than LCs. When the LC arrived, its somewhat crippled data bus presented bottlenecks, and the code had to be rewritten.

2. The design grid was changed to 512X384, and the first releases of software under Windows 3.1 two years later inherited this change.

3. All graphics were redrawn for 256 colors, which also was used in the Windows machines.

4. The Apple server did not cache files, so the software department had to write their own caching programs to avoid slow startups of a large number of machines on the server. This was a surprise to the development team, but reflected how the world had not yet understood the importance of networking.

The reception of the Apple LC was good but not overpowering. CCC marketing reps had for over a decade clamored for Apple hardware, but by the time it arrived, many schools were turning to first MS-DOS, then Windows, because of those systems' overall success in the marketplace. Some districts were known to be "Apple districts," but it turned out that places that favored Apples were not necessarily drawn to the integrated learning system approach of CCC in the first place.

6.10 Video for CCC Courses

CCC had investigated using video in instruction for some years. In fact, IMSSS had used film as a part of the IBM-based 1500 Instructional System in 1967. So the utility of video presentation was well established.

CCC always had an aversion to one-off educational products, however, and felt the need to create substantial courses like the MCS course. So, experiments tested the possibilities of building something substantial.

In 1989, CCC built a demonstration of video based on the computer-controlled Pioneer Laserdisc player with a separate monitor. The quality was excellent, but the overall platform had a large footprint. This was productized in the next two years into a survival skills course developed for the Dade County Schools.

Beginning in 1989, CCC investigated a huge number of video cards, software packages, and technologies. It was some time before computers had enough computational power, memory, and graphics equipment to support video without extra hardware. CCC looked at a large number of software-only solutions for videos, including early versions of Apple's QuickTime.

6.11 Platform Adoptions

The inclusion of MS-DOS and Macintosh hardware platforms from 1989 forward quickly brought about the acceptance of industry-standard hardware for CCC's products, as well as other educational software vendors.

The vintage graph in Figure 72 shows the speed of the adoption of MS-DOS/Windows and Macintosh platforms through 1993. In 1989, CCC sold about 10% IBM hardware, with the Atari platform at 90%. The lack of an audio solution for MS-DOS in 1989 inhibited sales, but by 1990 IBM had jumped to 45%. The Macintosh LC was introduced in 1991 and had less than 10% sales, while the Atari share had reduced to 35%.

By 1992, MS-DOS sales (combined manufacturers) accounted for about 60% and Macintosh for about 40%. This trend reversed in 1993, with Macintosh nearly 60%; MS-DOS had been replaced by Windows 3.1 by 1993, and combined manufacturers were down to about 40%.[13]

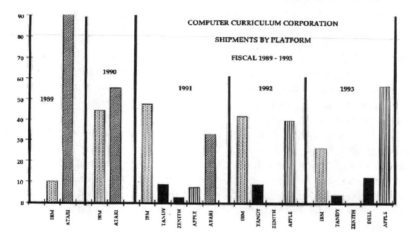

FIGURE 72: CCC Platform Shipments 1989–1993

With the true advent of industry-standard hardware from multiple vendors and with multiple support options, CCC lost revenue and profits from selling hardware and providing support. It is important to note that sales reps received commissions from selling Atari hardware but none from selling MS-DOS or Apple computers. Sales reps had stories of how bad they felt when customers would quote the educational prices from Apple and IBM, knowing that they would no longer receive a commission from the hardware portion of the sales.

This had impacts across the company. The CCC Engineering team was much smaller and now a part of general product support, and Manufacturing was long gone. Field Service had to scramble to obtain maintenance agreements on hardware that was no longer proprietary to CCC.

By the middle 1990s, CCC was selling a substantial amount of Dell equipment, and CCC had obtained agreements from Dell with some commissions for hardware sales. CCC found selling the hardware support to be easier than they had thought because they supported both the Dell hardware and CCC software together.

---

[13] Apparently, the ratios of Windows to Macintosh went up and down over the years, but no additional numbers are available.

6.12 Courses Offered at CCC Throughout the Years

A series of tables at the end of this chapter (page 227) show the evolution of CCC courses in a number of subject-matter areas, starting with Table 9 though Table 15. Each platform sold between the CCC-17 in 1977 and the Windows platform in 1992 has a column indicating the status of a given course for the platform and year. When audio and graphics were added, the notation "A" and "G" respectively are included for the course. This illustrates the continuity of the products over the years together with the variety of courses. Most platforms were supported as long as there were customers using them who paid for support, although some special arrangements were made to upgrade customers' systems.

In the late 1990s, many of the courses were dropped, especially courses like Logic and Science Discovery that ventured beyond the "basic skills" focus for which CCC became famous. Suppes recently commented that in early years, customers expected CCC to supply a broad range of courses, but with the coming of industry-standard hardware, schools had many more choices for courses and could mix different vendors.[14]

6.13 Acquisition of CCC by Paramount Communications

CCC had been looking for an acquisition partner since about 1985. Starting in that year, a number of companies looked at CCC, with some coming close to purchase (see page 199).

In 1987, Suppes had narrowed the acquisition process down to a few companies he thought might really know what to do with CCC. In 1988, Paramount Communications's publishing subsidiary, Simon and Schuster, held negotiations with CCC. Like other publishers, they were eager to enter the high-tech world with computer-assisted instruction. After many discussions, they expressed concerns about lack of industry-standard hardware; this was no surprise, and Suppes told them of the MS-DOS plans and commitment to Apple once Apple had a suitable product. The "due-diligence" team from Simon and Schuster was very sharp and professional; unfortunately they did not believe CCC's plans and schedule for IBM/MS-DOS development. They agreed to stay in contact.

In 1989, when the IBM platform was released to customers on schedule, Paramount returned, and a deal was struck. In late 1989, the Simon

---

[14]Historical documentation such as this was maintained by Barbara Tingey for many years and passed along for this volume by Alice Bauder in 2016.

and Schuster staff also became aware of the new Macintosh LC and the new SOLO platform, and were delighted to hear that CCC had received Apple's endorsement.

In March, 1990, CCC became a subsidiary of Simon and Schuster.

Patrick Suppes left the firm to return to Stanford University to do research and, as it turned out, create a new world of educational software known as EPGY.

Suppes was somewhat surprised and, he later allowed, even disheartened that Simon and Schuster did not want his ongoing involvement in CCC. It seemed, however, to be their corporate policy to distance themselves from the founders of the companies that they acquired.

Ron Fortune stayed on as president for nearly a decade after the acquisition and left in 1999. Robert Smith became Executive Vice President and stayed until 1992, missing Pat more than most. Nancy Smith became consultant until 1995 as IPS was winding down then went to Oracle. Sanders later became Executive Vice President and remained until late 1997, building a new product development process. Mario Zanotti and Kim Sheehan remained, along with many other people. In Suppes's absence, Zanotti took on a larger portion of the research and evaluation responsibilities.

Simon and Schuster brought in many additional managers and executives, especially in marketing and sales, with many more graphics illustrators, software engineers, and curriculum people hired than could ever have been envisioned in the old company. Many long-term employees left, although in the curriculum group and to some extent software, people remained.

Sanders sums up the integration of Suppes's ideas into the new company in the following way:

> Simon and Schuster poured many millions of development dollars into the company to bring a more modern and engaging look and feel to the Suppes-developed courses while also developing new comprehensive courses with significant individualization in the Suppes style. While each individual old-timer embraced the enhancements to CCC products in different ways, they held on to Pat's teachings and integrated them into the ongoing media rich products in development. In particular, the influx of development money allowed vast quantities of engaging audio, image and video media to be added to the courseware in instructionally relevant ways that enhanced the student's learning.[15]

In a few years, Viacom purchased Simon and Schuster along with the rest of Paramount. According to Ron Fortune, this did not change

---

[15] Personal communication.

the company very much. However, when Viacom sold its educational properties to Pearson Education, things did change. In the early 2000s, the facilities in Silicon Valley were shut down. Development was first moved to India, but moved to Arizona in a few years when the India experiment did not work as intended.

CCC is still owned by Pearson and markets new versions of the CCC products under the name SuccessMaker, an imprint that had been adopted in the early 1990s by CCC.[16] The name "Computer Curriculum Corporation" is now but an historical marker in the history of online instruction.

---

[16]See http://www.pearsonschool.com/successmaker for details.

TABLE 9: Course Evolution (Mathematics)

Subject	1977–1980 CCC-17	1981–1983 Audio	1984–1986 Mhost	1987 Graphics	1988	1989 MS-DOS	1990	1991 Mac	1992 Windows
Math Strands 1-6	✓	✓							
Math Strands 1-6, Spanish	✓	✓							
Math Strands 7-8	✓	✓							
Math Skills 1-8			✓			✓			
Math Concepts and Skills K-8				N(G)	✓	✓+ (G, A)	✓+	✓	✓+
Math Concepts and Skills, Spanish (K-2)									N(G, A)
Problem Solving 3-6	✓	✓	✓	✓	✓	✓	✓	✓	✓
Math Enrichment Modules 7-8	✓	✓	✓	✓	✓	✓	✓	✓	✓
Intro. to Logic			N	✓	✓	✓(G)	✓	✓	✓
Intro. to Algebra	✓	✓	✓	✓	✓				
Algebra Topics	✓					N(G)	✓+	✓	✓

Legend   ✓ : present   ✓+ : additions made   N: new   G: graphics   A: audio

TABLE 10: Course Evolution (Reading Skills)

Subject	1977–1980 CCC-17	1981–1983 Audio	1984–1986 Mhost	1987 Graphics	1988	1989 MS-DOS	1990	1991 Mac	1992 Windows
Reading Readiness						N(G, A)	✓	✓	✓
Basic Reading		N	✓	✓	✓				
Basic Sentences	✓								
Audio Reading		N(A)	✓	✓	✓				
Initial Reading						N(G, A)	✓	✓	✓
Reading, Grades 3–6	✓	✓							
Reading for Comprehension	✓	✓							
Reading for Comp., Rev.			✓						
Reader's Workshop				N(G)	✓	✓	✓+	✓	✓
Practical Reading Skills			N	✓	✓	✓	✓	✓	✓
Critical Reading Skills	✓	✓	✓	✓	✓	✓	✓	✓	✓
The Reading Network							N(G, A)	✓+	✓
Reading Investigations									N(G, A)

Legend   ✓: present   ✓+ : additions made   N: new   G: graphics   A: audio

TABLE 11: Course Evolution (Language Arts)

Subject	1977–1980 CCC-17	1981–1983 Audio	1984–1986 Mhost	1987 Graphics	1988	1989 MS-DOS	1990	1991 Mac	1992 Windows
Spelling Skills 2–8			N✓	✓	✓	✓	✓		N(G, A)
Language Arts Strands 3–6	✓	✓	✓	✓	✓	✓	✓	✓	✓
Language Arts Topics 3–6	✓	✓							
Writer's Express 3–6					N(G)	✓	✓	✓	✓
Writing: Process & Skills 7–9				N	✓	✓	✓	✓	✓
Fundamentals of English	✓	✓	✓	✓	✓	✓	✓	✓	✓
Discover English Apple-3									N(G, A)
English as a Second Language	✓	✓	✓	✓	✓	✓	✓	✓	✓

Legend   ✓: present   ✓+ : additions made   N: new   G: graphics   A: audio

Table 12: Course Evolution (Computer Science)

Subject	1977–1980 CCC-17	1981–1983 Audio	1984–1986 Mhost	1987 Graphics	1988	1989 MS-DOS	1990	1991 Mac	1992 Windows
Computer Literacy, Elementary					N	✓	✓		
Computer Literacy					N	✓	✓		
BASIC Programming		N	✓	✓	✓	✓	✓		
Intro. to Pascal			N	✓	✓				
Intro. to Cobol			N	✓	✓				
Intro. to Unix			N	✓	✓				

Legend ✓: present ✓+ : additions made N: new G: graphics A: audio

TABLE 13: Course Evolution (Courses for Adults)

Subject	1977–1980 CCC-17	1981–1983 Audio	1984–1986 Mhost	1987 Graphics	1988	1989 MS-DOS	1990	1991 Mac	1992 Windows
Adult Arithmetic Skills	✓	✓							
Adult Reading Skills	✓	✓	✓	✓	✓	✓			
Adult Language Skills I & II	✓	✓	✓	✓	✓	✓	✓	✓	
GED Curriculum	✓	✓							
GED Preparation							✓+		
Success in the Workplace									N
Exploring Careers	✓	✓							

Legend ✓ : present ✓+ : additions made N: new G: graphics A: audio

TABLE 14: Course Evolution (Dial-a-Drill)

Subject	1977–1980 CCC-17	1981–1983 Audio	1984–1986 Mhost	1987 Graphics	1988	1989 MS-DOS	1990	1991 Mac	1992 Windows
DIAL-A-DRILL Mental Arithmetic			✓	✓	✓				
DIAL-A-DRILL Reading			✓	✓	✓				
DIAL-A-DRILL Practical Reading			✓	✓	✓				
DIAL-A-DRILL Spelling			✓	✓	✓				

Legend   ✓ : present   ✓₊ : additions made   N: new   G: graphics   A: audio

TABLE 15: Course Evolution (Other)

Subject	1977–1980 CCC-17	1981–1983 Audio	1984–1986 Mhost	1987 Graphics	1988	1989 MS-DOS	1990	1991 Mac	1992 Windows
Survival Skills 9–12/A		✓	✓	✓	✓	✓	✓		
Essentials for Living and Working 9–12/A								N(G)	✓
Science Discovery							N(G)	✓+	✓+

Legend   ✓: present   ✓+ : additions made   N: new   G: graphics   A: audio

7

Research at Stanford and Founding of Educational Program for Gifted Youth 1980–2013

By 1980, Suppes had completed most of the computer-assisted instruction research that he felt was appropriate to do at Stanford. His attention had shifted to commercialization at CCC. However, there were some remaining opportunities at Stanford, mostly with support from the NSF for "transporting" courses to other universities; these projects led in the 1990s to a new round of research focused on gifted students, followed by another commercialization.

7.1 Transporting Stanford Courses to Other Schools

7.1.1 Transportable Logic

The IMSSS research performed in the 1970s had focused on university-level instruction. The *Logic* course had received the most use at Stanford, with the course being taught for three quarters per year for many years. Many other universities were interested in running this course in symbolic logic on a computer. Naturally, they mostly had different computers and displays, and the Stanford course had not been built for running on systems other than the PDP-10 at Stanford. Hence, the NSF became interested in the idea that the logic course could be converted to run on other machines and thus "transported" to other schools.

Tryg Ager was a tenured professor at SUNY Binghamton who was by his own admission bored with teaching philosophy to undergraduates. He had written a logic course using APL on an IBM 370 running CMS. The course dealt with propositional logic, including truth tables and elementary proofs. Ager learned of Suppes's efforts at Stanford and came out to California during his sabbatical year. At Stanford, he studied the logic and set theory courses and became aware of the amount of programming that was necessary to support a full-fledged course. He also noted that the facilities to run such courses only existed at places like Stanford, and began working to find support to build a logic course that could be "transported" to other schools.[1]

The NSF had a program called FIPSE (Fund for Improvement in Secondary Education), which funded Ager's proposal in 1978. Ager had made himself indispensable in other ways at IMSSS during this period. His wife, Mary Ager, who had taught English at Binghamton, joined CCC as a writer and editor. She edited generations of curriculum and publications for CCC, and was equally indispensable there.[2]

Technical Considerations in Transportability

By 1978, the logic course had progressed to the point that there were many issues involved in transporting it.[3]

- The Stanford software was programmed in LISP and SAIL, both artificial intelligence programming languages developed at Stanford for the Digital 10/20 systems. LISP existed in many other dialects and versions, none of which were particularly compatible.
- REDUCE, a symbolic algebra system, was used to simplify algebraic formulas for some portions of the course.[4]
- VOCAL, an interpretive, LISP-like language developed as a part of the earlier project, was used for the curriculum presentation to the students. See [50].

The first plan was to rebuild everything in a subset of LISP, a language that—it was believed—could be found on different machines in versions similar enough to this subset to make the course work. Once the LISP layer supported the proof checking, exercise presentation, and evaluation functions, the REDUCE and VOCAL components could also run in LISP.

Conversion to a subset of LISP began in 1979, with the first target being the IBM CMS operating system running on the IBM 370 hard-

---

[1] Typical of many people at Suppes's organizations, he taught himself about programming and computer technology, inspired by this goal.

[2] Hiring Tryg and Mary Ager into his projects is an example of something that Patrick Suppes was always very good at across a broad number of areas: recognizing someone who would do much better in a different area than he/she was currently working in, and providing assistance to help them make the transition. Of course, he was able to get some of their most enthusiastic efforts during this period of change.

[3] Ager had the assistance of a number of people on this project including Jim McDonald and Robert Maas.

[4] See http://reduce-algebra.com/documentation.htm.

ware and the LISP system running under CMS. The team discovered many issues, including core problems in the implementation of strings.[5]

After some months of effort on the cores of the various LISP systems, Ager found the work of Tony Hearn of the University of Utah and the Rand Corporation on transportability.[6] Hearn had developed REDUCE originally, and he had the same issues in transporting REDUCE to other universities. To solve this problem, Hearn's team at Utah was to build a new LISP system called Portable Standard LISP, or PSL for short.[7]

PSL was based on the Stanford LISP system from a language perspective and copied many general algorithms, but used the smallest possible "kernel" for LISP, with as much of the system as possible programmed in LISP. Thus, a more hierarchical system was created that required a minimum of work for each port to a new machine. Customarily, the LISP compiler on a machine is written to generate to a "LAP" (LISP Assembly Program) program that is in the assembly language of the target machine. PSL, however, compiled everything into C (a subset of standard C with a lot of conventions for how it is used). By 1980, C was a standard programming language which had been ported to almost every current system and worked nearly the same way everywhere because of its own architecture.

By converting the Stanford Logic Course into PSL, the problems of transporting were largely solved in a single step, since everything was converted into C. Suppes's group at IMSSS collaborated extensively with Hearn's group at Utah, and eventually Stanford assumed some distribution duties for REDUCE. Since UNIX was written in C and came with very standard C compilers, it was a natural target for PSL and also the Stanford Logic Course.

The Stanford Logic Course was sent to a number of universities, including Carnegie-Mellon University where it was used until Prof. Wilfried Sieg developed a replacement course; see page 298.

7.1.2   The DFx Transportable Calculus Course

The NSF was pleased with the progress on the transportable Stanford Logic Course. Ager remembers that he and Suppes talked to Andy Molnar of NSF in 1985 about new projects.[8] Molnar suggested that they would entertain a proposal to do a transportable calculus course

---

[5]Interactive CAI courses need good text handling capabilities.
[6]See [49] for details.
[7]See Wikipedia "Portable Standard Lisp" [208] for details.
[8]Molnar was one of the great supporters of computers in education in the Federal government during this period.

using some of the technology developed for the Stanford Logic Course. A proposal was written and rejected quickly. A new proposal, however, was successful, and the project began in 1986. It was called DFx.[9]

Given the success with PSL for the *Logic* course, the obvious decision was to use PSL and REDUCE for the calculus course.

The Naturalness of Mathematical Language

An important psychological distinction is the difference between algebraic solutions obtained by most symbolic manipulation programs, and the kinds of solutions that students would normally find in the course of working such exercises. Ager and his team noted that there were by 1985 a number of successful symbolic mathematical systems, including MACSYMA, REDUCE, and Maple, but these tools did not directly understand how students solve problems or the language that students use to describe those solutions (see [135] p. 26).

This distinction is similar psychologically to the nature of proofs in the set theory course a decade earlier. There, the goal had been to allow students to express proofs in a natural style, but to check them rigorously. Here, the same quality of naturalness was desired, together with mathematical correctness.

7.1.3 Curriculum Content and Presentation

The curriculum was based on the Educational Testing Service's recommendations for an AB advanced-placement calculus course. There were about 20 lessons, and the minimum time expected for completion was about 30 hours. Since exercises could also be assigned by the instructor, the minimum amount of time could double or even triple (see [135] pp. 21–22). The course presentation included text, graphics, and a variety of question types. Figure 73 shows a sample screen.

7.1.4 Interface to the Calculus Derivation Engine

The steps of working a calculus problem in the DFx course were taken using commands to an interactive symbolic engine called EQD. EQD accepted interactive commands that were intended to correspond to the steps a student would take to solve a calculus problem. EQD called REDUCE to assist with symbolic manipulations, but added a level of rigor as well as a more natural user interface.

---

[9] Ralph Kimball developed a CAI calculus course for his PhD thesis at Stanford in 1973. Kimball focused on instructional strategies, using calculus as an example, and did not have the ability to support the content required for a full course. Kimball's work appears to be the earliest effort to teach calculus with a computer. See [58].

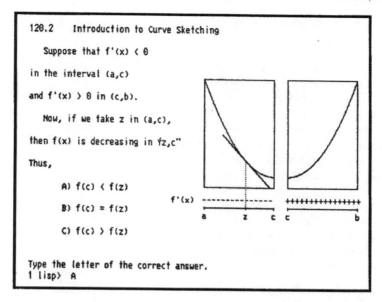

FIGURE 73: Sample Exercise Screen from the DFx Calculus Course

Level of Rigor in DFx

Ager argued that the problems of rigor in the calculus course were the problems of "characterizing explicitly and precisely the domain of definition of the functions being used. For example, if a function of a real variable is introduced, we cannot take the square root of this function if the values of the function are negative for some arguments in the domain .... Similar care must be exercised in taking logarithms, and in dividing by zero." Ager notes that "calculus textbooks vary greatly in the extent to which they make the appropriate restrictions a matter of explicit attention" ([135] p. 27).

Since it is necessary to build an interactive computerized system where these restrictions must be implemented, at least internally, the approach has been to build all restrictions into the system, "but not to bring all of these restrictions to the student's attention" ([135] p. 27). Specifically, proving what the entire domain is in which a function could be defined would be an onerous requirement on the student that would keep the student from progressing with the material.

For example, suppose the student begins with the identity function:

$$f(x) = x$$

and multiplies the function of the equation by $(1 - x)/(1 - x)$. The result would be the following:

$$f(x) = (x * (1 - x))/(1 - x)$$

but with the noted restriction that for all x, x is not equal to 1.[10]

This is a simple case, but it is suggestive of the underlying mathematical issues that happened as the student manipulated expressions in the system.

Ager noted: "Our teaching tools must embody the expertise that is presumed in the users of REDUCE [or commercial calculators]. So for our task, the difference between natural mathematical style on the one hand, and completely detailed deductions on the other, doesn't offer us a choice. We must do both" ([135] p. 30).

Figure 74 shows a sequence of steps in a DFx derivation (slightly abstracted). The problem is to differentiate the given formula with respect to x. The solution requires the polynomial differentiation rule, the chain rule, and some algebra. The EQD system must apply these rules but keep track of restrictions that arise.

x**3 + y**3 - 3xy = 0	given
3x**2 + 3y**2(dy/dx) - d(3xy)/dx = 0	differentiate
3x**2 + 3y**2(dy/dx) - 3y - 3x(dy/dx) = 0	chain rule
3x**2 - 3y + 3y**2(dy/dx) - 3x(dy/dx) = 0	rearrange terms
3(x**2 - y) + 3(y**2 - x)(dy/dx) = 0	collect terms now in standard form

FIGURE 74: Sample Student Steps with DFx to Differentiate a Function

7.1.5 Hardware Platform

IBM had gifted a significant amount of hardware to Stanford, including a 4381 mainframe, 3270 terminals, and RT workstations. The latter were effectively Berkeley UNIX machines. The hardware and system software were adequate to the overall task, but the user interface offered great challenges.

While fixed graphics could be displayed, there was a critical need for a "GUI" interface, including a pointing device such as a mouse. The lack of such a facility made selecting subformulas and activating commands tedious.

---

[10]The difficulty, of course, is that the new expression is not defined when $x = 1$ because there is now a division by zero.

7.1.6 Trial of the DFx Calculus Course

The stated goal of the project was to provide a calculus course for schools that could not offer a calculus course on their own. Small rural schools were intended to be a major target. Suppes was always interested in using computers to deliver courses that had little demand in any given local setting but large demand in the aggregate. He believed that computerized delivery could keep low-demand courses alive. See discussion of "productivity" in section 4.10.3.

The first trial of the course was in 1989–1990 in schools in San Jose, San Carlos, and Palo Alto, all on the San Francisco peninsula. The students were typical 11th- or 12th-grade students at these schools. IBM RT stations were set up at the schools, and tutors went to the buildings on a regular basis.

"It did not go well," according to Ager.[11]

Ted Alper was a tutor at the Andrew Hill School in San Jose, working with two groups of five students enrolled in the DFx AB calculus course. The problems he noted included the following:

- The DFx software and curriculum had a lot of bugs. Many of these were activated by "unusual" arguments or sequences of commands that the students tried but had not been tested during the QA process.
- The efforts at creating a mathematically rigorous system were not completely hidden and confused the students.
- The absence of a classroom instructor was felt by the students, whose motivation declined rapidly.

7.1.7 Another Try of DFx

By 1990–1991, it was time for another try of DFx with students. A large number of bugs and confusions had been removed from the course and software. In addition, this time a very different population was selected: gifted students.

Alper recalls that Cymra Haskell at Foothill College was teaching a course to 15 accelerated middle-school students. Each of their middle schools—seven schools in all–was given an IBM RT UNIX system for the delivery of DFx.

Alper visited each school twice a week. Ray Ravaglia who also worked on the course believes that "Ted's tutoring provided 'human energy' with a structure and expectation on the student which is what turned around the success of the program." Many of these students were indeed very successful: thirteen 5s and two 4s on the AP calculus test!

---

[11]Private communication.

242 / Computers in Education

This brought about a change in the target audience for the course and effort as a whole: gifted students who were looking to accelerate their progress.

This was exactly the opposite of the intent of the project. The DFx course was supposed to be used in settings where students were somewhat underserved, such as rural or inner-city communities. Instead, gifted middle-school students being taught at a junior college became the success story.

7.2 EPGY: Educational Program for Gifted Youth

Suppes spoke with Julian Stanley[12] of Johns Hopkins University[13] about the prospects in the marketplace of CAI courses for gifted students. Ravaglia[14] remembers that Stanley was enthusiastic and, at that point, Suppes decided to move forward with gifted education. In a few years, EPGY would be marketing its courses through Johns Hopkins.

The NSF contract for the development of DFx was set to expire. Suppes spoke with NSF about a new contract for education to the gifted, but NSF was not interested. This marked the end of Suppes long connection to funding from NSF, and it was a moment for personal reflection.

After the sale of CCC, Suppes was becoming restless, and the possibility of entering the gifted marketplace brought him back into full swing.

7.2.1 Previous Work in Home and Gifted Instruction

In fact, Suppes had a longstanding interest in both gifted students and home-based courses, including the earlier Dial-A-Drill in New York; see [12]. In addition, Dial-A-Drill had been tried commercially at CCC in 1982–83; see page 160.

In 1973, with funding from the NIE and NSF, IMSSS had conducted research on home-based courses and subsequently implemented a home-based experiment with identified gifted students from local schools based on intelligence test scores. This greatly foreshadowed the work of the 1990s:

In the fall of 1973 the Institute for Mathematical Studies in the Social

---

[12]See Wikipedia "Julian Stanley" [189].

[13]Contemporaneous machine records from 1973 at IMSSS show that terminals offering a full range of courses had been placed at Johns Hopkins during that time period so this was not a new relationship between Suppes and Johns Hopkins!

[14]Ray Ravaglia took courses from Suppes as a Stanford undergraduate and began working at IMSSS after graduation in summer of 1987. From then until 2013, his history is closely intertwined with that of EPGY.

Sciences (IMSSS) began an experimental home-based CAI program for gifted junior high school students. The students were able to receive courses in elementary and college logic, computer programming, and foreign languages via Teletypewriters placed in their homes and linked by the home telephone line to the IMSSS computer. With the exception of proctor help, which was available by telephone during certain limited hours, the students were entirely dependent on the computer for course instruction and the presentation and correction of problems and exercises. (See [69] p. 2.)

Parents were kept well-informed but were "encouraged not to urge their children to work on the teletypes; instead, students were to pace themselves and work as much or as little as they wished" ([69] p. 72). Interestingly, the role of proctor (later to be known as "tutor") was also featured in this early experiment.

A proctor was available at IMSSS 4 days a week during scheduled times so students could telephone for help. Some students, who indicated they felt too shy to telephone, were telephoned once a week by the proctor to see if they were having any problems. ([69] p. 72)

7.2.2 New Approach to Gifted Students

Suppes always believed that gifted students were somewhat ignored by the educational system. He also strongly believed in compensatory education. But, the experience with the DFx course gave him reason to think that the work he wanted to do might be better suited for gifted students. The reasons included the following:

- Suppes was interested in creating instructional materials for advanced courses. He wanted to create sophisticated, comprehensive courses and advanced software as a part of these courses. The courses should move toward having a dialogue with the students and would represent multiple instructional modalities. Such courses were partly experiments. Gifted students, it seemed, might be more willing to participate in experimental courses and provide thoughtful feedback about how to make improvements.
- Gifted students might be less interested in flashy products and more concerned with educational value, allowing Suppes and his group the freedom to pursue the features they thought were important rather than the media-driven trends of the general educational marketplace.
- Suppes would obviously need a source of funds to pay for the project. Organizations like the NSF and ONR had been the bulk of the funding of the Stanford projects over the years, but products for gifted students seemed more likely to attract funding from foundations and private individuals, as well as from parents for use by their students.

Suppes had sold CCC to Simon and Schuster in 1990, and was becoming eager to get back into courseware development. This surprised some who thought he would focus on the philosophy of science and other more academic areas. Suppes did, however, like the Stanford environment and didn't want to get into another purely commercial enterprise in which he would be constrained to not be too experimental. He had discovered at CCC that the only way he was able build the company up to be ready for sale was to focus completely on development of products customers wanted immediately rather than thinking about what was possible.

Rick Sommer puts it this way: "With no further funding, but a desire to get back into computer-assisted instruction, Pat and Ray Ravaglia came up with a tuition model."[15] The marketing plan was as follows:

- The courses would be branded as a part of Stanford University. They selected the acronym "EPGY," standing for "Educational Program for Gifted Youth." The theming for the products was deliberately selected to look somewhat old-school, suggesting educational quality. The appearance of being too game-oriented or frivolous was avoided. This appealed to many parents who felt, rightly or wrongly, that curriculum materials were being watered down to "engage" students in learning rather than teaching the rigorous content they remembered (or at least thought they remembered.)

- Suppes also had a non-compete agreement with Simon and Schuster for a period of time based on the sale, but he could do educational research at Stanford. By selecting advanced courses like calculus, he was able to remain within the confines of this non-compete.[16]

- The pricing model was based on "tuition." This was not simply a pay-as-you-go approach for individual courses, but rather a quarterly tuition that allowed students to take as many courses as they could, one at a time. Some students were able to take several in the same year, others would take a while to complete a course. This model took several years to implement seriously since a number of courses were needed.

- The tuition model helped give students and their parents a sense of belonging. They had been accepted into a program at Stanford and were taking an ongoing set of courses "at Stanford." Since many

---

[15] Private communication. Ray Ravaglia was a force of nature who pushed through the implementation of many things Suppes was interested in doing at Stanford from 1987 to 2013. Ravaglia eventually became Associate Dean and Director, Stanford Precollegiate-Studies, and now works for the New York Times.

[16] At one point in the late 1990s, CCC considered marketing the EPGY courseware to schools for their gifted students.

of the students were home-schooled, this association with a famous private university was more than welcome.

- To underscore the "gifted" model, students were given IQ tests through the mail, or were allowed to submit their own scores. This helped to confine the program to serious applicants, as well as creating a sense of exclusivity. See Figure 75 with a portion of a 1996 brochure sent to prospective students and parents, explaining in formal prose the various ways the student could demonstrate his/her gifted status.[17]

- From the outset, tutors were available to help students with their work. Email and phone conversations became a standard part of the process. The presence of tutors provided parents with the comforting feeling that there was help available. Tutors were often able to help gloss over problems with the content or delivery technology. As Ray Ravaglia said, "Any defect can be fixed by a tutor."[18]

- There was always some funding available for students who qualified but could not afford the tuition.

7.2.3 EPGY Courseware Development 1992–1996

Reactions to Previous Development

The development of courses at EPGY took a distinctly different approach than Suppes had taken in the past, in part influenced by what CCC was doing (both as a positive and negative influence on his thinking) and also taking advantage of the newest technological opportunities.

By 1991–1992, CCC was firmly in the camp of industry-standard hardware, featuring the Apple Mac and also Windows 3.1. The Mac had become inexpensive enough to be considered for schools, and Windows 3.1 had enough software stability to make it a success in the marketplace.

Thus Suppes agreed that it was time to focus on systems that people would be buying for multiple purposes, not just to run Stanford's courses. He considered the "transportable" logic course and the DFx calculus course to embody an outmoded idea of software development because newer and less expensive machines could, he believed, be programmed more easily. By 1992, it was possible to develop software for computers that were commonplace by choosing to use the Windows platform, which was supported by many hardware manufacturers.

---

[17]Today, many private schools have elaborate procedures including tests and interviews for qualifying students, even in elementary programs. Creating a sense of exclusivity is part of marketing.

[18]Private communication.

Qualifying for EPGY

A more detailed discussion of EPGY Admissions Policy is available on the EPGY world wide web site.

In order to serve the wider community of GATE students, EPGY is offering two programs of courses: (1) EPGY's Accelerated GATE Program and (2) EPGY's GATE Program. The former is designed for students whose ability is in the top 2-3% of the population, while the latter is designed for students whose ability is in the top 10-15%. Placement into these programs is determined by the student's standardized test scores and, as appropriate, his or her performance on EPGY's Mathematical Aptitude Test.

Students 14 and older. Students applying to take EPGY courses must submit the results of an AHSME, AJHSME, ACT, PSAT, PLUS, ERB, SCAT, or SAT. (For information on the SAT call (609) 771-7730.) Advanced Placement Examination scores may be used in place of SAT scores by students taking college level courses. Students applying to take Expository Writing courses must also submit a writing sample. Additional supporting materials may be submitted with the application if desired.

Students 13 and younger. Students under age 11 years old should submit the results of either a Weschler Intelligence Scale for Children Report (WISC) or an individualized Stanford-Binet evaluation. Students who have not taken such an exam may submit a nationally normed achievement test. Students who are 11-13 years old must submit the results of an ACT, PSAT, PLUS, SCAT, or SAT. (For information on the SAT call (609) 771-7730.) Students applying to take Expository Writing courses must also submit a writing sample. Additional supporting materials may be submitted with the application if desired.

Students who do not have any test score reports can still qualify for EPGY mathematics by submitting a teacher recommendation and by taking the EPGY Mathematical Aptitude Test.

FIGURE 75: EPGY Qualification Process (ca. 1996)

However, Suppes was disconcerted by the new product development process at CCC after his departure. Simon and Schuster saw the existing CCC product development process as being too chaotic and wanted a more rigorous process with the full workflow of requirements, specifications, test plans, and schedules. Elaborate internal proposals were written before any work was done. Suppes wanted something more efficient and flexible.[19]

Simon and Schuster also put a huge premium on graphical excellence and "look and feel" of the courseware. CCC hired about 70 graphics illustrators in 1990 to redraw every graphic in every course. This was probably a good idea considering the advances made in the hardware and escalating customer demands, but Suppes wanted the focus to be more on course content and educational results.

7.2.4 Support from the Sloan Foundation for Adult Math Courses

Tuition would be part of the funding model, but development and sustaining funds were still needed. In the spring of 1992, Suppes and Ravaglia made a proposal to the Sloan Foundation for funding to create beginning algebra and other pre-calculus courses for *adult* studies at Foothill College and other venues. The funding came in quickly and in the summer of 1992, development began, this time using Windows 3.1,

Ravaglia remembers that in the fall of 1992, the adult students came to Ventura Hall at Stanford, picked up a Windows PC with a CD-ROM (on loan), and started the beginning algebra course. Intermediate algebra followed in the winter, and a new calculus course in the spring.

Courseware Development, Software Platform, and Tools

Suppes came up with the idea of essentially recording authors giving lectures. Since full-motion video was not practical in 1990, EPGY settled for a tool that allowed an author to write on a tablet and talk at the same time. The tool recorded the tablet's state and synchronized the author's speech. At runtime, a software module would play it back on a Windows PC. The general flow of the lesson was a short lecture followed by a series of exercises about the content of the lecture. The tablet content was encoded using the Windows WMF format, and the audio was in the WAV format.[20] The main programming language was

---

[19]Today's "AGILE" software development style—which is very popular among Web-based companies—is closer in spirit to what Suppes always did.

[20] In later years, the tablet content was replaced by text and drawings for some courses, but the lecturer's audio was generally maintained.

Microsoft C, which by this time had an excellent development environment.

Suppes always felt that it was important to get things out into use and make incremental improvements. Unfortunately, it can be argued in 2016 that new software companies really only have a few chances to establish themselves and cannot afford to introduce a product that isn't compelling, but Suppes didn't like that approach. In any event, getting a set of courses developed quickly and inexpensively appealed to his biases.[21]

Having a small but effective staff was also appealing. At EPGY, Suppes had very little management structure. Ravaglia was in charge of the general development, but generally with Suppes's mentoring and approval. Suppes would often call impromptu meetings in his office to review either something he was especially interested in or to challenge something he thought wasn't right. This was an approach he had wanted to use at CCC but the size of the organization and the commercial nature of the company made it more difficult. At Stanford, he had freer rein.

A key programmer named Marianna Rozenfeld[22] joined the team. She had initially worked with Suppes on artificial intelligence, but was moved to programming for EPGY. She wrote a delivery tool named Psyche (in Microsoft C). This tool could present the recorded lectures and exercise content as well as control the flow of presentation. Psyche went through several iterations, initially in 16-bit Windows and later converted to 32-bit.

Other technical improvements in courses like calculus included the following:

- An equation editing module (called "structural input")[23] allowed interactive editing of equations, making corrections and substitutions, and selecting parts of formulas. This replaced the unintuitive editing conventions of the DFx calculus course, and was made possible by using the GUI interface and mouse input.
- Algebraic manipulations and simplifications were handled by the Maple system, replacing the older REDUCE;[24]

---

[21] It's also the case that this method of starting students on the first course in a sequence and then hurrying to keep the subsequent course development ahead of the students was a common practice throughout the years.

[22] Marianna Rozenfeld is a Russian mathematician and computer scientist who went through many generations of computer systems at EPGY and mastered all of them.

[23] [89] contains a good discussion of how the mathematical systems incorporated in the courseware worked (and didn't work).

[24] see https://www.maplesoft.com/solutions/education/.

- Course delivery to students was by CD-ROM mailed to their homes. Generally, there was a "system CD" that contained the software, and also a "course CD." Students were asked to install both. Somewhat surprisingly, neither the course nor the software CDs had to be replaced with new versions very frequently.
- Student performance data was emailed to Stanford for the first years. The student was generally assumed to have an Internet connection for data transfer and also communication with the tutors. In the 1990s, a dialup modem was adequate for this purpose.

EPGY Advanced Courses through 1996

By 1996, the advanced courses in Table 16 were available to EPGY students at the high-school level.

7.2.5 Marketing Relationships

- In 1994, Computer Curriculum Corporation bought a license that allowed CCC to sell the EPGY courses, and also gave EPGY access to the SuccessMaker courses which they could use to fill their gap in elementary mathematics with MCS. In 1996, CCC decided they did not want to continue the relationship, in part because states like Michigan and Florida were developing their own virtual schools so the market for EPGY courses had changed.
- A marketing relationship began with Johns Hopkins Center for Talented Youth (CTY) in 1996 as a part of their gifted student program. CTY listed the EPGY courses, kept 1/3 of the proceeds, and EPGY did the tutoring. Later, CTY did the tutoring. Things went well for a number of years, generating about $200,000 per year for EPGY, but eventually they wanted to make their own modifications and started doing their own development.[25] However, CTY continued to use the EPGY K7 Math course until 2014 when the agreement lapsed as CTY wanted to produce their own courses or work with vendors that would white label courses for them to sell under their brand.[26]

7.2.6 The K7 Math Course

In 1995, Suppes's non-compete agreement with Simon and Schuster expired. Moreover they were no longer wanting him to license MCS from them so he was also in need of a new course. He saw an opportunity to create an elementary math course intended for gifted students built without compromises due to the marketplace.

---

[25]Private communication from Ravaglia.

[26]Private communication from Jeanette Cook.

TABLE 16: EPGY Advanced Courses as of 1996

Code	Description
Secondary Mathematics	
M011	Beginning Algebra
M012	Intermediate Algebra
M013	Precalculus
Advanced Placement Mathematics and Physics	
M040	Calculus A
M041	Calculus B
M042	Calculus C
P051	Physics C: Mechanics
P053	Physics C: Electricity and Magnetism
P054	Electricity and Magnetism Lab
College Level Mathematics and Physics	
M043H	Linear Algebra
M044H	Multivariate Calculus
M045H	Differential Equations
M152	Elementary Theory of Numbers
M157	Introduction to Logic
P055A	Optics
P055B	Thermodynamics
P070	Modern Physics
P110, P111	Intermediate Mechanics
English Language and Expository Writing Courses	
W004, W005, W006	English Language Arts
W011A, B, C	Fundamentals of Expository Writing
E001A, B, C	Advanced Placement Expository Writing

"Sets and Numbers" for the Curriculum

For the curriculum, he started with the presentation and content of his Sets and Numbers textbook series from the 1960s, making many changes to satisfy new standards and technical opportunities. Suppes always believed that Sets and Numbers represented the best way to teach elementary mathematics.[27] The underlying approach of using set

---

[27]There was a very interesting comment in an 8/30/1966 letter from NSF regarding Suppes first use of Sets and Numbers at IMSSS: "The problem will then arise how to allocate observed differences between the experimental and control groups to (a) use of machine teaching, and (b) use of the sets-and-numbers curriculum in place of the traditional."

theoretical concepts appealed to his philosophical interests, and now this approach seemed very appropriate for gifted students.

Software Development Environment for K7

By 1995, a number of authoring environments were available for the Windows platform. His team looked at Authorware, Macromind Director, Supercard, and ToolBook. They decided on ToolBook.

ToolBook was developed by Asymetrix Corporation, founded by Microsoft founder Paul Allen. It was similar to GUI-based tools for creating software applications such as Microsoft Visual Basic and Powerpoint, but was intended for creating courses instead of stand-alone programs. The ToolBook layout tool included templates and answer-processing primitives. ToolBook had an event-driven programming language called "Openscript" and could easily be interfaced to external software.[28]

Suppes developed a workflow not unlike those from the early days of CCC but if anything more cost-effective.

- A few graphics designers laid out the templates and assembled libraries of images. Paul Dimitre did most of this for K7. Suppes enjoyed working directly with Dimitre because the designer could capture his ideas in a few iterations.

- One or two programmers would write the needed code to handle special answer processing and course motion as well as infrastructure details such as saving student performance data. Yong Liang did most of this for K7 in the early years.

- A large group of curriculum developers wrote the curriculum. These were mostly part-time Stanford students in 1995–1996. Suppes remarked that the process was one of the fastest that he had ever seen under his direction. Later, Betsy Macken, who had been Vice President of Curriculum at CCC and also Director of the Center for Study of Language and Information (CSLI) at Stanford, took over the extension and rewrites of the course.[29]

- A new feature of the courseware starting with K7 was that Suppes recorded virtually all of the audio himself. Dimitre set up a recording studio near Suppes's office where he spent many hours recording the audio for the lectures. The process was that he had a script for how to describe the concept that was being taught, but he always seemed

---

[28]See Wikipedia "ToolBook" [229] for details about the history of ToolBook. While it has been updated to use HTML for online delivery, other competitors have entered this space. In the 1990s, ToolBook was an important authoring system.

[29]Macken was one of Suppes's most senior associates in CAI. She was extremely detail-oriented and thorough, and also very effective at specifying software.

to add his own spin with frequent extemporaneous additions to their content![30] His voice was well-known and generally very well-received by all the EPGY students although in later years there were requests for more varied age and gender voices.

K7 Courseware Motion

Suppes's courses almost always had an algorithm for deciding what the student should do next. He called this *course motion*. Courses that contained multiple strands generally contained sets of exercises called *classes* (or *concept classes*). A class would contain more exercises than a student would be expected to do. So, there was an algorithm that would determine *mastery* of a class.

When a student mastered a class, the instruction would proceed to the next class in the strand. If the student took all of the exercises without mastery, then the student would return to the previous class, or alternatively take some diagnostic or review.

The two important decisions were: when is a class considered mastered, and when does the system switch to another strand? At CCC, a variety of algorithms were considered for determining mastery, but at EPGY, Suppes developed one model with some parameters.[31]

The idea is that a value q is associated with each class in the course and is interpreted to mean that the class is **not** mastered. q is modified with each exercise in the class that the student attempts; it is decreased if the student gets it right, and increased if the student gets it wrong.

If the student answers correctly on exercise number n in the class, the new value of q is given by

$$q_{n+1} = (1 - \omega) \times \alpha \times q_n$$

If the student answers incorrectly, the new value of q is given by:

$$q_{n+1} = (1 - \omega) \times \alpha \times q_n + \alpha \times \omega$$

The class is considered mastered when the value of q is less than the parameter m.

The values of the parameters are the subject of experimentation. One set of values is as follows:

$$q_0 = 0.5$$
$$\alpha = 0.9$$
$$\omega = 0.1$$
$$m = 0.23$$

---

[30]When releases were behind schedule, the developers liked to blame Suppes for being behind on his recordings.
[31]See [134] and [157] for details.

It is easy to illustrate the effect of these formulas and parameters. Consider the three sample scenarios in Table 17a. Each of these shows a different sequence of exercises performed by a student, up to six exercises. The checkmark by an exercise means the student has answered correctly, and the X means incorrectly. The value q—which starts at 0.5—increases or decreases with each exercise. Mastery will be achieved when the student reaches m.

- In Scenario #1, the student gets four exercises correct in a row. Q changes to 0.2152, which is less than m, so the student has mastered the class.

- In Scenario #2, the student answers incorrectly on Exercise E2, but "recovers" and answers correctly for the next three exercises. This is an important scenario, because it illustrates a property that Suppes looked for: he believed students should be "forgiven" initial errors as a part of the learning process, and he took the correct responses on the last three exercises to indicate that the student has mastered the class, and doesn't need any additional exercises.

- In Scenario #3, the student gets four out of eight exercises correct, but the order is chaotic, indicating that the student really hasn't mastered the class.

Of course, the attribution of mastery is only probabilistic and may be wrong. The overall curriculum structure provides for this by containing both organized review and rules that take the student back to earlier material if problems start to develop.

It is also possible that the student has mastered the skill for the time being but will fall back later. The course also had review opportunities to make sure the skill remained mastered.[32]

Math Races

Suppes wanted to use educational games throughout his career. He believed that gaming was useful but did not want to compromise educational quality.

An important educational element that games could do well, he believed, was to provide sustained practice of skills already learned in order to increase "automaticity" of performing a task or applying a concept. Suppes believed that students needed to practice—and keep practicing—skills in the same manner that a musician keeps practicing music.

The Math Concepts and Skills course at CCC (MCS) had contained a series of games called "Speed Games" that emphasized automaticity of

---

[32]There is a good deal more to be said about this. See [157].

TABLE 17: Scenarios for Illustrating K7 Motion

(A) Scenario 1

Exercise	Correct	q value
E1	✓	0.4050
E2	✓	0.3281
E3	✓	0.2657
E4	✓	0.2152
E5		
E6		

(B) Scenario 2

Exercise	Correct	q value
E1	✓	0.4050
E2	X	0.4181
E3	✓	0.3386
E4	✓	0.2743
E5	✓	0.2222
E6		

(C) Scenario 3

Exercise	Correct	q value
E1	✓	0.4050
E2	X	0.4181
E3	✓	0.3386
E4	X	0.3643
E5	✓	0.2951
E6	X	0.3290
E7	✓	0.2665
E8	X	0.3059

the elementary operations. In the K7 course, Suppes expanded this idea to "Math Races," which had an interactive visual component of racing into which the mathematics was embedded as well as a much wider array of skills. The gaming component was a race, either swimmers or cars (the student could choose). Getting an exercise correct would speed up the student's avatar in the race; an incorrect answer would slow it down.

The Math Races contained practice in a number of very challenging skills, including ones not normally assumed to benefit greatly from automaticity.

Educational games often restrict the domain to small parts of the content in order to have compelling games. Suppes thought that you have to start with the curriculum itself and hold that as a constant while trying to develop a more engaging educational context. This is not an easy problem to address.

K7 Course Acceptance

Distributed on CD-ROM beginning in 1996–97, the K7 course became the most successful product from EPGY. It was used by gifted students who were working at their own grade level but moving through the course very quickly, allowing the students to move into the algebra sequence and other courses designed for high school students.

As Ray Ravaglia put it, the course was "relentless."[33]

Early Uses of the Internet

By 2000, EPGY took a modest step towards using the Internet. The K7 course was instrumented so that student performance data was sent back to Stanford automatically through an Internet connection. Previously, performance data was sent manually by the student in email messages. At Stanford, these data were used for both formative and efficacy studies.

At that time, Suppes believed that the Internet was largely about advertising and media and did not see it as useful for interactive courseware. He was wary of bandwidth limitations and the lack of powerful client-side programming capabilities. These obstacles were, of course, rapidly being addressed, even though they remain concerns in 2016.

7.2.7 Growth of the Business

EPGY was now getting foundation support and other donations, but it was also dependent on tuition.[34] The pricing model became: a three-month period of time would cost $390, and the student could be enrolled

---

[33]Private communication.

[34]A number of models were used over the years.

in one course at a time.[35] If the student finished quickly, he/she could proceed to another course. If the student worked slowly, it might take several quarters. This method of charging by time periods worked much better than charging by the course.

In 1993–94, this brought in about $200K. By 1996, the amount was close to $1M. Steady increases brought this to about $3M per year by 2000.[36]

7.2.8 Highlights of Other Courses

- In 1992–93, courses in physics mechanics and physics electricity and magnetism were created; see [90].
- In 1993, EPGY developed a high school AP English Language and Composition course with evaluation by human tutors. These were "synchronous" courses where all students were at the same place.
- In 1994, linear algebra and multivariate calculus were taught in a virtual classroom model using a tool called Intel Pro-Share, an early online video service. EPGY shifted to Centra and was one of the first groups to use it. EPGY won a "Centra Pioneer Award" in 1996.[37]
- In 1994–96, the Atlantic Philanthropies provided funds for the development of English courses.[38]
- In the late 1990s, the computer science courses were developed.
- Composer David Brynjar Franzson designed and built an AP course in Music Theory. Marianna Rozenfeld developed the presentation software. This course had only a small number of students. Nancy and Robert Smith helped test the course, and felt that it was one of the most refreshing and beautiful CAI courses they had ever seen. In some exercises, students could actually add notes onto screens of musical notation, and hear the results dynamically generated on the server; Rozenfeld's algorithms could judge the correctness of the results.[39]

7.2.9 University-level Math Courses

EPGY received more support from the Sloan Foundation, this time for the development of university-level courses. Marc Sanders says that the earlier course development model was not as impressive as it could have been due to both the vision and the process with not as much time as needed for detailed work by the math department. He recalls:

---

[35]The $390 was increased to $480 by 2004.
[36]Private communication from Ray Ravaglia.
[37]Private communication from Ray Ravaglia.
[38]For a description of Atlantic Philanthropies see Wikipedia [172].
[39]Private communication from Rozenfeld.

I came to EPGY in 1998 to develop a suite of university-level math courses, pursuant to a Sloan Foundation grant that EPGY received. ...I came on-board, developed some new courses using a new development approach which was much more time-consuming but gave a better result, and then re-developed some old courses using this new approach. The courses were (roughly in order): Differential Equations, Complex Analysis, Multivariable Differential Calculus, Multivariable Integral Calculus, Real Analysis, Linear Algebra, Abstract Algebra (with Prof. Ralph Cohen), and Partial Differential Equations (with Prof. Rafe Mazzeo). (personal communication)

Marc Sanders[40] also notes that the annual enrollments in the university-level courses, which included some with which he had not been involved, have reached about 500 students. All of these courses are still being used at Stanford Pre-Collegiate Studies.[41]

7.2.10 A Proof Environment for Teaching Mathematics: Geometry Course

In 1998–2000, Rick Sommer and Greg Nuckols with programming by Dave McMath and Marianna Rozenfeld developed a new proof environment for teaching mathematics and applied it to a geometry course; see [105]. This followed in the tradition of work at IMSSS during the 1970s but was considerably updated. This was also funded by the Atlantic Philanthropies.

The goal was "to approach 'standard mathematical practice' both in how the final proof looks and in the techniques students use to produce them" ([105] p. 227). This was covered in part by using a modern Windows interface with menus and the use of the mouse. See Figure 76 for a sample screen. The EPGY Theorem Proving Environment also contained a theorem prover named Otter[42] and the Maple symbolic algebra system.[43] The Verify command, shown in Figure 76, called the theorem prover with the current proof context to prove another statement. For further details of the theorem-proving environment, see [77].

From a logical perspective, a key feature of the system was the maintenance of a list of "proof obligations." These are side issues that must be dealt with before the proof can be finalized. For example, division by a term necessitates the obligation that the dividing term is not 0. Sometimes, the prover can automatically discharge such "obligations" ([105] p. 238–239).

---

[40]Sanders is now Senior Director of Digital Learning Strategy at the Office of the Vice President of Teaching and Learning at Stanford.

[41]See https://ohsx.stanford.edu/university-math.

[42]See [76] and Wikipedia "Prover9" [213]

[43]See https://www.maplesoft.com/solutions/education/.

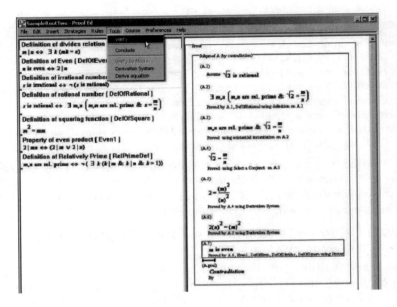

FIGURE 76: Screen from the Proof Environment for the Geometry Course

Regarding the choice of Otter, the authors note that "since Otter works in first-order logic and since the logic of student interaction is a higher-order logic with partial functions, Otter will not always be the best choice" ([105] p. 257). Sommer and Nuckols also felt that the theorem prover needed to provide more help to the student in the case of failed derivations, perhaps suggesting a different intermediate goal ([105] p. 254).

The course was initially offered in April 2000 (distributed on CD-ROM). Over 170 students worked proof exercises using the system in some version, and 43 completed the 2001 course version. To finish the course, students were each required to complete 22 proof exercises ([105] pp. 247–248).

7.2.11 Hand-held Computers: Mobile Math

In 2000, Ronald Fortune and Robert Smith began thinking about delivering courses on hand-held devices. They saw that students would be carrying around cell phones that would be suitable for educational use, and they wanted to build comprehensive courseware for these devices. They began conversations with Suppes about the prospects of working with EPGY.

They chose the Palm products for their GUI, active screen with a stylus, and programmability, and constructed a prototype with about 50 different exercises types. The devices did not yet have Internet capability, so they devised a "syncing" method that used a Windows PC. They were anticipating devices like the Palm Treo or BlackBerry that would be programmable cell phones connected to the Internet.

Fortune and Smith discussed this on numerous occasions with Suppes, who agreed that there was an opportunity but felt it was too early. (This is ironic because Suppes was generally too early himself!) After refining the concept, they spent a great deal of time in New York and Sand Hill Road talking to investors.

Mobile Math Development

Suppes decided to make an investment and also ask Stanford to license the EPGY K7 math course for porting to handhelds. The licensing agreement process with Stanford took a year, by which time they had worked out many technical details. Edumetrics Learning was formed!

Smith formed a small engineering team. The engineers extracted the content from the K7 course's ToolBook files, converted it to a more modern XML, and built the Mobile Math system. It contained about 70% of the then-existing K7 content, could sync 32 Palm's to a PC at the same time, and had a complete management system running on the PC. They solved the problems of how the motion scheme would work on a small device, and of how the Palms would be synced and recharged.

A typical exercise is shown in Figure 77, and the management system's dashboard is shown in Figure 78.

Outcomes of Mobile Math

The Mobile Math product worked and generated some interest, but the funding ran out before Smith and Fortune felt it had a real chance. The company clearly needed more time to establish itself.

It was also during this period that Apple Computer introduced its first iPhone. While too expensive for student use, it clearly foreshadowed the mobile revolution that soon followed.

However, it is not clear that comprehensive educational products are compatible with cell phone use. There are now many educational applications running on iPads for example, and many games on cell phones, but there are few comprehensive courses being delivered on small devices. The impressive audio-visual capabilities of a modern cell phone are certainly more than adequate for the delivery of courseware. It may simply be that people want more casual use of their cell phones rather than comprehensive educational content.

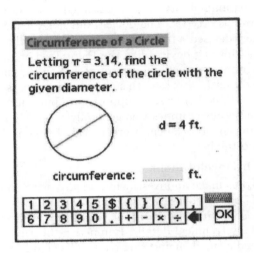

FIGURE 77: Typical Mobile Math Exercise–Compute Circumference

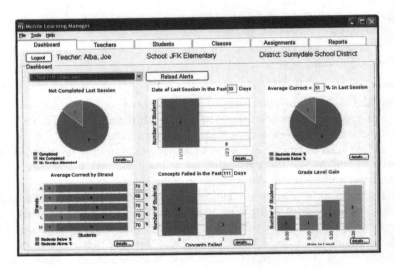

FIGURE 78: Mobile Math Management System Dashboard

Suppes and EPGY benefited in several ways from the Mobile Math experience.

- The most important was that Fortune was able to convince Suppes that the EPGY courses, especially K7, could be successfully used in schools as well as home-based, gifted settings. Suppes undertook to create a separate version for general use. This was done with a different set of outline and motion parameters pulling from the same content base, where the outline specifies which exercises are to be available at which content/grade level and the motion parameters control the pace of the course and mastery criteria, see page 266.
- At that point, EPGY's courses were still delivered via CD-ROM. Fortune convinced Suppes that CD-ROM delivery was no longer attractive for schools, and that the Internet was the future. Smith overcame Suppes's technical objections, and some of the software and techniques developed for Mobile Math were used by EPGY in converting the K7 course for Internet delivery.
- Fortune made a substantial sale to Memphis, TN of the new Internet-based courseware. This launched EPGY's success in the school marketplace. Approximately 70,000 students were enrolled in the EPGY math program each year, and approximately 25,000 students in language arts and writing.

7.2.12   EPGY and Sales to Schools

The sale to Memphis in 2005 was followed by an effort to expand EPGY to schools. Courses like K7 were adapted for use in schools, and a new management system was developed that supported the needs of teachers and schools.

At that time the following key roles were established in the development of the school programs: Dave McMath[44] and Rozenfeld took over the programming of the K7 course, especially after Yong Liang left the project; Macken continued to enhance the course and do evaluations; Smith became consultant to EPGY working on project management for course development as new courses were coming online and older courses needed revision for robustness with more students; and Ravaglia took over the Memphis relationship.

More sales to schools were to come, see page 266.

---

[44]Dave McMath is a prodigiously capable programmer as well as being a creative architect, and the software developed at EPGY was greatly shaped by him. Suppes always believed that particular individuals stand out to get the job done, and McMath is such a person.

7.2.13   English Grammar and Style of the Sentence (EG20)

A number of writing courses were developed in the 1990s using online courses with tutor evaluation or synchronous courses in virtual classrooms. Suppes and others had a deep dissatisfaction for these earlier courses where there was a lag between the "stimulus and the response," i.e., how long it took to get corrections back to students.

In 2002–2003, the EG20 course was created with Conrad Scott Curtis as the author and Dave McMath as the programmer. This was the first web-based course at EPGY so the technology was new, as was the idea of using the tutor to build a database of correct answers during their initial grading so that later the course could handle the answer evaluation mostly automatically. Other new tools were also developed including an authoring language and tools for handling parse trees in a flexible grammar.

The EG20 grammar course for grades 7–12 and the W9/10/11 instructor-lead writing courses for high school students were available and could be taken concurrently. So the next need was for preparing elementary students for these sequences. This would be the Language Arts and Writing course for grades 1–6.

7.2.14   Language Arts and Writing (LAW)

Suppes began a course in Language Arts and Writing in 2002. Blair Kaneshiro, Tamara Woodson, Olivia Solis, Susan Awbrey Arnold, and a team of writers worked on the content, which used new courseware delivery software developed by Rozenfeld.

The important innovation was a parser that checked free-form student input for syntactic correctness and gave useful advice. This meant that students could type free-field input and have their responses dynamically checked. The parser was initially the work of Kaneshiro and linguist Michael Boettner, but substantially more progress was made when Dan Flickinger, a computational linguist working at Stanford, took over as project manager.

Flickinger changed the parser to a framework that is still being developed by him and worldwide collaborators in the DELPH-IN research consortium in computational linguistics.[45] He also extended it to parsing paragraphs as well as sentences. Mathematician and computational linguist Jiye Yu worked closely with Flickinger on processing paragraphs and on developing a combination of symbolic and statistical methods for evaluating the correctness of meaning for sentences composed by students.[46]

---

[45]See http://www.delph-in.net.
[46]As of 2016, this research is still underway at Redbird Advanced Learning.

Suppes had long wanted students to be able to have genuine dialogs with computerized software, and this was his most sophisticated and successful attempt. In his last years working with EPGY courseware, he spent more time working with this language arts course than any other research project in online instruction.

7.2.15 Conversion of CD-ROM-based Courses to Online Delivery

Beginning in about 2006, EPGY began the conversion of the older CD-ROM courses to Internet delivery. The high school math courses received the most attention, with Rozenfeld and Nuckols doing most of the work.

Content improvements and new software were developed to upgrade the courses as well as port them to the Internet. Content was upgraded to the most recent standards. The Maple algebraic conversion engine was replaced by Maxima, a shareware version of the Macsyma system developed in the 1960s at MIT;[47] Maxima ran on the web server. It was interesting to see that what was formerly a high-end project created by mathematicians and computer scientists could now so readily become a part of a high school math course.

7.2.16 The Summer Institutes

Several other related programs were developed by EPGY and are still in operation including the Summer Institutes and the Online High School. In 2001, Ray Ravaglia, Gary Oas, and Marc Sanders tried an experimental summer program called "Summer Institute in Math and Physics" (SIMP). It was a notable success, and Suppes and Rick Sommer decided to make it something much bigger, and succeeded.[48] The program was part of a general effort by Stanford (and other universities) to use their dormitories and classrooms during the summer. This program has grown to the point where there is no more space available. International students are now coming in greater numbers. Generally, the Summer Institutes courses are short but intensive courses organized to stimulate interest among students. Table 18 shows the list of courses offered in summer 2015.[49]

---

[47]See Wikipedia "Macsyma" [196].

[48]Personal communication from Marc Sanders.

[49]As soon as this was going, Suppes had little direct involvement, leaving most issues to Sommer and his team.

7.2.17 The Online High School (OHS)

In 2004, Suppes and Ray Ravaglia founded a new entity called the Online High School (OHS).[50] Support of $3.3M for this was provided by the Malone Family Foundation. Members of the Malone family had used the EPGY courseware for gifted students and were sufficiently impressed with those courses to want to support a new program. The OHS has become self-sustaining.[51]

As Ravaglia explains it, one of Suppes's major contributions to the school was his conception of the core curriculum being based on certain topics related to philosophy. Here is how this is currently described by the OHS.

> Our four-year interdisciplinary Core Sequence equips our students with exceptional skills in careful reading, critical thinking, and oral and written argumentation. More than any brief course in logic or reasoning, our sequence gives students broadly applicable experience in evaluating data and scientific theory formation, and in thinking about claims and concepts in politics, ethics, and the study of identity. ([110])

An obvious idea was to use the existing high school and college courses as a part of the OHS. Ravaglia soon discovered that the courses that worked for self-paced individualized instruction for gifted students were not well suited as a part of the OHS. So, the OHS today does not use any traditional CAI materials, but instead uses collaboration software where the courses are taught live in a "virtual classroom" shared online by teacher and students in real time.[52]

Jeffrey Scarborough and Ray Ravaglia have written a book entitled *Bricks and Mortar* ([95]) about their experiences; Scarborough was an early headmaster of the school. They summarize their book thus:

> This is not a book about technology. While technology certainly figures prominently within this book, it is first and foremost about a school. That the school exists only because of the technology is true, though this is not the most interesting thing about the school. Rather, what is interesting is the realization that compared to the importance of getting the interaction between teachers and students right, and providing them with a rich and fertile environment in which this interaction can occur, the technology is only a small part of the puzzle. ([95] p. 1.)

---

[50]Ravaglia took over much of the planning and development; see [109] for the press release. Jan Keating was the head of the school for some years and did significant development work that made the school a reality.

[51]See Wikipedia "Stanford University Online High School" [226].

[52]The OHS now uses the Adobe Connect tool for online collaboration. It used SABA for some of the early years.

TABLE 18: Summer Institute High School Program Courses, 2015

Field	Grades	Course
Business	9–10	Topics in Business & Entrepreneurship
	9–10	Topics in Decision Leadership & Negotiation
	10–11	Investigations in Business & Entrepreneurship
	10–11	Investigations in Decision Leadership & Negotiation
Computer Science	10–11	Artificial Intelligence
	9–10	Computer Simulations & Interactive Media
	8–9	Java and Robotics
Mathematics	9–10	Cryptography
	9–10	Discrete Mathematics
	10–11	Topics in Number Theory
	10–11	Investigations in Number Theory
	8–10	Logic & Problem Solving
	8–9	Mathematical Puzzles and Games
	9–10	The Mathematics of Symmetry
Science & Engineering	9–11	Cosmology
	9–11	Environmental & Earth Science
	9–10	The Frontiers of Physics
	10–11	Investigations in Bioscience & Biotechnology
	10–11	Investigations in Engineering
	9–11	Particle Physics
	10–11	Quantum Mechanics
	10–11	Theory of Relativity
	9–10	Topics in Bioscience & Biotechnology
	9–10	Topics in Engineering
	8–9	Topics in Physics
Writing & Humanities	9–11	20th Century Humanities
	8–11	Creative Writing
	8–11	Expository Writing
	9–11	Screenwriting
	9–11	Why Music Matters
Social Science	10–11	International Relations
	10–11	Investigations in Legal Studies
	9–11	Topics in Anthropology
	9–11	Topics in Legal Studies
	9–11	Topics in Politics & Public Policy
	9–11	Topics in Psychology
	9–11	Topics in Sociology

The book deals with a number of issues involving organizing extra-curricular activities, supporting student "meetups," developing a culture of seminar-like classes. Few of the actual issues discussed in the book are technical.

The OHS has grown at a steady pace since 2006 and as of 2016 has about 620 students including full- and part-time students, with 388 full-time equivalents. Students live in many states and countries, and some of them are even traveling with their families. Students come to Stanford for a summer program and also for graduation.

7.2.18 Evaluation Studies and Growth of School Programs

Evaluation of the efficacy of the EPGY courses was an ongoing project but funds were needed to pay for substantial efforts. In 2006, funds were obtained for a two year study in elementary schools followed by another four year study in middle schools. Jeanette Cook provided the following description of these school programs and their results.

Preparing K7 for School Programs

During the six years that the K7 Math course was the basis for evaluation with low performing students, a special version of the course was created, internally named "reinforcement," which underwent many changes designed to improve the course's ability to adapt to these students' learning style, which Suppes believed was different in many aspects from the gifted students for which the course was originally developed. These changes increased the amount of scaffolding (or "reinforcement") in both the content and in the motion system's presentation of the content.[53] Additionally, some enhancements were made to increase student engagement, such as adding short music clips ("Math Tunes") and enhancing the Math Races user interface to encourage students to use it more often to develop automaticity in calculations.

Elementary School Study

In 2006, the first efficacy study was begun with a $1.2M grant from the Silicon Valley K-12 Education Foundation. It was a two-year study in which the K7 Math course was used in eight elementary schools with a high percentage of Title I (federal free lunch program) students and low mathematics achievement levels as measured by the annual California state test (CST). The foundation's donors had a particular interest in helping these low performing schools, and in addition the No Child Left Behind legislation required that these schools show improvement each year or face serious consequences so there was also a strong incentive for schools to participate.

---

[53]See page 259 for further details.

In the first year of the elementary school evaluation of K7 Math, a randomized treatment method was used where students were matched as "pairs" and then split and randomly assigned to the treatment or the control group. Students in the treatment group were expected to use the K7 Math program at least 100 minutes each school week, while students in the control group received their usual instruction. Schools were provided with onsite support and training from Stanford site instructors. The site instructors were also tasked with monitoring usage to make sure that each student in the treatment group at their assigned school(s) was using the course as expected. This was a continual struggle due to class schedules and technical problems that were mostly related to the school's computing environment. Suppes met with the team of site instructors each week to review progress and issues, frequently brainstorming solutions with the group.[54]

The results after the first year were promising, with the treatment group showing significant gains in their year-end math exams compared to the control group. With these positive results, schools lobbied to have the control and treatment groups merged for the final year, since this would make their class scheduling easier, and Suppes eventually agreed to this change. After this, the evaluation focus changed to measuring the impact of the amount of course use on test scores, since all students had access to it.

Middle School Study

In 2008, the Institute for Education Sciences (IES, a part of the US Department of Education) awarded a $3M grant to evaluate EPGY courses.

The IES project was a four-year study of middle school students, again focusing on schools with high percentages of Title I students who for the most part were struggling to achieve grade level competence in mathematics. These middle school students were even further behind than the elementary students in the prior study, so Suppes pushed to get the schools to commit to 200 minutes per week for each student, instead of the 100 minutes in the elementary study. To help make this possible, the grant included computer equipment for the schools, as well as the support of site instructors. Each participating school was provided with a complete computer lab which was set up and maintained by Stanford staff. All the schools needed to provide was space, power and Internet access. The project began with a small group of schools and at its conclusion included participation from over 1400 students at 13 schools.

---

[54]It was during these weekly sessions that Suppes met his fourth wife Michelle Nguyen.

The results for both of these evaluations showed that the greater the amount of work done, the greater the gain on the tests; students that were initially further behind grade level received more gain.

During the years of the IES study, data was also available from Memphis City Schools, where over 65,000 students per year in grades K-12 were using the K7 Math course and taking the Tennessee state test annually. The same analysis was done with these larger data sets, and again positive results were shown for students who used the course more often and in a more productive way.

More Analysis of the Data

After analyzing correlations between K7 Math curriculum variables and student test score changes, Suppes came up with a measure of productive use called "correct-first-attempt." This curriculum variable indicated that the student was engaged and focused while using the course and correlated strongly to test score improvements. The total number of correct-first-attempts that the student completed was the measure of their "usage" for the analysis, and the analysis consisted of measuring the effect size of this usage rather than a simple comparison of a treatment to a control group.

In 2013, a final analysis including both the IES and the Memphis data was completed and published in the *Journal of Computers & Education* with the unwieldy title of "Positive technological and negative pre-test-score effects in a four-year assessment of low socioeconomic status K-8 student learning in computer-based Math and Language Arts courses" ([150]).[55]

Lessons to be Learned from Study Schools

These study school projects exhibit three of the most common themes from throughout Suppes's projects:

- Strong focus on evaluation.
- Excellent support to the schools through the use of site instructors (equivalent to consultants at CCC) to ensure program success.
- Ability to find both government and non-government funding (which Suppes was still doing almost right up to the close of EPGY at Stanford).

7.2.19 Changing Structure of the Organization

The number of school sites had increased dramatically with Memphis, the study schools, a number of new school districts such as San Francisco, and a new program called District Open Enrollment (DOE) where

---

[55]Most of this section was written by Jeanette Cook in a private communication in 2016.

a group of parents in a school district that did not have a license with EPGY could organize, provide a site instructor and create their own "school."

In 2007, Jeanette Cook[56] moved up from her initial position as school site instructor to work with Ravaglia to manage the "Schools Programs" and head the large staff in the field. Without an official sales or marketing department, those duties also all fell to Ravaglia and Cook.

Nancy Smith was also hired in 2007[57] to work directly with Suppes as project coordinator for the growing organization.

With Cook and Smith onboard, Suppes made a very unusual management change for him where he established a Program Management Office (PMO) in 2008:

> Effective management of programming projects is critical to the success of our major programs: the Schools Program and related studies, OHS, Summer Institute and the Gifted Individual Program. We are pleased to announce the formation of a new Program Office to manage the prioritization, scheduling, resource assignments and quality levels for all programming projects at EPGY. The office will be led by Nancy Smith and Jeanette Cook, in addition to their current responsibilities. Dave McMath and Carolyn Fairman will continue as the technical leaders for the combined programming group. Together Nancy, Jeanette, Dave and Carolyn form the matrix management team for the programming organization at EPGY. Please join me in supporting them in this new role. Pat

Carolyn Fairman was senior system administrator for a very large operation at headquarters in the client-server model which included physical and virtual servers running Redhat/Linux for: course delivery (including webserver to cache student state on disk for performance), Oracle database, math expression evaluation, grammatical expression parsing, course development, testing, release and version control, report processing, and handling for content proxy servers located remotely at the schools.

Massive revisions and extensions were underway particularly to K7 where every grade was reviewed by Macken over a several year period according to the collected data on student answer responses. This necessitated a frequent cycle of development, test, and system release coordinated over many courses and several departments. Suppes monitored the release schedule and progress quite closely!

---

[56] Jeanette Cook was an excellent interface between customers and all the groups at Stanford. She represented everyone honestly and fairly making each group's case to the others as the usual tensions occurred between management, marketing, and product development.

[57] This was her third stint working for Suppes.

This PMO group (Smith, Cook, McMath,[58] Fairman) continued to meet weekly from 2008 to 2013.

7.2.20   Licensing the EPGY Courseware 2010–2013

In about 2010, Suppes and Stanford made the decision to license the EPGY courseware to an outside firm. They agreed that EPGY had largely succeeded in forming a business whose principal purpose would no longer be to advance research, and the future of the products could best be assured by spinning it off to a company.[59]

The Stanford Office of Technology Licensing (OTL) developed an offering and found a surprising amount of interest. At the time of the offering, the courses being licensed had an annual revenue of $7 million to Stanford, with over 100,000 students using the courses per year (mostly from large school districts).

Established, large companies such as Pearson, small but established companies, and newly conceived startups participated in the due diligence and negotiation process. In the summer of 2012, a deal was formulated between Rocket Learning of Miami, FL and Stanford, with financing provided by the Perot Foundation as the financial base for their startup, named Redbird Advanced Learning.[60]

A year was spent doing very detailed planning, including informing customers, setting up plans to move servers and sorting through many technical issues and human resource issues. The technical tasks included moving the web servers to cloud storage from the locations at Stanford, reorganizing the files, and converting the database from Oracle to Postgres; these were largely handled by Carolyn Fairman and Dave McMath. Smooth transfer of existing customers and marketing policies was handled by Jeanette Cook. Human resource issues and compliance with a multitude of requirements and policies were handled by Ray Ravaglia and Nancy Smith.

In July of 2013, the licensing occurred, and a good portion of the EPGY staff left to join Redbird Advanced Learning. In 2015, the Office

---

[58]Within the year, McMath moved his family to Fayetteville, Arkansas where he could be viewed daily on WebEx and came back to headquarters for one week each month while Smith became co-head of programming

[59]Suppes was not entirely happy with the way this was handled, in particular believing that the University had failed to note the research value of having courses in operation in multiple schools and subjecting the results to constant evaluation. Suppes was for a time very concerned that the University was discarding something of intrinsic value.

[60]The name "redbird" is very likely a clever substitute for "cardinal," which is the name of Stanford's sports teams, although it refers to the color not the bird. See https://redbirdlearning.com/.

of Technology Licensing honored EPGY for the more than five million dollars of royalties that Stanford had thus far received from Redbird.

Suppes noted at the time that many of his concerns about the process were alleviated by the attitude of the principals involved in the purchase. He was particularly pleased with the selection of Matthew Mugo Fields as president of the new company, and spent a good deal of time meeting with him. Fields noted that he was eating at Suppes's house at least once a week during this period. Suppes was also pleased by the fact that Redbird wanted to continue a research relationship with Stanford, which was in tune with his long-term views about the combination of research and commercialization that was needed.

7.3 The End of Patrick Suppes's Research in Computers in Education

Stanford placed the remaining parts of EPGY, including the Summer Institutes, the Online High School, and the online college level courses under the banner of "Stanford Pre-collegiate Studies," or SPCS, which expanded to include other relevant programs at the University. Ray Ravaglia was appointed director, and Rick Sommer took over that role at the end of 2015 when Ravaglia joined The New York Times. The name EPGY went along to Redbird.

Starting July 2013, Redbird Advanced Learning was adapting and marketing the EPGY courses under the EPGY name for the school courses and GiftedandTalented.com for the tutored courses.[61] Matthew Mugo Fields, a founder of Rocket Learning, was president of the company, Dave McMath was vice president of product and technology, Carolyn Fairman was director of information technology, and Marianna Rozenfeld was a senior software engineer (presently converting the high school courses for gifted students to yet another authoring environment!).

On September 30, 2016, McGraw-Hill Education acquired Redbird Advanced Learning.[62] Fields said that Redbird had not simply bought the technology and customers, but wanted a continuing relationship with Stanford University, and that McGraw-Hill wanted to continue the relationship. This included the ongoing work on the LA&W course as well as course evaluation. Suppes had been very pleased with this relationship.

Fields said that Redbird had developed a new elementary math

---

[61] See https://giftedandtalented.com/.

[62] Robert and Nancy Smith interviewed Redbird's president, Matthew Mugo Fields, about the current state of Redbird, its future, and what Suppes's reaction to these events might have been.

course beginning in late 2013 after the licensing. Fields allowed that he and Suppes had talked—even had a "vigorous debate"—about the development of this new mathematics course at Redbird during 2014. The course included much of the instructional content of Suppes's K7 course, and an adapted motion system, but it was built on modules that contained games and projects. Suppes's concern was that these things would weaken the overall effect of the system if not introduced with care and evaluation of the results. Fields says that he argued that because of the Common Core and other new standards, it had become a marketing necessity to move immediately in this direction while there was still an opportunity. Fields noted that Suppes was also a businessman who understood marketing priorities, just as he had done at CCC with respect to color and graphics. Fields said that Redbird's new math program had won awards and is now used by over 200,000 students and was one of the reasons that McGraw-Hill Education had bought the company.

Fields says that Redbird is also building tools for teachers, embedded in the Redbird Learning Center, following Suppes's long interest in blended learning, and is continuing to work with various Stanford departments. He sees challenges on more "personalization," more focus on the problems and opportunities of Internet delivery and implementation issues. Like Suppes, he believes that the school environment will be transformed in the coming years.

Fields himself is moving to McGraw-Hill's offices in New York City to work on new challenges.[63] He noted that there has been a "Cambrian explosion" of new edtech companies, and McGraw-Hill (now a privately held company) is taking a startup-like approach to competing in this new business environment. Redbird will continue as a company within McGraw-Hill, and the staff is being transferred to work at other McGraw-Hill centers.

So what would Suppes have thought about the sale to McGraw-Hill? Fields felt that he would have been very pleased, especially since McGraw-Hill is eager to continue the research relationship with Stanford. Fields also noted that McGraw-Hill Education thinks of itself as a "125-year-old startup."

The McGraw-Hill acquisition means that Suppes's two major commercialization efforts (CCC and EPGY) now are owned by the top two educational publishers in the US (Pearson and McGraw-Hill respectively). Suppes had always wanted the major publishers to move into online instruction, and he would be very happy with the outcome.

---

[63] On the personal side, he said that he had kept ownership of his house in Brooklyn and is happy to be moving near his family.

8

Summation and Thoughts about the Future

What are Suppes's accomplishments in his fifty years in what is now called "edtech," what are the principal objections to his approach, and what did he think the future might bring?[1]

8.1   The Singular Accomplishment

In 1979, economist Dean Jamison wrote an article entitled *Suppes's Contributions to Education* in a volume on Suppes's work. Jamison gives the overall summary of this work:

> ... what perhaps most characterizes Suppes's work in CAI is the tenacity and long term character of his commitment to production of operational CAI curriculums, and his success in doing so. ([56] p. 190)

At the time Jamison wrote this, in 1979, Suppes had been working on CAI for 16 years. The shocking fact is that he continued to work on CAI as his principal occupation for the next 34 years, well into the new millennium.

Suppes was certainly capable of a bit of obsession, and furthermore he hated not finishing things he started. But this long-term effort must be seen as something beyond those traits of character.

During the years between the opening of the IMSSS lab in 1963 and the capitalization of CCC, the worlds of both computing and education went through a Cambrian explosion of new theories, technologies, and artifacts. Suppes saw a long-term set of goals, most clearly stated

---

[1]Patrick Suppes had planned to write this chapter by himself when the entire project was nearly done. Unfortunately, this did not happen. Robert Smith completed the work using Suppes's ideas from conversations about the chapter, but with many changes and additions, especially concerning the assessments of Suppes's work by others.

in his *Scientific American* article (see page 32). His unique perspective was that education needed a combination of theory, research, and hard-nosed evaluation of cost-effectiveness in order to bring about educational improvements.

Suppes saw that to test the various theories and tools that would come along, it was not sufficient to have a short period of development followed by some deployments. It was necessary to create entire comprehensive courses in a broad range of subjects, and to deploy and test them over time for many kinds of students and learning situations.

He saw quickly that he would need at least two platforms for his work: one a university-setting where theories could be created and new ideas developed and given initial tests; and the second a commercial company that would develop and deploy courses based on the research for broad segments of the population. The trajectory of both IMSSS and CCC in the '60s and '70s illustrates this duality of focus for his work: theory and practice.

When Suppes read Jamison's article on his work in education in 1979, he was very surprised that the article focused almost entirely on economic issues. For example, Jamison claimed that a key benefit of CAI would be reducing the time needed for the student to learn a curriculum.

Jamison perhaps crystallized Suppes's contribution in this way:

> Suppes's lasting contribution [to education] will have been *to enlarge the set from which choice is possible*. The simple economics of the situation makes the eventual widespread adoption of CAI inevitable. Suppes's work is recognized as the first substantial pioneering of that technology. ([56] p. 202)

8.1.1 "Near First" Contributions

No accounting of achievements can fail to have a list of "firsts": things done before anyone else. Yet, primacy can be very difficult to verify in a community where many people are working on similar things, communicating in a variety of ways (including new tools like email), and when "ideas are in the air," as the expression goes. Joshua Lederberg recognized this in the founding of his SUMEX-AIM project, an ARPANET-based computer system at Stanford dedicated to scientific collaboration.[2]

Primacy may not actually be that important in all cases. Sometimes perfecting and deploying an idea can be a significant part of the overall contribution.

---

[2]See [36], a retrospective written by long-time director Thomas Rindfleisch.

Table 19 lists "near-firsts" of Patrick Suppes and his teams. Some of these may actually be "firsts," but most of them were carried out over a significant period of time.

TABLE 19: "Near-First" Accomplishments

Accomplishment	Date	Location
Computer-based lessons given to a child	Dec. 1963	IMSSS
Lessons given in a school	Spring 1964	IMSSS
Full-year implementation of a course in a school—Grant School, Cupertino	1965–66	IMSSS
Full-screen, WYSIWYG text editor—TVEDIT	1965	IMSSS
Comprehensive math course—Grant School, Cupertino	1965–67	IMSSS
Use of phone lines to a school—Grant School, Cupertino	1965–67	IMSSS
Commercially available computer instruction system located in a school district—Brentwood School, East Palo Alto	1966–68	IMSSS
Comprehensive reading course with audio—Brentwood School, East Palo Alto	1966–68	IMSSS
Multiplexed telephone lines used for computer courseware delivery to a school	1967	IMSSS
Comprehensive college course taught by computer—Russian (Joe Van Campen)	1968	IMSSS
Home-based computerized instruction—Dial-A-Drill	1968	IMSSS
Company dedicated to computers in education—Computer Curriculum Corporation	1967	CCC
Commercialization of home instruction—Dial-A-Drill, New York City	1969	CCC
Large instructional network of schools—(The "Deaf Project")	1970	IMSSS

Continued next page

Accomplishment	Date	Location
Dedicated computer for comprehensive math instruction to multiple students—M8 system	1971	CCC
CAI delivered over satellite	1971	IMSSS
Programming instruction (AID) uses interface between content and the interpreter	1971	IMSSS
Stand-alone instructional system with multiple courses for up to 16 simultaneous users—A16	1971–73	CCC
University logic course delivered completely on-line for over a decade	1973–1992	IMSSS
"Interactive Radio Math" initially in Nicaragua	1974–1979	IMSSS
Advanced university mathematics course delivered completely online for several years—Axiomatic Set Theory	1975–79	IMSSS
Proof checker for axiomatic mathematics with a natural computer interface—EXCHECK	1975–79	IMSSS
Stand-alone instructional system with multiple courses for up to 96 students at a time—CCC-17	1977	CCC
Comprehensive courses delivered on a microcomputer—SONY SMC-70	1982–83	CCC
Speech synthesis system for cost-effective, intelligible, dynamically-generated speech	1976/1982	IMSSS and CCC
Comprehensive first-year calculus course for local school delivery	1986	IMSSS
Evaluation system that predicts individual performance over time supporting teacher interventions—IPS	1986	CCC
Advanced Placement Calculus (AP) AB	1988	IMSSS

Continued next page

Accomplishment	Date	Location
Sale of a computer courseware company to a major publisher—CCC sold to Simon and Schuster	1990	CCC
Comprehensive courses on the first cost-effective Macintosh (begun by Suppes)	1991	CCC
Comprehensive courses on the Windows 3.1 system (begun by Suppes)	1992	CCC
Advanced CD-based courses for gifted students in the home—Multiple EPGY courses.	1992	EPGY
Comprehensive elementary math course for gifted students delivered on CD with tutoring—K7	1996	EPGY
Comprehensive elementary math course for both gifted and mainstream students with and without tutoring—K7	2004	EPGY
Internet-delivered elementary math course—K7	2005	EPGY
Comprehensive math course operating on a cell phone—Mobile Math on the Palm Treo (with Edumetrics)	2005	EPGY
Online high school operated by a major university—Stanford OHS	2006	EPGY
Internet delivered language arts course with automated grammatical analysis system—LA&W	2009	EPGY
Comprehensive math course articulated to Common Core standards	2011	EPGY
University licensing of a large set of online courses to a private firm	2013	EPGY

8.2   Other Voices, Concerns, and Directions

Over the years, there have been many reactions to both Suppes's specific work and his overall vision. In this section, we consider some of these.

8.2.1   Oettinger's *Run Computer, Run*

In 1969, Anthony G. Oettinger wrote a book entitled *Run Computer, Run* [83]. The book deals with the general idea of innovation in education, with particular emphasis on computers.

Oettinger is a computer scientist and expert on computer information resources, and a professor emeritus at Harvard University.[3] While some people believed that he was a detractor of work on computers in education, this is not the case. He was, however, asking questions.

The 1960s was a time when exuberance about solving social, racial, and educational problems through government and technology hit its apex. Oettinger wrote in 1969, when doubts about efforts like computers in education began to emerge. Speaking about computerization generally, Oettinger noted:

> Troubles, as we shall see, arise from cost, amount, reliability, maintenance, complexity, comfort, standardization, integration, and content. ([83] p. 170)

He noted the following possible problems:

- *Limits of individualization:* "The real bottleneck [to the effective use of individualization] is our inability to foresee more than a very few of the most common possible learner responses." He does agree that algorithms for such things as spelling and syntax correction can improve this situation. ([83] p. 181)

- *Initial successes may not be sustainable:* Acknowledging that students were rising "to impressive levels of intensity and concentration" while working with CAI, Oettinger suggested that this may at least in part be due to the "Hawthorne effect" in which people perform better in experiments using new things than they will do in steady-state usage. ([83] p. 183)

- *School organization:* Noting the design of the lab at Brentwood, Oettinger suggests that integrating CAI into a school and its operation may be very difficult.

- *Size and level of staff required:* Oettinger observes that a large staff was available at Brentwood, of varied levels of background, experience, and salary. He suggests that this is not scalable and calls the environment created at Brentwood "sheltered." ([83] p. 185)

- *Economic arguments:* Oettinger presents a variety of economic arguments. For example, he quotes an official of RCA Instructional Systems estimating that "the equipment which RCA would release

---

[3]See Wikipedia "Anthony Oettinger" [170].

would be leased for about $50 per year per student"; at the time, the district involved was spending about $4 per year for all textbooks.[4]

Despite his concerns, Oettinger stated that he believed in the general concept. He says:

> More subtle qualities, however, make computers capable of profoundly affecting science and education by stretching human reason and intuition, much as telescopes or microscopes extend human vision. I suspect that the ultimate effects of this stretching will be as far-reaching as the effects of the invention of writing. ([83] p. 200)

As an example of the stretching of imagination, Oettinger details work being done at Harvard on developing interactive computerized simulations of mathematical concepts and processes ([83] pp. 200–214).

Computer simulations have, of course, become very common in educational materials, including some of Suppes's later work at CCC and EPGY.[5]

8.2.2 The People's Computer Company

Between 1966 and 1972, a sea-change had taken place in American life. Institutions were not trusted as they had been in the years shortly after the Second World War. Computers were seen as large, expensive systems owned and controlled by large corporations or government bureaucracies. The idea that computers would be used in education was, while still promising, now seen as frightening if not controlled by "the people." This was particularly true when the computers were providing seemingly mindless drill-and-practice instead of enhancing creativity. People needed to control their machines, not the opposite.

Just a short distance from Suppes's IMSSS labs at Stanford, the People's Computer Company opened its doors in Menlo Park. This was a group of hobbyists and visionaries who published newsletters, made computer time available, and promoted the BASIC language.[6]

The People's Computer Company's real accomplishments were not technical or traditionally educational, but rather the conception and promulgation of a philosophy. The group believed that computers could be good if people controlled them directly. They promoted computer

---

[4]The curriculum that RCA was using was developed by Patrick Suppes at IMSSS (see [19]). RCA did not succeed in this business.

[5]Suppes much admired the work of Alfred Bork of the University of California at Irvine, who developed courseware in physics with especially good simulations. See [29] for a 1999 interview with Bork, and also [13] for a book about personal computers in education.

[6]See Wikipedia [206] for the People's Computer Company and [63] for background about the role that "hackers" had in the computer revolution.

use, especially for use in education, and operated a storefront where people could come to use their PDP-8 computer for a small fee. Computers belonged to the people, they proclaimed, not the government or big business.[7]

One of the principal individuals in the hacker community and also the People's Computer Company was Bob Albrecht.[8]

In 1973, *Saturday Review* published an article entitled "Computer Confrontation" in which Suppes, Albrecht and a representative of Seymour Papert's General Turtle company are all included; see below for more about Seymour Papert. See [136] for the quotations below.

This "confrontation" was largely a miscommunication.

- Suppes called Albrecht a "romantic" and said "I think the real problem with romantics is that their intellectual level is so poor. You get things in education that you don't find in any other field. Nobody would seriously listen to someone who built better televisions just on the basis of watching television,"

- Albrecht comes from his own experience watching people use computers as mediated by his underlying philosophy. "Kids who continually interact with a computer in a situation where all the control is on the computer's side, where all they do is respond and the computer says you're right or you're wrong, are likely to become susceptible to computer control. Drill and practice programs where the computer is in full control are all right as part of the learning environment—if you teach kids how to control computers."

- The Papert representative says that Papert "believes that children learn by doing and by thinking about what they can do." See description below.

In retrospect, these three points of view are hardly irreconcilable. Suppes was interested in how people learn, how learning can be optimized and individualized in a cost-effective way. Albrecht may be interpreted as saying that we need more data about what people will expect out of computers before we can see all of the learning possibilities and people should be in control. Papert is going in a quite different direction of promoting discovery learning.

8.2.3 Seymour Papert and the LOGO Language

Seymour Papert was an MIT professor and one of the early proponents of computers in education, but in a very different way.[9] A student

---

[7]See [63] pp. 165-170 for more details.

[8]See Wikipedia "Bob Albrecht" [175].

[9]Papert passed away on July 31, 2016; see Wikipedia "Seymour Papert" [221].

of Jean Piaget, Papert advocated for student-directed learning with the computer as an aid to the student's creativity. Cynthia Solomon writes:

> He [Papert] sees most of present-day school mathematics as denatured and alienating and outside of a child's concerns. He sees the computer as a way to create new learning conditions and new things to learn. He envisions the computer as a 'mathland'. ([104] p. 103)

For this "mathland," Papert, together with Wallace Feurzeig, Daniel Bobrow, Richard Grant, and Cynthia Solomon, designed the LOGO language at Bolt Beranek and Newman in 1965; see [38]. The language was an implementation of LISP using a syntax somewhat like BASIC, the other language competing for educational uses in the 1960s.

The enduring image of the LOGO language is the "turtle," a real or simulated device that could move around a grid and draw lines. With suitable commands, many figures and images could be created.

Papert never seems to have advocated an actual curriculum for teaching with LOGO. He was more interested in mentoring and stimulating students to creativity.[10] Hal Abelson of MIT together with Andrea diSessa wrote a book about "turtle geometry" that Suppes praised for its mathematical sophistication. There was no shortage of things you could create with LOGO. See [1].

In some ways, Suppes and Papert were diametrically opposed, at least in the common mind. But Suppes always had the idea of picking up anything that worked and using it. For example, a course in Computer Literacy built at CCC in 1985 contained a section on turtle graphics with a simplified language with a curriculum of exercises.

Papert had a LOGO lab at MIT that was an interesting place to visit. Outfitted with the best equipment one could buy, new furniture, and staffed by MIT graduate students teaching the children of MIT professors with very favorable teacher-to-student ratios, the lab created some impressive results.

Suppes had three main concerns about the LOGO approach:

- *Scalability:* Suppes could see some of the benefits of this creative approach for certain students, but he felt that scaling to the general population of schools, teachers, and students would be very difficult. Papert's attitude was often not supportive of teachers in more typical classrooms, Suppes believed.

- *Objectives and standards:* Education generally assumes that teachers are teaching to certain objectives. Papert really didn't seem to have

---

[10] Two of Suppes's graduate students, Alex Cannara and Steve Weyer, tried LOGO teaching with some curriculum materials; see page 138.

any specifics about objectives, and in fact openly disdained them.

- *Evaluation:* Suppes believed that educational programs should be evaluated both to make improvements and to measure effectiveness. Papert's attitude was very different. As Solomon says,

> Much of Papert's thinking sees LOGO as something other than an instrument whose purpose is to help specific learning. ...Papert believes that changes in children's learning are demonstrable not through testing different pieces of curriculum but by looking at the whole child and the whole classroom. ([104] pp. 130–131)

Suppes felt that this simply takes the issue of evaluating whether or not LOGO and Papert's ideas "work in practice" into a realm where evaluation is not possible.

More extensive notes about Suppes's views on Piaget's work may be found in [126].

Solomon's Critique of Suppes

Solomon's thesis contained an intellectual critique of Suppes and his work in education. She said that Suppes's ideas are a part of a tradition founded by the work of Alfred North Whitehead and Bertrand Russell entitled *Principia Mathematica* in which mathematics is reduced to logic.[11] Solomon writes:

> We see in Suppes's curriculum the influence of the PM [*Principia Mathematica*] point of view. Suppes dissects mathematics into component skills. His underlying philosophy supports the same old methods of teaching, in which the teacher gives knowledge to the children in discrete components. ...Seymour Papert breaks radically with this reductionist view of reform in mathematics education. ...([104] p. 115)

Suppes's philosophical ideas about mathematics were very different from Russell's and also what Solomon describes. Suppes was not a logicist or a formalist, but rather believed in an empiricist foundation for mathematics. He often suggested that mathematics was created to support explanation and prediction in the sciences, with calculus being a prime example. Suppes was not a reductionist, although he often found reductions to be useful or illustrative.[12]

The structure, scope, and sequence of Suppes's curriculums were generally based on the long traditions in curriculum design and teaching and not on any *a priori* ideas. Suppes would have his developers look at standards from many states, textbooks from different publishers, and historical materials. While he tried to improve on what he found by making the connections more explicit, the resulting courses were

---

[11]See Wikipedia "Principia Mathematica" [210]

[12]See his book *Representation and Invariance* [133].

always developed in a highly *empiricist* style. These courses also were immediately recognizable to teachers, who would be able to integrate them into their practice.

As the years went by, Suppes's courses evolved to meet the updated expectations of teachers and schools for content and presentation style. One of the last projects he worked on in the math curriculum was helping Betsy Macken create a correlation between the EPGY K7 course and the new Common Core standards; this was in 2011–12.

Suppes's empiricism did not stop with standards. His courses were always being updated based on student usage data. From 2010 to 2012, Betsy Macken added many new tutorials to the K7 course to respond to issues students were having as demonstrated by the data. A few years earlier, Suppes had completely revamped the content of the "Math Races" for advanced students, after he was presented with student performance data showing that some of the content was too difficult.

It should also be noted that Suppes's work on the teaching of axiomatic mathematics was an explicit rejection of formalism in mathematical expression. He wanted proof checkers that could deal with informally stated proofs, and felt it important for students to understand the key points of a proof while not having to be explicit about every detail. See page 116.

8.2.4 "Personal Dynamic Media"

In 1975, Alan Kay and Adele Goldberg of Xerox PARC published an article entitled *Personal Dynamic Media* [57]. Here is how they describe a book-sized computer called the *Dynabook*:

> Imagine having your own self-contained knowledge manipulator in a portable package the size and shape of an ordinary notebook. Suppose it had enough power to outrace your senses of sight and hearing, enough capacity to store for later retrieval thousands of page-equivalents of reference materials, poems, letters, recipes, records, drawings, animations, musical scores, waveforms, dynamic simulations, and anything else you would like to remember and change. ([57] p. 394)

They summarized the potential educational benefits in this way:

> Second, the kids love it! The interactive nature of the dialogue, the fact that they are in control, the feeling that they are doing real things rather than playing with toys or working out "assigned" problems, the pictorial and auditory nature of their results, all contribute to a tremendous sense of accomplishment to their experience. Their attention spans are measured in hours rather than minutes. ([57] p. 394)

The Dynabook was never built as such. However, the authors "simulated" tasks it might do on a Xerox Alto system. A number of interactive applications were programmed as concept pieces for the Dynabook, including editing, drawing, animation, music, and simulations.

This article has been the model for smaller, more powerful, and more media-featured devices for over thirty years. Everything from PCs, notebooks, tablets, handhelds, and cell phones has been claimed to be inspired by the Dynabook.

The Dynabook itself did not envision the Internet; communications is a large part of today's devices that otherwise may be similar to the Dynabook. The credit for the concept of the Internet generally goes to Vannevar Bush's 1947 idea of the "Memex," a conceptual device for search and viewing hypertext.[13] On the other hand, the Dynabook was supposed to arrive with programming tools such as SmallTalk that students would use to create things like simulations and games. Today's Apple and Android devices are not meant to be directly programmable.

Kay and Goldberg were interested in education, and were deeply influenced by Seymour Papert and others at MIT and BBN. They distanced themselves from Suppes's ideas to a considerable degree, wanting to create enthusiasm and foster creativity rather than teach a specific curriculum or set of skills and concepts.

It should be noted that Kay, Goldberg, and Papert all knew each other and Suppes, and all got along well together. Following Pat's love of argument, they certainly could argue. Goldberg had worked at IMSSS in the 1970s and wrote her dissertation primarily with Pat; see page 102. She was one of Suppes's star collaborators. Seymour Papert and his associate Marvin Minsky knew Pat for many years and had a lot of very general ideas in common, including a belief that computer technology would change education *somehow*, even if they didn't know how.

Robert and Nancy Smith remember a dinner in 1973 at Suppes's house with Minsky and Papert. Papert had just been learning Chinese, and practiced by ordering over the phone (in Chinese!) at a restaurant favored by the Stanford computer hackers. Smith was dispatched to pick up the food and negotiate the exact dishes with the proprietor. It was all good, as they all agreed over Chinese food and wine, that government funding for computers in education should increase. Papert was expounding his ideas about hand-held devices, and Suppes was promoting the idea of computer networks. Both were right, it turns out.

8.3 Computers as Media Devices in Education

While it is universally recognized that Suppes was an effective pioneer and promoter of computers in education,[14] there is disagreement about

---

[13]See Wikipedia "Memex" [198].
[14]See for example [72].

the value of his specific ideas. The strongest disagreement is about the entire idea of directly teaching anything with the computer other than perhaps mentoring students as they try to create new things. Underlying this is, of course, some degree of dissatisfaction with systematic education including curricula, classrooms, lectures, assignments, and tests.

The vision of media as providing students with endlessly reconfigurable worlds to manipulate and explore is appealing. To what extent is this really feasible? Does it work, and how do we know it works?

8.3.1   Television: A Cautionary Tale

No previous electronic medium was more enthusiastically anticipated for its possible uses in education than television. Many of the inventors of television who worked in the 1920s and 1930s thought that they were creating an educational tool. The most important person in the early development of television was Philo T. Farnsworth, who was known to be critical of the uses being made of the product he helped invent. In 1996, Farnsworth's wife Elma commented to an interviewer about his reaction to seeing the landing on the moon on TV in 1969: "We were watching it, and, when Neil Armstrong landed on the moon, Phil turned to me and said, 'Pem, this has made it all worthwhile.' Before then, he wasn't too sure" ([59]).

Early broadcasts in the 1950s included programs with a high degree of educational content. By the 1960s, educators were predicting that exposure to television was making students far more advanced than any previous generation.

By the end of the decade, however, the opposite was clear: television was not helping students; if anything, programming was of lower educational quality than it had been; and parents should limit the amount of television that their children consumed. The television became known as the "boob-tube."[15]

In the 1970s, cable television was becoming popular, and many communities added systems. Channel space was now much larger, and television visionaries began talking about "narrow-casting." The idea was that channels would be aimed at small populations, and education would be part of the purpose. The Federal government changed the rules about franchising to require funding of so-called PEG channels ("public, education, and government") so that educational institutions would have an opportunity to deliver their programming.[16]

---

[15]There is now a large literature about the effects of television on children and learning. One example is [47]. Suffice it to say that this is not a simple issue.

[16]See Wikipedia "Public-access television" [214].

Over the decades, however, less has happened than one might have hoped. "Narrow-casting" is something of a reality, but channels that used to have some educational focus (The History Channel and Discovery Channel, for example) have moved towards the mainstream with their programming and reduced the educational content. The funding for and interest in PEG channels has greatly decreased, especially with new franchising rules. Viewers have hundreds of increasingly similar channels with little educational content.

The Internet is now the hope of those wishing to have educational content and media available. There is a lot of educational content for those who look for it, and one could earn many college degrees simply using the Internet's resources. But how common is it for our students to consume educational content?

There are no clear measures of this, but parents are now treating "time on the iPad" in a way similar to the way parents used to treat "time watching the tube." The publication *Variety* recently reported that a single provider, Netflix, was consuming 37% of the prime-time downstream bandwidth in the United States. Other web sites with high prime-time bandwidth included: YouTube 15.6%, general browsing 6%, and Facebook 2.7%. There is certainly some educational content on YouTube but no clear notion of how much is being used by students. See [108].

One extreme measure is to avoid any use of electronic media in education, even not allowing children any access. Todd Oppenheimer's 2003 book *The Flickering Mind* is one example ([84]). Oppenheimer is very critical of all technologies, even traditional textbooks. He ties technology to standardized tests, which he feels undermine creativity. His strongest praise is for direct interaction between teachers and students and shared activities.

Overall, there seems to be a growing consensus that online access, like television, is often not likely to result in any educational gains, and that some sort of direction needs to be applied to what students are doing. Simply making the media available doesn't help most students. But what does help?

8.3.2 Current Trends in the Use of Media in Education

What are some of the current trends in the uses of media in education, and how do Suppes's ideas connect with them?

In the recent report *Using Media to Support At-Risk Students' Learning* by Linda Darling-Hammond, Molly B. Zielezinski, and Shelley Goldman at the Stanford Center for Opportunity Policy in Education ([28]), the recommendations would not have met with Suppes's complete endorsement, although the actual difference between Suppes's ideas and the ideas of the authors is less than one might think. There is plenty of common ground.

Suppes would have agreed with the general call for equity in education and its importance to the nation's future. He always supported measures such as enhanced bandwidth and availability of computers for at-risk students.

The report emphasizes student creativity and involvement in authentic experiences rather than drill and practice, which the authors consider ineffective:

> ...early versions of computer-based instruction (CBI) were structured much like electronic workbooks, moving students through a transmission curriculum in a fairly passive manner. Often programs have been geared toward improving student performance on minimum-competency tests, like high school graduation exams, that cover similar material in a similar format.

> Results from these efforts have been largely disappointing. In some cases, students demonstrated improved outcomes on tests of similar information tested in a similar format; in most, they performed about the same as students taught by teachers during the same time period. One recent study, for example, used rigorous methods of random assignment to evaluate the impact of a variety of math and reading software products across 132 schools in 33 school districts, with a sample of more than 9,400 students, and found no significant difference on student test scores in classrooms using the software as compared to classrooms not using the software. ([28] p. 6)

The authors recommend interactive instruction but don't have a high-level definition of what that means:

> ...unlike "computerized workbooks" that march students through material they learn through rote or algorithm, [such] interactive CBI systems can diagnose students' levels of understanding and customize the material they engage with, offer a more interactive set of instructional activities, and provide feedback to students, as well as more detailed information about student progress. Programs like these, with teachers supplementing instruction to explain concepts and coordinate student discussion, have been found in several studies to be successful ... ([28] p. 7)

Suppes's courses often contained drill material, but he was certainly trying to customize the material for individual students and provide detailed feedback to students as well as actionable reports to teachers.

The authors remark further:

One of the benefits of well-designed interactive programs is that they can allow students to see and explore concepts from different angles using a variety of representations. For example, one study of at-risk high school students in Texas found that they learned significantly more using an interactive instructional environment to study quadratic functions than those in a control group who studied the same concepts via traditional lecture ... ([28] p. 7)

Suppes agreed with the value of simulations and built such environments into many of the courses developed by his teams. By today's standards and with today's tools, Suppes's earlier courses were primitive, but they were quite innovative for their time.

There are some differences between the approach advocated by Darling Hammond et al., as follows:

- Suppes always believed that he found elements of drill and practice in any curriculum outlines or objectives. He believed that computers could do that well because of the immediate feedback, optimization, and tutorial intervention. He never endorsed mindless drill; he wanted drill that was focused, individualized, and efficient. He did feel that some contemporary educators did not appreciate the need for some drill.

- Darling-Hammond and her team refer to stimulating creativity and interaction between students and their media. Suppes didn't tend to focus on those aspects in his work, although they are present. The recent Language Arts and Writing course from EPGY could evaluate and comment on students' writing, including both sentences and paragraphs. In his work about axiomatic mathematics, he was very concerned with allowing students to prove theorems their way and wanted the computer to have dialogues with the students about the theorems they were proving.

- Suppes always created lengthy and comprehensive courses. The basic skills courses would follow basal textbooks in having up to eight years of content in a single course.

- Suppes's use of the term "individualization" differs from that of the authors. Operationally, Suppes's courses largely had mastery criteria and used them to determine how much or how little content the student needed to see. Darling-Hammond is advocating for something more dramatic and intelligent, but her reference points for old-style computer-based instruction do not benefit from Suppes-style individualization.

- Suppes always tried to encourage teachers to use progress reports about individual students, but did not assume that teachers would have the time to do so in his designs. He believed in what is now called "blended learning" but felt it was hard to implement in practice.
- Darling-Hammond emphasizes students building their own teaching tools to illustrate things that they are learning. Suppes would be fine with this but would not expect to get materials that could be used very broadly with this approach. Organizing such an approach also places a heavy burden on the teachers and other staff.

8.4 Underlying Ideas about the Research and Development Process

Suppes had given a lot of thought to the issues that he believed were of underlying importance to future research in computers in education.

8.4.1 University Research and Commercial Deployment

Stanford University is famous for having bridged some of the gaps between academic research and commercial deployment, and has many success stories involving what is now called "Silicon Valley." Suppes was a part of this but nevertheless had some doubts about how it works.

The classical model is that research at a university reaches a certain point at which it can be commercialized. Then, either by placing the results in the public domain or licensing them, private firms take over the further development and start marketing the new product or service. Suppes pointed out the ways in which this could have problems:

- University research might bring an idea to the point of being very interesting but still not really ready for the rigors of the marketplace. Today, in contrast to Suppes's years at IMSSS, research funds may be only for a small number of years, and the faculty member may end up publishing the results without really having enough time to prepare for commercialization.
- Finding a commercial partner may be difficult. Suppes tried partnerships with IBM and RCA, and found that they were not prepared for a long-haul effort, even though they clearly had the resources. He had really wanted a publisher, but it took nearly thirty years of conversations to get Simon and Schuster to buy into the idea.
- Building your own company can be treacherous. Suppes and his partners did not take any outside investment for CCC. This meant many years of small contracts, loaning the company money, fighting to make the payroll. Taking startup investment can be even more diffi-

cult: investors are looking for impressive results, not slow, tortuous growth. Today, most new "edtech" startups obtain investor funding. Investors expect returns quickly. Suppes always said that if he had founded CCC with investor capital, the company would have been shut down on any number of occasions as investors grew impatient.

- Once you are started, you need to keep doing research. Paying for "basic research" inside of a small startup is difficult. Companies like AT&T and IBM were successful with research, and today Google, Microsoft, and Tesla are doing an impressive job. But Xerox failed to capitalize on its impressive research in the 1970s, and RCA eventually shut down their formerly impressive research facilities.

The approach that he chose to take was to keep one foot in each camp by continuing new research at Stanford while commercializing at CCC. Later EPGY was an attempt to do both research and commercialization at Stanford. However, this effort was constrained by university polices when university officials did not want more deployments of the EPGY courses in schools. EPGY was licensed to a private firm with the hope of doing evaluations with that firm. Suppes was very disappointed with this decision from Stanford but worked to make it a successful transition.

8.4.2 Evaluation

Suppes felt that curricula and software needed to be evaluated and tested over a period of time and in a variety of circumstances.

- He believed that educational interventions need to be tested in many kinds of environments, not just a few. Local ecology is very important.
- Evaluations should also occur after a period of familiarization by the teachers and staff. Too many commercial companies try to schedule product evaluations during the first year of deployment at a customer's site.
- Suppes felt that evaluations should have both formative and efficacy aspects and often should do both at the same time. He pioneered the idea of collecting student performance data and bringing it back to the lab for evaluation, long before the Internet made this easy.

8.5 Suppes's Important Ideas about Courseware Development and Implementation

8.5.1 Comprehensive Courses

Suppes generally wanted courses to follow the current practices of schools and teachers and to be comprehensive courses, even though they were mostly used as supplementary materials. A semester was generally the shortest length, and elementary courses were sometimes several years long.

He thought that it was important to have continuity in the delivery to students in order to see long-term effects in the same courses.

Suppes noted that many edtech companies today do not seem to have a commitment to comprehensive courses. Midian Kurland, a former CCC staff member and most recently CTO of a large software publisher, commented that many companies don't have courses, they have "features."[17]

8.5.2 Student Choice

Allowing students individual choices was a passion. For example, in courses that used audio at IMSSS in the 1970s, he gave students the choice in whether or not to have audio together with the course. See page 126 for details.

Suppes knew that student choice could be carried much further than he had taken it but he was also concerned about the cost of producing courses with more features of this kind.

8.5.3 Teacher Choice

This was also very important to Suppes as teachers are critical to learning and need to be able to use the courseware comfortably in order to help their students succeed. His early models of the management system including many settable parameters and a wide variety of reports for teachers which were well ahead of their time. New report types were added at CCC to the point that eventually a report-writing language was developed so that CCC consultants and the teachers they supported could have "101 reports."[18]

8.5.4 Support

Suppes found that CAI products needed to be supported. This includes support for the delivery hardware, for the teacher and other staff members, and the individual student. While the hardware and software changed dramatically, a common theme from the Grant School program in the 1960s to using EPGY courses by gifted students was the need for support.

---

[17]Private communication.

[18]This was a favorite of Robert and Nancy Smith who offered a contest at CCC to users to see who could suggest the most useful reports; the result was productized with both built-in reports and a report authoring language, and was used for many years. This happened before the use of modern relational databases in the product.

8.5.5 The Internet

The Internet has certainly become the distribution platform for many kinds of information, including education. However, Suppes was not completely satisfied.

He remembered that in the late 1990s, for the first time, he felt that he had a hardware/software platform that was adequate to his research interests and was also cost-effective: PCs with local-area networks and a connection to a distant server for data collection.[19]

PCs were inexpensive, becoming more powerful, and there were excellent "desktop" development systems like C++. There were many "engines" that one could incorporate on the PC, such as the symbolic-algebra program Maple.

While the Internet seemed to make deployment simpler, in some ways it did not. Programming the client side was difficult and awkward. He tried both client-side Java and Flash, both of which had their problems and are fading from use. Browser-side Javascript with frameworks like JQuery seems to be the only solution as of today.

Suppes felt that the time that needed to be spent on the conversion to the Internet had cost him some forward momentum in working on his current agenda of tutorial and dialogue issues.[20]

Of course, he knew these problems would be resolved eventually, making the Internet more workable than previous platforms.

8.5.6 Economics and New Platforms

Suppes believed that economics would determine the use of computers in education. Now, with a delivery system that was unthinkable only a few years ago, Suppes was puzzled by what would get students more interested in using devices like cell phones and tablets for learning (without being told to do so). He recognized that the capabilities of a cell phone (including speech recognition such as Siri on the iPhone) represented an amazing platform if students could be motivated.

8.5.7 Artificial Intelligence

Suppes had many near-encounters with artificial intelligence research. His early claim that students would "in a few years" have a computerized tutor comparable to Aristotle clearly would require significant "AI."

---

[19]This was the same idea as IPS use of UNIX dialups in the 1980s but actually was working much more smoothly now.

[20]He had wanted to put writing into the K7 math course, asking the students to explain what they had learned. He was also experimenting with speech recognition, and found a few tools to be very promising.

He had some issues with the way AI was promoted during the '60s and '70s, believing that it was too faddish and promised too much. AI found application in several projects at IMSSS during the 1970s, as Suppes noted in [131].

Many times, Suppes would see a certain AI system, get excited about it, and then realize that the techniques involved would be much too expensive to implement in a *scalable* manner suitable for inclusion in a large course.

8.5.8 Blended Learning

Suppes is known for building CAI systems that ran on "automatic pilot." To many teachers, this was a good thing: students could be taken to the lab for 20 minutes of CAI three times a week, with the assurance that something reasonable was happening. To other teachers and educational reformers, the CAI experience was too disconnected from the classroom and the teacher.

Part of this was quite deliberate on Suppes's part: he wanted courses that were responsive to the individual needs and choices of each student in a reasonable way. But he also saw the need for better connection to the teacher.

From the outset at Grant School, Suppes tried a variety of reports. Those reports were rarely if ever accessed (see page 21). Later at CCC, he tried "progress reports" and various "alerts" that would try to involve the teacher.

IPS (see page 175) was a major effort to create "blended learning"[21] that would allow teachers to monitor the progress of individual students and intervene to their advantage. As noted beginning on page 184, there were many logistical problems in making IPS work effectively. Many of them could be solved using technological improvements, including using the Internet to provide more automated reporting more quickly. However, the limitation of the time, training, and willingness of the teachers to involve themselves was very real. CCC countered this by providing staff support to IPS.

At EPGY, however, he did see a pattern of commercial success with the tutors that supported the courses. Many of the first EPGY courses were advanced mathematics and physics, and the availability of the tutors made a huge difference, resulting in what could be called an early successful application of the later concept of "blended learning." This effect was carried over into courses such as the K7 math course. It is likely that the combination of tutors supplied by Stanford University,

---

[21]The term is newer than IPS.

the high prices charged, and the up-scale EPGY student population have all helped to make this a success.

8.6 The Future

As *Life* magazine said of Suppes in 1967,

> Pat Suppes, on the other hand, is continually trying to push his machines into the outer limits of research and beyond. "You know, with technology you always have a gleam in your eye about what you're going to do next," he says. ([14] p. 81)

So what did he think the future would bring?

8.6.1 Are Schools Going Out of Style?

Suppes was beginning to think that the survival of schools in general and universities in particular was in peril. Most people who express this concern focus on escalating costs combined with technical innovations such as online courseware.

Suppes added to that his alarm over the growth of bureaucracy in education. He often noted the ease with which his own work was done in the 1960s compared to the growing complexity of university and government rules.

Interviewed by Kevin Carey for his book *The End of College* [23] about the changes coming, here is what Suppes had to say:

> "It's going to be painful," he said, when that day finally, inevitably comes. "The consequences of really teaching everything you can do well with computers were terrifying for a lot of us once we thought about it carefully." For college education, he said, "we probably should expect a revolution." ([23] p. 159)

Suppes had concerns about the implications of the breakdown of schools. He felt that universities serve an important role in research, one that he had himself benefited from, and he felt that advanced courses, seminars, and the like were very valuable. He understood that universities and their academic units depended heavily on the dollars they received from running introductory undergraduate courses and "service" courses. These courses provided the ability to hire faculty members who would largely focus on research and the training of graduate students.

He himself had contributed to using computers to "displace" faculty members at Stanford with his CAI course in logic, which ran for almost twenty years with Suppes as the instructor of record.

When Suppes "retired" in 1992, the new logic instructor assigned to the course did not want to use a computer component. Similarly, Richard Schupbach also commented that the very successful computerized Russian course of 1968 was not continued by other faculty members; he speculated that this was because of faculty concerns about jobs (see page 134).

With regard to Suppes's computerized logic course, it should be noted that there were some very good teaching assistants who were available to help the students; they kept hours at times convenient for students in the labs, and knew the curriculum thoroughly.[22]

Moreover, many of the TAs and course developers felt that the best course would be one that combined some lectures with the on-line course. They believed that the conceptual and philosophical issues within logic would benefit from the teachers, while the technical details benefited from the computerized instruction. This is, of course, "blended learning." The question of the future of educational institutions continues to be debated, although by 2016, it is beginning to appear that media technology will coexist with traditional schools.

8.6.2 MOOCs

Massive open online courses ("MOOCs") have attracted considerable media attention in the past several years. MOOCs are offered online by Internet companies or universities (or some combined effort) generally free of charge (at the lowest tier).

A Brief History of MOOCs

At first, MOOCs attracted a large following, and were seen as a threat to established schools. Soon, it was discovered that only a few people who signed up for a course even took a lesson, and many fewer still finished a course. While a target area for MOOCs was people under-served by the educational establishment, it turned out that about 70% of the participants already had one or more college degrees. Many such discoveries led to considerable reassessment.[23]

Suppes's Views of MOOCs and their Creators

Suppes was very happy to see this development, claiming it vindicated his long-held positions about the future, but was also very annoyed. For one thing, the people building the MOOCs had followed very little of the history of computers in education or learning theory in general.[24]

More concretely, Suppes also criticized the simplicity of the course delivery tools used by the MOOC authors. MOOCs tend to rely heavily

---

[22]Very similar to the use of tutors at EPGY.

[23]There is too much to say about MOOCs to include here. Just google "MOOC" and see what you find. By the time this is published, it will have changed.

[24]See [23] p. 158. Carey seems to present a somewhat more annoyed point of view in his book than Suppes actually had, on balance.

on video lectures and have few significant interactions with students, he felt. He believed that authors were simply creating courses as quickly as they could with little regard for quality and no concern for evaluation of the courses or techniques used to build them. He noted the absence of finesse and the lack of considering what has been learned in the last half century.

Suppes's long-time collaborator Richard C. Atkinson expressed concern about the lack of individualization of the instructional process. He said, "My argument through all of this would be, what's key to the future is being able to individualize the instructional process—and that, to do well, requires a sophisticated psychological theory" (quoted in [96]).

Suppes also cited his belief that students need to have "some skin in the game" in order to be willing to persevere. Psychologist Robert A. Bjork is quoted making this point in more depth:

> "There's an important dimension of MOOCs that's relevant here," Bjork said. "They're free, but they also have the property that you can just quit." He worries that if MOOCs incorporate desirable difficulties—such as frequent testing, spacing or alternating instruction on separate topics, and varying the conditions of learning rather than keeping them constant and predictable— many students will quit in frustration when they perform poorly on early assessments, perhaps even blaming instructors for the apparent inadequacy of the course design. Instructors who teach according to best scientific practices may be punished on teaching evaluations by students who drop out early in the courses, before the benefits of introducing desirable difficulties become apparent. (quoted in [96])

Former Dean of Education at Stanford Richard Shavelson (see [98]) thinks that MOOCs may find a "niche" for people in developing countries. He said this would be analogous to the continuing success of interactive radio math that Suppes and his team developed in the 1970s.[25]

In any case, MOOCs are certainly with us for the duration. The rational assessment as of 2016 appears to be that both the hype and the fear about MOOCs have reduced considerably, but what the MOOCs have done is to show us the kind of scale that is possible in online courseware delivery.[26]

---

[25]Personal communication.

[26]The last two years since Suppes last spoke have brought changes to the MOOC catalogs. Many high-quality, university-level offerings are now available from prestigious universities with carefully designed curriculums, quizzes, and peer review of assignments, but still not the interactive features as described here. They are their own product with their own merits.

New Yorker Article on IMSSS and MOOCs!

An article in the *New Yorker* in 2014 entitled "Will MOOCs be Flukes?" discussed problems with MOOCs where the author considered the problems with these courses. Looking into history, she said:

> So what's the solution? How can MOOCs live up to their promise? One possibility is to go back in order to go forward. The MOOC movement started off in a tech whirlwind; the people who pushed it forward were so caught up in its technological possibilities that they scarcely considered decades of research into educational psychology. They might, for instance, have looked at the work of the researchers Patrick Suppes and Richard Atkinson, who in 1962 were charged with designing a course that would use the latest computer technology to teach mathematics and reading to children in kindergarten through third grade. Suppes, a Stanford psychologist and philosopher who had been trained in mathematics, decided to use something called 'control theory' as the basis for his approach. Students in his computer-based class wouldn't all receive the same instruction. Instead, their materials and the order in which those materials were presented would shift according to their past performance and other learning metrics—much like the G.R.E.'s adjusted sections, which become harder or easier depending on how you're doing. Some students might get stopped every fifteen minutes for a reassessment and summary of materials; others might go for an hour before they reach a stopping point. The approach combined leveling (in which the same material is presented at different learning and reading levels, depending on the student) with dynamic learning (which involves playing around with the manner and order in which information is presented, so that students don't get bored or frustrated).

> The Suppes-Atkinson courses proved so successful that they were soon expanded to include multiple subjects for many age levels. A company called the Computer Curriculum Corporation (which is now a part of Pearson) started distributing them globally. ([61])

8.6.3   Instruction for the Gifted

Over the years, Suppes became more concerned about education for the gifted; this was the motivation for starting EPGY at Stanford in the early 1990s. Former Stanford Dean of Education Richard Shavelson (see [98]) noted that some people had "outgrown" traditional CAI, but Suppes showed how effective it could be for gifted students by providing sophisticated courses and encouraging the students to go as fast as they could go, learning a lot of content very quickly.

When Stanford licensed the EPGY courseware to Redbird Advanced Learning, Redbird formed a subsidiary, GiftedandTalented.com, that continues the gifted program with some of the same developers and tutors still working at Redbird.

Shavelson said that he himself believes that "there is no one learning theory," and also notes that what works today in a certain setting may not work in the future in similar settings. For example, gifted students may no longer find Suppes's comprehensive online courses challenging or exciting and opt for some other choice.

8.6.4 The Role of Video

A surprising recent speculation that Suppes made in 2014 was that the future of education would make great use of "interactive video." He felt that video was one of the areas that should be most explored for storing and transmitting knowledge. "No one wants to read anymore!" he exclaimed.[27]

One explanation for this is Suppes's belief that when there is a confluence of interest in something with many people and groups working on it, there would be some good results. It should be emphasized that he expects something quite different than we have seen before.

8.7 Products Developed by Suppes Still in Use

The courses and management system developed by Computer Curriculum Corporation are still sold by Pearson under the name Success-Maker. Many modifications have been made since 1990 when Suppes sold CCC, and less-used courses dropped from distribution, but the main math and language arts courses are still identifiable.[28]

The EPGY courses were licensed to Redbird Advanced Learning by Stanford University in 2013. As of 2016, Redbird has replaced the math course with a derived work that includes interactive simulations and environments for problem-solving. The other courses, including the advanced courses with tutorial support, have been ported to new delivery environments.[29] In 2016, Redbird was sold to McGraw-Hill Education.

One currently used course is a methodological descendant of the work done at Stanford during the 1970s in the sense that it follows the approach Suppes recommended for university-level online courses. This is the *Logic and Proofs* course at Carnegie-Mellon University, built by Wilfried Sieg, a professor in the Department of Philosophy. Sieg describes his course as an "introduction to modern symbolic logic—with all of the necessary syntactic and semantic details, not to mention a

[27]Private communication.
[28]See http://www.pearsonschool.com/successmaker.
[29]See https://redbirdlearning.com/.

quite different logical calculus [than Suppes's VALID logic course]. I do think, however, that it approximates Pat's vision for such a course."[30]

Sieg was a graduate student at Stanford and a teaching assistant for the *Logic* course developed at IMSSS in the 1970s. He worked on an experiment to use the EXCHECK system to teach a course on Gödel's incompleteness theorems.[31] As his page on the CMU website says, "Sieg carries on Suppes's legacy as the Patrick Suppes Professor of Philosophy" and is a part of the university's online initiative ([111]).

Sieg recalls that CMU was using the VALID course developed at Stanford as a part of the transportability project. In about 2002, Sieg decided that he could create a new and more modern course with Internet delivery. He says that a "rough" version of the course was deployed in 2003, but it was not considered acceptable. The first year of actual use was 2004, with some lectures given by Sieg, but eventually the course was complete and no classroom was needed. There were teaching assistants. Support was obtained from the NSF as well as other foundations. See [65] for details.

The proof checker was designed to provide hints and dialogue to the student using the student's own evolving proof. It follows the developments of Goldberg's thesis (see page 102) and also the EXCHECK program (see page 105).

The model for the development of Sieg's course matches almost exactly the model Suppes used in his research at Stanford during the 1970s, most importantly in that the course was a comprehensive course, was designed to be available to students at other locations, and had a significant dialogue component. Sieg kept in close contact with Suppes and met with him whenever possible.

Between 2003 and 2011, 3,908 students took the *Logic and Proofs* course; for some years this was mainly at CMU.

Sieg observed with amusement that Kevin Carey, in his 2015 book *The End of College*, had questioned how much use his course would get.

> Sieg assumed that other universities would adopt his course en masse. ...He was wrong. ...Most of higher education proceeded as if the course simply didn't exist. ([23] p. 112)

However, in the last year or so, things have changed. New contracts with the University of Washington and the University of Maryland, as well as other schools, have brought many more students. In 2015–2016, 300 CMU students took the course, and 1,000 non-CMU students. Sieg

---

[30]Private communication.
[31]See page 116.

is in hopes that this growth will continue and make the course no longer dependent on foundation support.

Incidentally, some other schools are paying $80/student for being able to take the course, and the completion rate is 98%. This confirms the views of Suppes and others that MOOCs need to charge and give credit in order to have students take them seriously.

Suppes had kept in very close contact with Sieg throughout the years. Unfortunately, he could not have known of the recent developments with the student population of *Logic and Proofs*.

8.8 Suppes's Influence Today On Research into Computers in Education

Suppes is one of the most important of the contributors to the use of computers in education. You can see Suppes's influence everywhere in online learning systems, and adaptive survey and testing tools. Shavelson notes, for example, that Khan Academy looks a lot like Suppes's work.[32]

So what is the influence of Suppes and his work to researchers in the educational use of computers and media today? Shavelson says: very little. His name is seldom invoked; he is an important part of history but not a part of the current conversation in most academic settings, including the Stanford Graduate School of Education.

Here is a list of some of his top priorities that could/should be considered by future developers, whether or not they adhere to his specific ideas.

- *Evaluation:* Edtech products and ideas should be tested to evaluate their effectiveness, in different environments and at different times. The results of the evaluations should be considered in the next development cycle. In 1990 Suppes wrote:

    My prediction of 'important consequences for all students in the immediate future' was certainly too sanguine. It is not only a matter of not using data to revise and improve ordinary texts and workbooks. It is even a problem of extensive use of data to improve computer-assisted instruction. The problems of having good data feedback and good analytical and statistical methods for using the data for improvement have not really been satisfactorily solved, and we are in terms of global results, not too much better off than we were 20 years ago. All the same. I am still hopeful. ([130] p. 251)

---

[32]Khan Academy is a foundation that provides multiple courses online providing a "free, world-class education for anyone, anywhere." See Wikipedia "Khan Academy" [191]. The courses have gained a lot of use and interest because of the low cost of usage.

- *Comprehensive Courses:* Suppes believed that courses that covered a scope and sequence fully would get the most long-term use and appropriate modification.
- *Individualization:* Students should receive the instruction and help that they most need as individuals.
- *Appropriate Drill and Practice:* Drill and practice are important and should be efficiently and engagingly delivered. He often pointed out that athletes, musicians, dancers, and computer programmers (among others) need to practice skills in order to improve and maintain them.
- *Tutorial and Dialogue:* The educational computer system should diagnose difficulties that the student is having, engage them in conversations, and answer questions.
- *Needed Background Research:* Continued research in learning theory, brain science,[33] and artificial intelligence are all needed.
- *Cost-effectiveness:* CAI products must be demonstrated to be worth their cost and effort of implementation.

8.9   Whence Cometh Aristotle?

In 1966, Suppes wrote that students would have a personal tutor like Aristotle within a few years. This prediction was often quoted and modified along the way. In 1979, Dean Jamison said that it might take until the turn of the century, which is now 16 years past us.

Suppes recently declined to use any reference to Aristotle, but he did say that he felt it would take more than a hundred years to resolve the issues that he had been working on in the use of computers in education.

Sometimes, even when you live to 92 and work very hard, there are jobs you cannot finish yourself, but have to entrust to others.

---

[33] In the last decade of his life, Suppes had a large team of researchers working on brain science, with many publications. He was trying to find connections between observed brain activity and cognitive processes to form better models of learning.

Online Resources

In constructing the references for this book, the authors have tried to use online references as much as possible. This includes articles at the Patrick Suppes legacy library, which will contain more materials in the future.

References to related topics (e.g., the history of the PDP-1 computer) point to articles at Wikipedia. The authors checked these articles for general accuracy and to make sure that they contained the information that was relevant to the text.

At the present time, these URLs access the indicated materials. It is possible that some of these may move in the future.

- Patrick Suppes's complete archive:
  http://suppes-corpus.stanford.edu/.
- All IMSSS technical reports:
  http://suppes-corpus.stanford.edu/imsss.html.
- All articles published by Patrick Suppes concerning computers in education:
  http://suppes-corpus.stanford.edu/browse.html?c=comped.
- Articles written by Richard C. Atkinson about computers in education during his career at Stanford:
  http://rca.ucsd.edu/selected-stanford.asp.
- Selected articles by Richard C. Atkinson about computers in education:
  http://rca.ucsd.edu/selected-CAI.asp.

References

[1] Abelson, Harold and Andrea diSessa, 1981. *Turtle Geometry: The Computer as a Medium for Exploring Mathematics.* Cambridge, MA: MIT Press. [cited on page 281]

[2] Allen, John, 1977. A modular audio response system for computer output. In *1977 IEEE International Conference on Acoustics, Speech, and Signal Processing*, pp. 507–582. doi:10.1109/ICASSP.1977.1170218. [cited on page 126]

[3] Atkinson, Richard C., 1967. Instruction in initial reading under computer control: the Stanford project. Psychology and Education Series 113, IMSSS. URL http://suppes-corpus.stanford.edu/techreports/IMSSS_113.pdf. [cited on page 120]

[4] Atkinson, Richard C., 1968. The computer as a tutor. *Psychology Today.* January, (Republished in *Readings in Psychology Today*, Del Mar, CA: CRM Books, 1969 (1st ed.), 1972 (2nd ed.), 1974 (3rd ed.); *Readings in Developmental Psychology Today*, Del Mar, CA: CRM Books, 1970; *Readings in Educational Psychology Today*, Del Mar, CA: CRM Books, 1970.). [cited on page 50]

[5] Atkinson, Richard C., 1968. A reply to Professor Spache's article, 'A reaction to computer-assisted instruction in initial reading: The Stanford Project'. *Reading Research Quarterly*, 3(3): 418–420. doi: 10.2307/747012. URL http://www.jstor.org/stable/747012. [cited on page 50]

[6] Atkinson, Richard C., J. D. Fletcher, E. J. Lindsay, J. O. Campbell, and A. Barr, 1973. Computer-assisted instruction in initial reading. *Educational Technology*, 13(9): 27–37. [cited on page 120]

[7] Atkinson, Richard C. and Duncan N. Hansen, 1966. Computer-assisted instruction in initial reading: The Stanford project. Psychology and Education Series 93, IMSSS. URL http://suppes-corpus.stanford.edu/techreports/IMSSS_93.pdf. [cited on page 50]

[8] Atkinson, Richard C. and H. A. Wilson, 1968. Computer-assisted instruction. *Science*, 162(3849): 73–77. doi:10.1126/science.162.3849.73.

305

URL http://science.sciencemag.org/content/162/3849/. [cited on page 50]

[9] Bailey, Gerald D. (ed.), 1993. *Computer-Based Integrated Learning Systems*. Englewood Cliffs, NJ: Educational Technology Publications. [cited on page 199]

[10] Barr, Avron and Marian H. Beard, 1976. An instructional interpreter for BASIC. Psychology and Education Series 270, IMSSS. URL http://suppes-corpus.stanford.edu/techreports/IMSSS_270.pdf. [cited on page 137]

[11] Becker, Henry Jay, 1992. Computer-based integrated learning systems in the elementary and middle grades: A critical review and synthesis of evaluation reports. *Journal of Educational Computing Research*, 8(1): 1–41. doi:10.2190/23BC-ME1W-V37U-5TMJ. URL http://jec.sagepub.com/content/8/1/1.abstract. [cited on page 186]

[12] Beech, R. P., S. D. McClelland, G.R. Horowitz, and G. Forlano, 1970. Final report: An evaluation of the Dial-A-Drill program. Technical report, New York: State Education Department. [cited on page 242]

[13] Bork, Alfred, 1985. *Personal Computers for Education*. New York: Harper and Row Publishers. [cited on page 279]

[14] Bowen, Ezra, January 1967. The computer as a tutor. *Life*, 62(4): 68–81. URL https://books.google.com/books?id=aVYEAAAAMBAJ. [cited on pages 50 and 294]

[15] Brown, John Seely and Richard R. Burton, 1975. Multiple representations of knowledge for tutorial reasoning. In Daniel G. Bobrow and Allan Collins (eds.), *Representation and Understanding: Studies in Cognitive Science*. Academic Press. doi:10.1016/B978-0-12-108550-6.50016-1. [cited on page 100]

[16] Brown, John Seely and Richard R. Burton, 1978. Diagnostic models for procedural bugs in basic mathematical skills. *Cognitive Science*, 2(2): 155–192. doi:10.1207/s15516709cog0202_4. [cited on page 28]

[17] Brown, John Seely, Richard R. Burton, and Alan G. Bell, 1975. SOPHIE: A step toward creating a reactive learning environment. *International Journal of Man-Machine Studies*, 7(5): 675–696. doi:10.1016/S0020-7373(75)80026-5. [cited on page 100]

[18] Buck, George and Steve Hunka, 1995. Development of the IBM 1500 computer-assisted instruction system. *IEEE Annals of the History of Computing*, 17(1): 19–31. doi:10.1109/85.366508. URL https://uofa.ualberta.ca/-/media/digitallearning/ibm-1500.pdf. [cited on pages 37, 38, and 96]

[19] Bush, W. R., 1970. A review of the RCA experience in educational computing. *International Journal of Man-Machine Studies*, 2(2): 169–187. doi:10.1016/S0020-7373(70)80027-X. [cited on pages 76 and 279]

[20] Cannara, A.B., 1976. Experiments in teaching children computer programming. Psychology and Education Series 271, IMSSS. URL http:

//suppes-corpus.stanford.edu/techreports/IMSSS_271.pdf. [cited on page 138]

[21] Carbonell, J.R., 1970. AI in CAI: An artificial intelligence approach to computer-assisted instruction. *IEEE Transactions on Man-Machine Systems*, 11(4): 190–202. doi:10.1109/TMMS.1970.299942. [cited on page 99]

[22] Carbonell, J.R. and A.M. Collins, 1973. Natural semantics in artificial intelligence. In *Third International Joint Conference on Artificial Intelligence*, pp. 344–351. [cited on page 99]

[23] Carey, Kevin, 2015. *The End of College: Creating the Future of Learning and the University of Everywhere*. New York: Riverhead Books. [cited on pages 294, 295, and 299]

[24] Carroll, John B., 1963. A model of school learning. *Teachers College Record*, 64(8): 723–733. [cited on page 186]

[25] Christian Science Monitor, 1983. CCC-17 call home; an end to hooky, cooperative education. *Christian Science Monitor*. URL http://www.csmonitor.com/1983/0705/070505.html. July 5. [cited on page 164]

[26] Colossus: The Forbin Project. URL http://www.imdb.com/title/tt0064177/. [cited on page 125]

[27] Coulson, John E., 1962. Programmed learning and computer-based instruction. In *Proceedings of the Conference on Application of Digital Computers to Automated Instruction*. John Wiley and Sons. [cited on pages 5 and 12]

[28] Darling-Hammond, Linda, Molly B. Zielezinski, and Shelley Goldman, 2014. Using technology to support at-risk students' learning. Technical report, Alliance for Excellent Education / Stanford Center for Opportunity Policy in Education. URL https://edpolicy.stanford.edu/sites/default/files/publications/using-technology-support-risk-students%E2%80%99-learning.pdf. [Online; accessed 20-August-2016]. [cited on pages 218, 286, 287, and 288]

[29] Educause, 1999. The future of learning: An interview with Alfred Bork. *Educom Review*, 34(4). URL https://net.educause.edu/ir/library/html/erm/erm99/erm9946.html. [cited on page 279]

[30] EduTech Wiki, 2009. Programmed instruction — EduTech wiki, a resource kit for educational technology teaching, practice and research. URL http://edutechwiki.unige.ch/mediawiki/index.php?title=Programmed_instruction&oldid=21892. [cited on page 3]

[31] EdWeek, 1992. SuccessMaker partnership guarantee. *Education Week*. URL http://www.edweek.org/ew/articles/1992/12/16/15side.h12.html. December 16. [cited on page 175]

[32] EFA Global Monitoring Report team, 2015. *Education for All 2000-2015: Achievements and Challenges*. Education for All Global Monitoring Report. Paris: UNESCO Publishing, second edition. URL http://en.unesco.org/gem-report/report/2015/education-all-2000-2015-achievements-and-challenges. [cited on page 141]

[33] Elman, Harvey, 1970. Dial-a-Drill brings computerized instruction into home. *Computerworld*, 4(22): 27. URL https://news.google.com/newspapers?nid=v_xunPVOuKOC&dat=19700603&printsec=frontpage&hl=en. June 3, 1970. [cited on page 80]

[34] Entebbe Mathematics Workshop, 1964. *Primary Three Teachers' Guide*. Educational Services Incorporated. [cited on page 141]

[35] Farmer, Jim, 2013. MOOCs: A disruptive innovation or not? URL https://tagteam.harvard.edu/hub_feeds/2060/feed_items/245240. August 14. [cited on page 53]

[36] Feigenbaum, Edward A., 1979. SUMEX: Stanford University medical experimental computer resource: Annual report—year 06. Technical Report RR-00785, Stanford University School of Medicine. URL https://profiles.nlm.nih.gov/ps/access/BBGHML.pdf. Submitted to Biotechnology Resources Program, National Institute of Health. [cited on pages 59 and 274]

[37] Feurzeig, W., 2011. Educational technology at BBN. In David Walden and Raymond S. Nickerson (eds.), *A Culture of Innovation: Insider Accounts of Computing and Live at BBN*. East Sandwich, MA: Waterside Publishing. URL http://www.walden-family.com/bbn/feurzeig.pdf. [cited on pages 98, 99, and 100]

[38] Feurzeig, W., S. Papert, M. Bloom, R. Grant, and C. Solomon, 1969. Programming languages as a conceptual framework for teaching mathematics. Technical Report 1889, Bolt, Beranek, and Newman. [cited on pages 138 and 281]

[39] Fletcher, J.D. and Richard C. Atkinson, 1971. An evaluation of the Stanford CAI program in initial reading (grades K through 3). Psychology and Education Series 168, IMSSS. URL http://suppes-corpus.stanford.edu/techreports/IMSSS_168.pdf. [cited on page 120]

[40] Fletcher, J.D. and M.H. Beard, 1973. Computer-assisted instruction in language arts for hearing-impaired students. Psychology and Education Series 215, IMSSS. URL http://suppes-corpus.stanford.edu/techreports/IMSSS_215.pdf. [cited on page 70]

[41] Friedman, Michael, 2014. Patrick Suppes, Stanford philosopher, scientist and Silicon Valley entrepreneur, dies at 92. URL http://news.stanford.edu/news/2014/november/patrick-suppes-obit-112514.html. [Online; accessed 13-October-2016]. [cited on page xxiii]

[42] Friend, J., 1971. Instruct coders' manual. Psychology and Education Series 172, IMSSS. URL http://suppes-corpus.stanford.edu/techreports/IMSSS_172.pdf. [cited on page 68]

[43] Friend, J., 1989. Interactive radio instruction: developing instructional methods. *British Journal of Educational Technology*, 20(2): 106–114. [cited on page 145]

[44] Friend, Jamesine, Barbara Searle, and Patrick Suppes (eds.), 1980. *Radio Mathematics Project in Nicaragua*. Stanford, CA: Institute for Mathematical Studies in the Social Sciences. [cited on pages 143, 144, and 150]

[45] Gettinger, Maribeth, 1985. Time allocated and time spent relative to time needed for learning as determinants of achievement. *Journal of Educational Psychology*, 77(1): 3–11. doi:10.1037/0022-0663.77.1.3. [cited on page 186]

[46] Goldberg, Adele, 1973. Computer-assisted instruction: The application of theorem-proving to adaptive response analysis. Psychology and Education Series 203, IMSSS. URL http://suppes-corpus.stanford.edu/techreports/IMSSS_203.pdf. [cited on page 102]

[47] Gunter, Barrie and Jill L. McAleer, 1990. *Children and Television: The One Eyed Monster?* London, New York: Routledge. URL https://books.google.com/books?id=Ka8OAAAAQAAJ. [cited on page 285]

[48] Hansen, Duncan and Theodore S. Rodgers, July 1965. An exploration of psycholinguistic units in initial reading. Psychology Series 74, IMSSS. URL http://suppes-corpus.stanford.edu/techreports/IMSSS_74.pdf. [cited on page 42]

[49] Anthony Hearn, inventor of REDUCE and Portable Standard LISP. URL http://www.rand.org/content/dam/rand/people/h/hearn_anthony_c.pdf. [Resume, list of works]. [cited on page 237]

[50] Hinckley, M., J. Prebus, Robert Smith, and D. Ferris, 1977. VOCAL: Voice oriented curriculum author language. Psychology and Education Series 291, IMSSS. URL http://suppes-corpus.stanford.edu/techreports/IMSSS_291.pdf. [cited on pages 111, 124, and 236]

[51] Ho, Jennifer and Hetal Thukral, 2009. Tuned in to student success: Assessing the impact of interactive radio instruction for the hardest-to-reach. Technical report, Education Development Center, 1000 Potomac St. NW, Suite 350 Washington, DC. URL http://idd.edc.org/sites/idd.edc.org/files/EDC%20Tuned%20in%20to%20Student%20Success%20Report.pdf. [cited on pages 143 and 151]

[52] InfoWorld (editorial), 1983. A high-tech hickory stick? *InfoWorld*, 5(29): 36. July 18, 1983. [cited on page 164]

[53] Isaac, Alistair, 2014. RIP: Patrick Colonel Suppes, 1922–2014, eulogy and apologia. *Digressions&Impressions* (blog of Eric Schliesser), December 8, 2014. URL http://digressionsnimpressions.typepad.com/digressionsimpressions/2014/12/rip-patrick-colonel-suppes-19222014-eulogy-and-apologia.html. [Online; accessed 13-October-2016]. [cited on page xxiii]

[54] Jamison, D., Patrick Suppes, and S. Wells, 1972. The effectiveness of alternative instructional methods: A survey. Psychology and Education Series 196, IMSSS. URL http://suppes-corpus.stanford.edu/techreports/IMSSS_196.pdf. [cited on pages 77, 141, and 153]

[55] Jamison, Dean T., Barbara Searle, Klaus Galda, and Stephen P. Heyneman, 1981. Improving elementary mathematics education in Nicaragua: An experimental study of the impact of textbooks and radio on achievement. *Journal of Educational Psychology*, 73(4): 556–567. [cited on page 150]

[56] Jamison, D.T., 1979. Suppes' contribution to education. In R.J. Bogdan (ed.), *Patrick Suppes*, pp. 187–206. D. Reidel Publishing. [cited on pages 153, 154, 273, and 274]

[57] Kay, A. and Adele Goldberg, 1977. Personal dynamic media. *Computer*, 10(3): 31–41. [cited on page 283]

[58] Kimball, Ralph B., 1973. Self-optimizing computer-assisted tutoring: Theory and practice. Psychology and Education Series 206, IMSSS. URL http://suppes-corpus.stanford.edu/techreports/IMSSS_206.pdf. [cited on page 238]

[59] Kisseloff, Jeff, 2016. Elma "Pem" Farnsworth, interview. Archive of American Television. URL http://www.emmytvlegends.org/interviews/people/elma-pem-farnsworth. June 25, 1996, Salt Lake City, UT, part 10, 4:35 into the tape. [cited on page 285]

[60] Klatt, Dennis, 1976. Structure of a phonological rule component for a synthesis-by-rule program. In *IEEE Transaction on Acoustics, Speech, and Signal Processing*, volume 24, pp. 391–398. [cited on page 126]

[61] Konnikova, Maria, November 2014. Will MOOCs be flukes. *The New Yorker*. URL http://www.newyorker.com/science/maria-konnikova/moocs-failure-solutions. [November 7, Online; accessed 23-August-2016]. [cited on page 297]

[62] Lekan, Helen A., 1973. *Index to Computer Assisted Instruction*. Harcourt Brace Jovanovich, third edition. [cited on page 96]

[63] Levy, Steven, 2010. *Hackers: Heroes of the Computer Revolution*. Sebastopol, CA: O'Reilly Media, 25th anniversary edition. [cited on pages 279 and 280]

[64] Litman, George H., 1973. CAI in Chicago. In *Paper presented at the Association for Educational Data Systems Annual Convention*. [cited on page 75]

[65] Logic and Proofs from Carnegie-Mellon University. URL http://www.phil.cmu.edu/projects/apros/index.php?page=landp. [cited on page 299]

[66] Lorton, P. Jr. and J. Slimick, 1969. Computer-based instruction in computer programming: A symbol manipulation-list processing approach. In *AFIPS '69 (Fall) Proceedings of the November 18-20, 1969, fall joint computer conference*, pp. 535–544. doi:10.1145/1478559.1478623. [cited on pages 64 and 138]

[67] Mace, Scott, July 1983. Teaching computer phones and drills students. *InfoWorld*, 5(28). [cited on page 164]

[68] Mace, Scott, November 1985. ST targeted as school workstation. *InfoWorld*, p. 25. [cited on page 208]

[69] Macken, Elizabeth, R. van den Heuvel, Patrick Suppes, and T. Suppes, 1975. Study of needs and technological opportunities in home-based education. Psychology and Education Series 258, IMSSS. URL http://suppes-corpus.stanford.edu/techreports/IMSSS_258.pdf. [cited on pages 177 and 243]

[70] Macken, Elizabeth, Patrick Suppes, and Mario Zanotti, 1980. Considerations in evaluating individualized instruction. *Journal of Research and Development in Education*, 14(1). [cited on page 177]

[71] Malone, Thomas W., Patrick Suppes, Elizabeth Macken, Mario Zanotti, and Lauri Kanerva, 1979. Projecting student trajectories in a computer-assisted instruction curriculum. *Journal of Educational Psychology*, 71(1): 74–84. [cited on page 177]

[72] Markoff, John, 2014. Patrick Suppes, pioneer in computerized learning, dies at 92. *New York Times*, p. B16. URL http://www.nytimes.com/2014/12/03/us/patrick-suppes-pioneer-in-computerized-learning-dies-at-92.html?_r=0. December 3, 2014. [cited on pages xxiii and 284]

[73] Martin, William Ted, 1962. Mathematics in Africa: The Accra conference. *Educational Services Incorporated Newsletter*, 1(1). [cited on page 141]

[74] McCarthy, John, 1966. Information. *Scientific American*, 215(3): 64–72. doi:10.1038/scientificamerican0966-64. [cited on page 33]

[75] McCarthy, John, Dow Brian, Gary Feldman, and John Allen, 1967. Thor–a display based time sharing system. In *Proceedings of the Spring Joint Computer Conference*, pp. 623–633. [cited on page 60]

[76] McCune, W., 1994. Otter 3.0 reference manual and guide. Technical Report ANL-94/6, Argonne National Laboratory. [cited on page 257]

[77] McMath, David, Marianna Rozenfeld, and Richard Sommer, 2001. A computer environment for writing ordinary mathematical proofs. In Robert Nieuwenhuis and Andrei Voronkov (eds.), *Logic for Programming, Artificial Intelligence, and Reasoning: 8th International Conference, LPAR 2001 Havana, Cuba, December 3–7, 2001 Proceedings*, pp. 507–516. Berlin, Heidelberg: Springer. doi:10.1007/3-540-45653-8_35. URL http://dx.doi.org/10.1007/3-540-45653-8_35. [cited on page 257]

[78] McNeil, Sara. TICCIT (Time-Shared Interactive Computer Controlled Information Television). URL http://faculty.coe.uh.edu/smcneil/cuin6373/idhistory/ticcit.html. A Hypertext History of Instructional Design. [cited on pages 98 and 153]

[79] Nambiar, Archana, 2010. USAID interactive radio instruction in India. *Educational Technology Debate*. URL http://edutechdebate.org/ict-tools-for-south-asia/interactive-

`radio-instruction-iri-improves-indian-student-learning/`.
[cited on page 143]

[80] National Association for the Deaf. TTY and TTY relay services. URL `https://nad.org/issues/telephone-and-relay-services/relay-services/tty`. [accessed, January 23, 2017]. [cited on page 66]

[81] New York Telephone, 1971. Advertisement. *Saturday Review*, pp. 41–43. URL `http://www.unz.org/Pub/SaturdayRev-1971jun19:44`. [cited on page 80]

[82] Nowell, Richard and Joseph Innes, 1997. Educating children who are deaf or hard of hearing: Inclusion. *ERIC Clearinghouse on Disabilities and Gifted Education*. URL `http://www.ericdigests.org/1998-2/inclusion.htm`. [cited on page 68]

[83] Oettinger, Anthony G., 1969. *Run, Computer, Run: The Mythology of Educational Innovation*. Cambridge, MA: Harvard University Press. [cited on pages 278 and 279]

[84] Oppenheimer, Todd, 2003. *The Flickering Mind*. New York: Random House. [cited on page 286]

[85] PDP-1 restoration project. URL `http://www.computerhistory.org/pdp-1/`. [cited on page 15]

[86] Quillian, M.R., 1968. Semantic memory. In M. Minsky (ed.), *Semantic Information Processing*. MIT Press. [cited on page 99]

[87] Quine, W., 1959. *Methods of Logic*. Holt, Rinehart, and Winston. [cited on page 108]

[88] Raudebaugh, Charles, November 1959. First graders in Palo Alto learn geometry. *San Francisco Sunday Chronicle*, p. 11. [cited on page 7]

[89] Ravaglia, Raymond, Theodore Alper, Marianna Rozenfeld, and Patrick Suppes, 1998. Successful pedagogical applications of symbolic computation. In Norbert Kajler (ed.), *Computer-Human Interaction in Symbolic Computation*, Texts and Monographs in Symbolic Computation, pp. 61–88. Springer Vienna. doi:10.1007/978-3-7091-6461-7_5. [cited on page 248]

[90] Ravaglia, Raymond, J. Acacio de Barros, and Patrick Suppes, July/August 1995. Computer based instruction brings Advanced-Placement to gifted students. *Computers in Physics*, 9(4): 380–386. doi: 10.1063/1.4823419. URL `http://dx.doi.org/10.1063/1.4823419`. [cited on page 256]

[91] Rawson, F.L., 1973. Set-theoretical semantics for elementary mathematical language. Psychology and Education Series 220, IMSSS. URL `http://suppes-corpus.stanford.edu/techreports/IMSSS_220.pdf`. [cited on page 131]

[92] RCA Corporation. URL `http://www.computerhistory.org/brochures/companies.php?alpha=q-s&company=com-42bc220794e22`. [cited on page 75]

[93] Rodgers, Theodore S., 1967. Linguistic considerations in the design of the Stanford computer-based curriculum in intital reading. Psychology and Education Series 111, IMSSS. URL http://suppes-corpus.stanford.edu/techreports/IMSSS_111.pdf. [cited on page 42]

[94] Sanders, Sil, 2014. Reminiscences of 45 years of multimedia. URL https://www.linkedin.com/pulse/20140628031403-44567171-reminiscences-of-45-years-of-multimedia. [Online; accessed 27-September-2016]. [cited on page 53]

[95] Scarborough, Jeffrey and Raymond Ravaglia, 2014. *Bricks and Mortar: The Making of a Real Education at the Stanford Online High School.* Stanford, CA: CSLI Publications. [cited on page 264]

[96] Schroeder, Sarah, 2014. From principles of cognitive science to MOOCs. *Observer*, 27(6). URL http://www.psychologicalscience.org/index.php/publications/observer/2014/july-august-14/from-principles-of-cognitive-science-to-moocs.html. July 22, 2014. [cited on pages 55 and 296]

[97] Searle, Barbara, Jamesine Friend, and Patrick Suppes (eds.), 1976. *The Radio Mathematics Project: Nicaragua 1974-1975.* Stanford, CA: Institute for Mathematical Studies in the Social Sciences. [cited on pages 143, 145, and 150]

[98] Richard Shavelson, former dean of the Stanford school of education. URL https://ed.stanford.edu/faculty/richs. [cited on pages 296 and 297]

[99] Singer, Arthur L., 2009. Easy to forget, and so hard to remember: Memoirs of selected episodes. URL https://phe.rockefeller.edu/news/blog/2010/08/04/arthur-l-singer-jr-easy-to-forget-and-so-hard-to-remember/. January 1, 2009. [cited on page 141]

[100] Smith, N.W., 1974. A question-answering system for elementary mathematics. Psychology and Education Series 227, IMSSS. URL http://suppes-corpus.stanford.edu/techreports/IMSSS_227.pdf. [cited on page 131]

[101] Smith, R.L., 1972. The syntax and semantics of ERICA. Psychology and Education Series 185, IMSSS. URL http://suppes-corpus.stanford.edu/techreports/IMSSS_185.pdf. [cited on page 130]

[102] Smith, R.L., N.W. Smith, and F.L. Rawson, 1974. CONSTRUCT: In search of a theory of meaning. Psychology and Education Series 238, IMSSS. URL http://suppes-corpus.stanford.edu/techreports/IMSSS_238.pdf. [cited on page 131]

[103] Smith, Robert, 1975. TENEX SAIL. Psychology and Education Series 248, IMSSS. URL http://suppes-corpus.stanford.edu/techreports/IMSSS_248.pdf. [cited on page 64]

[104] Solomon, Cynthia, 1986. *Computer Environments for Children: A Reflection on Theories of Learning and Education.* Cambridge, MA: MIT Press. [cited on pages 281 and 282]

[105] Sommer, R. and G. Nuckols, 2004. A proof environment for teaching mathematics. *Journal of Automated Reasoning*, 32: 227–258. [cited on pages 257 and 258]

[106] Spache, George D., 1967. A reaction to 'Computer-assisted instruction in initial reading: The Stanford project'. *Reading Research Quarterly*, 3(1): 101–109. doi:10.2307/747206. URL http://www.jstor.org/stable/747206. [cited on pages 46 and 50]

[107] Spain, Peter L., Dean T. Jamison, and Emile G. McAnany (eds.), 1977. *Radio for Education and Development: Case Studies*, volume 1 of *World Bank Staff Working Paper 266*, chapter The Nicaragua Radio Mathematics Project. Washington, DC: World Bank. [cited on pages 144 and 150]

[108] Spangler, Todd, 2015. Netflix bandwidth usage climbs to nearly 37% of internet traffic at peak hours. *Variety*. URL http://variety.com/2015/digital/news/netflix-bandwidth-usage-internet-traffic-1201507187/. May 28, 2015. [cited on page 286]

[109] Stanford University, 2006. Stanford to offer first online high school for gifted students. Stanford News Service. URL http://news.stanford.edu/pr/2006/pr-ohs-041206.html. April 11, 2006. [cited on page 264]

[110] Stanford University, 2016. Online high school: Our curriculum. URL https://ohs.stanford.edu/academics/curriculum. [Online; accessed 23-August-2016]. [cited on page 264]

[111] Stimmel, Emily, 2015. Logic & proofs: Computer-supported learning and the philosophy of mathematics. *Dietrich College of Humanities and Social Sciences News Service, Carnegie Mellon University*. URL https://www.cmu.edu/dietrich/news/news-stories/2015/december/wilfried-sieg.html. December 14, 2015. [cited on page 299]

[112] Suppes, Patrick. Intellectual autobiography, 1922-1978. URL http://suppes-corpus.stanford.edu/autobiography.html. [cited on page 1]

[113] Suppes, Patrick, 1957. *Introduction to Logic*. Princeton, NJ: Van Nostrand. [cited on pages 6, 28, and 105]

[114] Suppes, Patrick, 1960. *Axiomatic Set Theory*. Princeton, NJ: Van Nostrand. [cited on pages 7, 105, and 109]

[115] Suppes, Patrick, 1962. Proposal for a computer-based learning and teaching laboratory. Unpublished, December 21, 1962, submitted to the Carnegie Corporation of New York; authors have a digitized copy. [cited on pages 9, 10, and 11]

[116] Suppes, Patrick, 1964. Modern learning theory and the elementary-school curriculum. *American Educational Research Journal*, 1(2): 73–93. doi:10.3102/00028312001002079. URL https://www.jstor.org/stable/1162072. [cited on page 4]

[117] Suppes, Patrick, 1966. The uses of computers in education. *Scientific American*, 215(3): 206–220. doi:10.1038/scientificamerican0966-206. [cited on pages 32, 36, 37, and 101]

[118] Suppes, Patrick, 1967. *Sets and Numbers*. Singer Co. [cited on pages 18 and 29]

[119] Suppes, Patrick, 1968. Computer-assisted instruction: An overview of operations and problems. In A. J. H. Morrell (ed.), *Information Processing 68.2. Proceedings of IFIP Congress, 1968, Edinburgh*, pp. 1103–1113. [cited on page 57]

[120] Suppes, Patrick, 1968–1971. NASA grant documents. unpublished. [cited on page 68]

[121] Suppes, Patrick, 1969. Radio entebbe proposal. unpublished. [cited on page 141]

[122] Suppes, Patrick, 1969. Stimulus-response theory of finite automata. *Journal of Mathematical Psychology*, 6: 327–355. [cited on page 28]

[123] Suppes, Patrick, 1970. *Collective choice and social welfare*. Holden-Day. [cited on page 116]

[124] Suppes, Patrick, 1970. Probabilistic grammars for natural languages. Psychology and Education Series 154, IMSSS. URL http://suppes-corpus.stanford.edu/techreports/IMSSS_154.pdf. [cited on page 130]

[125] Suppes, Patrick, 1971. Semantics of context-free fragments of natural languages. Psychology and Education Series 171, IMSSS. URL http://suppes-corpus.stanford.edu/techreports/IMSSS_171.pdf. [cited on page 130]

[126] Suppes, Patrick, 1972. Facts and fantasies of education. Psychology and Education Series 193, IMSSS. URL http://suppes-corpus.stanford.edu/techreports/IMSSS_193.pdf. [cited on pages 3 and 282]

[127] Suppes, Patrick, 1974. Congruence of meaning. Psychology and Education Series 229, IMSSS. URL http://suppes-corpus.stanford.edu/techreports/IMSSS_229.pdf. [cited on page 130]

[128] Suppes, Patrick, 1981. *University-Level Computer-assisted Instruction at Stanford: 1968-1980*. Stanford, CA: Institute for Mathematical Studies in the Social Sciences. [cited on pages 52, 54, 55, 103, 105, 107, 111, 113, 116, 117, 118, 120, 121, 122, 123, 126, 127, 133, 134, 135, 136, 137, and 139]

[129] Suppes, Patrick, 1984. *Probabilistic Metaphysics*. Basil Blackwell. [cited on page 117]

[130] Suppes, Patrick, 1990. Three current tutoring systems and future needs. In Frasson Gauthier and Giles Gauthier (eds.), *Intelligent Tutoring Systems: At the Crossroads of Artificial Intelligence and Education*, pp. 251–265. Norwood, NJ: Ablex Publishing. [cited on page 300]

[131] Suppes, Patrick, 1990. Uses of artificial intelligence in computer-based instruction. In V. Marik, O. Stepankova, and Z. Zdrahal (eds.), *Artificial Intelligence in Higher Education*, pp. 206–225. Springer-Verlag. [cited on pages 60 and 293]

[132] Suppes, Patrick, 1992. Estes' statistical learning theory: Past, present, and future. In Alice F. Healy (ed.), *From Learning Theory to Connectionist Theory: Essays in Honor of William K. Estes*, pp. 1–20. Lawrence Erlbaum Associates. [cited on pages 4 and 214]

[133] Suppes, Patrick, 2002. *Representation and Invariance of Scientific Structures*. Stanford, CA: CSLI Publications. [cited on pages xxvi and 282]

[134] Suppes, Patrick, 2006. Movement and mastery: EPGY math grades K-7 and language arts and writing grades 3-5 (LAW I-III). *[N/A]*. [cited on page 252]

[135] Suppes, Patrick, Tryg A. Ager, Paul Berg, Rolando Chuaqui, William Graham, Robert Elton Maas, and Shuzo Takahashi, 1987. Applications of computer technology to pre-college calculus: First annual report. Psychology and Education Series 310, IMSSS. URL http://suppes-corpus.stanford.edu/techreports/IMSSS_310.pdf. [cited on pages 238, 239, and 240]

[136] Suppes, Patrick, Bob Albrecht, and Caryl Rivers, April 1973. Computer confrontation: Suppes and Albrecht. *The Saturday Review*, pp. 48–50. URL http://www.unz.org/Pub/SaturdayRev-1973apr14-00048. [cited on page 280]

[137] Suppes, Patrick and Kenneth Arrow, 1955. Proposal to the ford foundation. unpublished. [cited on page 1]

[138] Suppes, Patrick and Richard C. Atkinson, 1960. *Markov Learning Models for Multi-Person Interactions*. Stanford, CA: Stanford University Press. [cited on page 4]

[139] Suppes, Patrick, J. D. Fletcher, and Mario Zanotti, 1975. Performance models of American Indian students in computer-assisted instruction in elementary mathematics. *Instructional Science*, 4: 303–313. [cited on page 177]

[140] Suppes, Patrick, J. D. Fletcher, and Mario Zanotti, 1976. Models of individual trajectories in computer-assisted instruction for deaf students. *Journal of Educational Psychology*, 68(2): 117–127. [cited on page 177]

[141] Suppes, Patrick, J.D. Fletcher, Mario Zanotti, P.V. Lorton, and B.W. Searle, 1973. Evaluation of computer-assisted instructiom in elementary mathematics for hearing-impaired students. Psychology and Education Series 200, IMSSS. URL http://suppes-corpus.stanford.edu/techreports/IMSSS_200.pdf. [cited on page 65]

[142] Suppes, Patrick and Rose Ginsberg, 1962. Application of a stimulus sampling model to children's concept formation with and without overt

correction responses. *Journal of Experimental Psychology*, 63(4): 330–336. doi:10.1037/h0047093. URL https://suppes-corpus.stanford.edu/article.html?id=38. [cited on page 4]

[143] Suppes, Patrick and Rose Ginsberg, 1962. Experimental studies of mathematical concept formation in young children. *Science Education*, 46(3): 230–240. [cited on page 151]

[144] Suppes, Patrick, Adele Goldberg, Grace Kanz, Barbara Searle, and Carolyn Stauffer, 1971. Teacher's handbook for CAI courses. Psychology and Education Series 178, IMSSS. URL http://files.eric.ed.gov/fulltext/ED054620.pdf. [cited on page 65]

[145] Suppes, Patrick and Newton Hawley, 1959. Proposal. unpublished. Request for $67,000 for experimental teaching of math in schools. [cited on page 7]

[146] Suppes, Patrick and Dean Jamison, 1971. NSF proposal. unpublished. [cited on page 68]

[147] Suppes, Patrick and Max Jerman, 1969. Computer assisted instruction at Stanford. *Educational Technology*, 9: 22–24. [cited on page 57]

[148] Suppes, Patrick, Max Jerman, and Dow Brian, 1968. *Computer-assisted Instruction: Stanford's 1965-66 Arithmetic Program*. New York: Academic Press. [cited on pages 21, 22, 24, 28, and 32]

[149] Suppes, Patrick, M. Léveillé, and R.L. Smith, 1974. Developmental models of a child's French syntax. Psychology and Education Series 243, IMSSS. URL http://suppes-corpus.stanford.edu/techreports/IMSSS_243.pdf. [cited on page 131]

[150] Suppes, Patrick, Tie Liang, Elizabeth E. Macken, and Daniel P. Flickinger, 2014. Positive technological and negative pre-test-score effects in a four-year assessment of low socioeconomic status K-8 student learning in computer-based math and language arts courses. *Computers & Education*, 71: 23–32. doi:10.1016/j.compedu.2013.09.008. URL https://suppes-corpus.stanford.edu/articles/comped/463.pdf. [cited on page 268]

[151] Suppes, Patrick and Mona Morningstar, 1972. *Computer-assisted Instruction at Stanford, 1966-68: Data, Models, and Evaluation of the Arithmetic Programs*. New York: Academic Press. [cited on pages 28, 37, and 39]

[152] Suppes, Patrick and Barbara Searle, 1975. The Nicaragua radio mathematics project. *Educational Broadcast International*. [cited on page 146]

[153] Suppes, Patrick, Barbara Searle, and Jamesine Friend (eds.), 1978. *The Radio Mathematics Project: Nicaragua 1976-1977*. Stanford, CA: Institute for Mathematical Studies in the Social Sciences. [cited on pages 143, 146, 148, and 150]

[154] Suppes, Patrick, Robert Smith, and Marian Beard, 1977. University-level computer-assisted instruction at Stanford: 1975. *Instructional*

Science, 6(2): 151–185. doi:10.1007/BF00121084. [cited on pages 133, 137, and 154]

[155] Suppes, Patrick, Robert Smith, and M. Léveillé, 1972. The French syntax and semantics of PHILIPPE, part I: Noun phrases. Psychology and Education Series 195, IMSSS. URL http://suppes-corpus. stanford.edu/techreports/IMSSS_195.pdf. [cited on page 131]

[156] Suppes, Patrick and Kalée Tock, 2013. The high dimensionality of gifted students' individual differences in performance in EPGY's K-6 computer-based mathematics curriculum. In Patrick Suppes (ed.), *Individual Differences in Online Computer-Based Learning: Gifted and Other Diverse Populations*, pp. 3–105. Stanford, CA: CSLI Publications. [cited on page 177]

[157] Suppes, Patrick and Mario Zanotti, 1996. *Foundations of Probability with Applications: Selected Papers 1974–1995*. New York: Cambridge University Press. doi:10.1017/CBO9781139172639. [cited on pages 177, 252, and 253]

[158] Suppes, Patrick, Mario Zanotti, and Nancy Smith, 1988. *Probable Relation Between Functional Gain and Time Needed for Math Concepts and Skills and Reader's Workshop*, pp. 1–6. Computer Curriculum Corporation. [cited on page 185]

[159] Swart, Edward R., 1980. The philosophical implications of the four-color problem. *The American Mathematical Monthly*, 87: 697–707. URL http://www.maa.org/programs/maa-awards/writing-awards/ the-philosophical-implications-of-the-four-color-problem. [cited on page 119]

[160] Taylor, Jonathan, 2016. Koko: The gorilla who talks to people. documentary, June 2016, BBC, also broadcast on PBS with the subtitle "The Gorilla who Talks". URL http://www.pbs.org/program/koko-gorilla-who-talks/. [cited on page 140]

[161] Trumbore, Anne, 2014. Automated and amplified: active learning with computers and radio (1965-1979). *International Journal of Designs for Learning*, 5(2): 20–28. [cited on pages 142, 148, and 151]

[162] United States Court of Appeals (Third circuit), 1994. Instructional Systems Inc. vs. Computer Curriculum Corp. September 16, 1994. URL http://digitalcommons.law.villanova.edu/ thirdcircuit_1994/135/. [cited on page 194]

[163] Wescourt, Keith T., Marian H. Beard, Laura Gould, and Avron Barr, 1977. Knowledge-based CAI: CINs for individualized curriculum sequencing. Psychology and Education Series 290, IMSSS. URL http: //suppes-corpus.stanford.edu/techreports/IMSSS_290.pdf. [cited on page 137]

[164] Weyer, S.A., 1973. Fingerspelling by computer. Psychology and Education Series 212, IMSSS. URL http://suppes-corpus.stanford. edu/techreports/IMSSS_212.pdf. [cited on page 72]

[165] Weyer, S.A. and A.B. Cannara, 1975. Children learning computer programming: Experiments with languages, curricula and programmable devices. Psychology and Education Series 250, IMSSS. URL http://suppes-corpus.stanford.edu/techreports/IMSSS_250.pdf. [cited on page 138]

[166] Wikipedia, 2013. School Mathematics Study Group — wikipedia, the free encyclopedia. URL https://en.wikipedia.org/w/index.php?title=School_Mathematics_Study_Group&oldid=571947281. [Online; accessed 11-August-2016]. [cited on page 29]

[167] Wikipedia, 2015. TICCIT — wikipedia, the free encyclopedia. URL https://en.wikipedia.org/w/index.php?title=TICCIT&oldid=677030711. [Online; accessed 11-August-2016]. [cited on page 98]

[168] Wikipedia, 2016. Agostini v. Felton — wikipedia, the free encyclopedia. URL https://en.wikipedia.org/w/index.php?title=Agostini_v._Felton&oldid=724047166. [Online; accessed 11-August-2016]. [cited on page 195]

[169] Wikipedia, 2016. Aguilar v. Felton — wikipedia, the free encyclopedia. URL https://en.wikipedia.org/w/index.php?title=Aguilar_v._Felton&oldid=724052082. [Online; accessed 11-August-2016]. [cited on pages 179 and 195]

[170] Wikipedia, 2016. Anthony Oettinger — wikipedia, the free encyclopedia. URL https://en.wikipedia.org/w/index.php?title=Anthony_Oettinger&oldid=730226166. [Online; accessed 15-August-2016]. [cited on page 278]

[171] Wikipedia, 2016. ARPANET — wikipedia, the free encyclopedia. URL https://en.wikipedia.org/w/index.php?title=ARPANET&oldid=731254041. [Online; accessed 11-August-2016]. [cited on page 59]

[172] Wikipedia, 2016. Atlantic Philanthropies — wikipedia, the free encyclopedia. URL https://en.wikipedia.org/w/index.php?title=Atlantic_Philanthropies&oldid=737833379. [Online; accessed 5-September-2016]. [cited on page 256]

[173] Wikipedia, 2016. Augmentation Research Center — wikipedia, the free encyclopedia. URL https://en.wikipedia.org/w/index.php?title=Augmentation_Research_Center&oldid=751311223. [Online; accessed 2-February-2017]. [cited on page 59]

[174] Wikipedia, 2016. Boards of Cooperative Educational Services — wikipedia, the free encyclopedia. URL https://en.wikipedia.org/w/index.php?title=Boards_of_Cooperative_Educational_Services&oldid=719323064. [Online; accessed 11-August-2016]. [cited on page 194]

[175] Wikipedia, 2016. Bob Albrecht — wikipedia, the free encyclopedia. URL https://en.wikipedia.org/w/index.php?title=Bob_

Albrecht&oldid=740566642. [Online; accessed 21-September-2016]. [cited on page 280]

[176] Wikipedia, 2016. Bucky bit — wikipedia, the free encyclopedia. URL https://en.wikipedia.org/w/index.php?title=Bucky_bit&oldid=724266424. [Online; accessed 16-August-2016]. [cited on page 62]

[177] Wikipedia, 2016. Coursera — wikipedia, the free encyclopedia. URL https://en.wikipedia.org/w/index.php?title=Coursera&oldid=730269858. [Online; accessed 10-August-2016]. [cited on page xxii]

[178] Wikipedia, 2016. Distance education — wikipedia, the free encyclopedia. URL https://en.wikipedia.org/w/index.php?title=Distance_education&oldid=734058632. [Online; accessed 11-August-2016]. [cited on page 2]

[179] Wikipedia, 2016. Donald Bitzer — wikipedia, the free encyclopedia. URL https://en.wikipedia.org/w/index.php?title=Donald_Bitzer&oldid=703713289. [Online; accessed 11-August-2016]. [cited on page 96]

[180] Wikipedia, 2016. Douglas Hofstadter — wikipedia, the free encyclopedia. URL https://en.wikipedia.org/w/index.php?title=Douglas_Hofstadter&oldid=733915744. [Online; accessed 11-August-2016]. [cited on page 140]

[181] Wikipedia, 2016. Edward Fredkin — wikipedia, the free encyclopedia. URL https://en.wikipedia.org/w/index.php?title=Edward_Fredkin&oldid=728663075. [Online; accessed 11-August-2016]. [cited on page 12]

[182] Wikipedia, 2016. Edward G. Begle — wikipedia, the free encyclopedia. URL https://en.wikipedia.org/w/index.php?title=Edward_G._Begle&oldid=707891705. [Online; accessed 11-August-2016]. [cited on page 29]

[183] Wikipedia, 2016. Four color theorem — wikipedia, the free encyclopedia. URL https://en.wikipedia.org/w/index.php?title=Four_color_theorem&oldid=729495821. [Online; accessed 11-August-2016]. [cited on page 119]

[184] Wikipedia, 2016. Graphical Environment Manager — wikipedia, the free encyclopedia. URL https://en.wikipedia.org/w/index.php?title=Graphical_Environment_Manager&oldid=733558572. [Online; accessed 11-August-2016]. [cited on page 205]

[185] Wikipedia, 2016. IBM 1500 — wikipedia, the free encyclopedia. URL https://en.wikipedia.org/w/index.php?title=IBM_1500&oldid=747525967. [Online; accessed 2-February-2017]. [cited on page 37]

[186] Wikipedia, 2016. J. C. R. Licklider — wikipedia, the free encyclopedia. URL https://en.wikipedia.org/w/index.php?title=J._C._R._Licklider&oldid=733041411. [Online; accessed 11-August-2016]. [cited on page 5]

[187] Wikipedia, 2016. John Dewey — wikipedia, the free encyclopedia. URL https://en.wikipedia.org/w/index.php?title=John_Dewey&oldid=734234497. [Online; accessed 23-August-2016]. [cited on page 3]

[188] Wikipedia, 2016. Jostens — wikipedia, the free encyclopedia. URL https://en.wikipedia.org/w/index.php?title=Jostens&oldid=730773398. [Online; accessed 11-August-2016]. [cited on pages 199 and 200]

[189] Wikipedia, 2016. Julian Stanley — wikipedia, the free encyclopedia. URL https://en.wikipedia.org/w/index.php?title=Julian_Stanley&oldid=735807018. [Online; accessed 23-August-2016]. [cited on page 242]

[190] Wikipedia, 2016. Kenneth Arrow — wikipedia, the free encyclopedia. URL https://en.wikipedia.org/w/index.php?title=Kenneth_Arrow&oldid=732278426. [Online; accessed 11-August-2016]. [cited on page 115]

[191] Wikipedia, 2016. Khan Academy — wikipedia, the free encyclopedia. URL https://en.wikipedia.org/w/index.php?title=Khan_Academy&oldid=731666612. [Online; accessed 11-August-2016]. [cited on page 300]

[192] Wikipedia, 2016. Logic in computer science — wikipedia, the free encyclopedia. URL https://en.wikipedia.org/w/index.php?title=Logic_in_computer_science&oldid=724544152. [Online; accessed 11-August-2016]. [cited on page 29]

[193] Wikipedia, 2016. Lotus 1-2-3 — wikipedia, the free encyclopedia. URL https://en.wikipedia.org/w/index.php?title=Lotus_1-2-3&oldid=733651084. [Online; accessed 11-August-2016]. [cited on page 202]

[194] Wikipedia, 2016. Macintosh II — wikipedia, the free encyclopedia. URL https://en.wikipedia.org/w/index.php?title=Macintosh_II&oldid=717265860. [Online; accessed 11-August-2016]. [cited on page 208]

[195] Wikipedia, 2016. Macintosh LC — wikipedia, the free encyclopedia. URL https://en.wikipedia.org/w/index.php?title=Macintosh_LC&oldid=722096154. [Online; accessed 11-August-2016]. [cited on page 220]

[196] Wikipedia, 2016. Macsyma — wikipedia, the free encyclopedia. URL https://en.wikipedia.org/w/index.php?title=Macsyma&oldid=730746465. [Online; accessed 11-August-2016]. [cited on pages 119 and 263]

[197] Wikipedia, 2016. Maxima (software) — wikipedia, the free encyclopedia. URL https://en.wikipedia.org/w/index.php?title=Maxima_(software)&oldid=720228815. [Online; accessed 11-August-2016]. [cited on page 119]

[198] Wikipedia, 2016. Memex — wikipedia, the free encyclopedia. URL https://en.wikipedia.org/w/index.php?title=Memex&oldid= 726060982. [Online; accessed 11-August-2016]. [cited on page 284]

[199] Wikipedia, 2016. Milacron — wikipedia, the free encyclopedia. URL https://en.wikipedia.org/w/index.php?title=Milacron&oldid= 729541596. [Online; accessed 11-August-2016]. [cited on page 82]

[200] Wikipedia, 2016. Mizar system — wikipedia, the free encyclopedia. URL https://en.wikipedia.org/w/index.php?title=Mizar_ system&oldid=730726257. [Online; accessed 11-August-2016]. [cited on page 120]

[201] Wikipedia, 2016. MS-DOS — wikipedia, the free encyclopedia. URL https://en.wikipedia.org/w/index.php?title=MS-DOS& oldid=733942106. [Online; accessed 11-August-2016]. [cited on page 166]

[202] Wikipedia, 2016. NAPLPS — wikipedia, the free encyclopedia. URL https://en.wikipedia.org/w/index.php?title=NAPLPS& oldid=736824284. [Online; accessed 2-February-2017]. [cited on page 204]

[203] Wikipedia, 2016. The Oregon Trail (video game) — wikipedia, the free encyclopedia. URL https://en.wikipedia.org/w/index.php? title=The_Oregon_Trail_(video_game)&oldid=728321281. [Online; accessed 11-August-2016]. [cited on page 203]

[204] Wikipedia, 2016. Osborne Computer Corporation — wikipedia, the free encyclopedia. URL https://en.wikipedia.org/w/index.php?title= Osborne_Computer_Corporation&oldid=729376288. [Online; accessed 11-August-2016]. [cited on page 172]

[205] Wikipedia, 2016. PDP-1 — wikipedia, the free encyclopedia. URL https://en.wikipedia.org/w/index.php?title=PDP-1&oldid= 726907721. [Online; accessed 11-August-2016]. [cited on pages 11 and 15]

[206] Wikipedia, 2016. People's Computer Company — wikipedia, the free encyclopedia. URL https://en.wikipedia.org/w/index.php?title= People%27s_Computer_Company&oldid=701288892. [Online; accessed 23-January-2016]. [cited on page 279]

[207] Wikipedia, 2016. Plato (computer system) — wikipedia, the free encyclopedia. URL https://en.wikipedia.org/w/index.php?title= PLATO_(computer_system)&oldid=719109037. [Online; accessed 11-August-2016]. [cited on pages 96, 97, and 199]

[208] Wikipedia, 2016. Portable Standard Lisp — wikipedia, the free encyclopedia. URL https://en.wikipedia.org/w/index.php?title= Portable_Standard_Lisp&oldid=710755917. [Online; accessed 11-August-2016]. [cited on page 237]

[209] Wikipedia, 2016. Presburger arithmetic — wikipedia, the free encyclopedia. URL https://en.wikipedia.org/w/index.php?title=

Presburger_arithmetic&oldid=729403846. [Online; accessed 15-August-2016]. [cited on page 103]

[210] Wikipedia, 2016. Principia Mathematica — wikipedia, the free encyclopedia. URL https://en.wikipedia.org/w/index.php?title=Principia_Mathematica&oldid=734867584. [Online; accessed 19-August-2016]. [cited on page 282]

[211] Wikipedia, 2016. Propositional calculus — wikipedia, the free encyclopedia. URL https://en.wikipedia.org/w/index.php?title=Propositional_calculus&oldid=730950278. [Online; accessed 11-August-2016]. [cited on page 107]

[212] Wikipedia, 2016. Prosody (linguistics) — wikipedia, the free encyclopedia. URL https://en.wikipedia.org/w/index.php?title=Prosody_(linguistics)&oldid=728828256. [Online; accessed 11-August-2016]. [cited on page 122]

[213] Wikipedia, 2016. Prover9 — wikipedia, the free encyclopedia. URL https://en.wikipedia.org/w/index.php?title=Prover9&oldid=715462317. [Online; accessed 11-August-2016]. [cited on page 257]

[214] Wikipedia, 2016. Public-access television — wikipedia, the free encyclopedia. URL https://en.wikipedia.org/w/index.php?title=Public-access_television&oldid=730284626. [Online; accessed 20-August-2016]. [cited on page 285]

[215] Wikipedia, 2016. Push-button telephone — wikipedia, the free encyclopedia. URL https://en.wikipedia.org/w/index.php?title=Push-button_telephone&oldid=729741181. [Online; accessed 10-August-2016]. [cited on pages 76 and 160]

[216] Wikipedia, 2016. RCA Spectra 70 — wikipedia, the free encyclopedia. URL https://en.wikipedia.org/w/index.php?title=RCA_Spectra_70&oldid=702710222. [Online; accessed 11-August-2016]. [cited on page 75]

[217] Wikipedia, 2016. Reader Rabbit — wikipedia, the free encyclopedia. URL https://en.wikipedia.org/w/index.php?title=Reader_Rabbit&oldid=733288510. [Online; accessed 11-August-2016]. [cited on page 203]

[218] Wikipedia, 2016. Resolution (logic) — wikipedia, the free encyclopedia. URL https://en.wikipedia.org/w/index.php?title=Resolution_(logic)&oldid=710632432. [Online; accessed 11-August-2016]. [cited on pages 103 and 107]

[219] Wikipedia, 2016. R.U.R. — wikipedia, the free encyclopedia. URL https://en.wikipedia.org/w/index.php?title=R.U.R.&oldid=743072516. [Online; accessed 7-October-2016]. [cited on page 50]

[220] Wikipedia, 2016. Score! Educational Centers — wikipedia, the free encyclopedia. Wikipedia, The Free Encyclopedia.

URL   https://en.wikipedia.org/w/index.php?title=SCORE!
_Educational_Centers&oldid=733789356.   [Online; accessed 16-August-2016]. [cited on page 174]

[221] Wikipedia, 2016. Seymour Papert — wikipedia, the free encyclopedia. URL https://en.wikipedia.org/w/index.php?title=Seymour_Papert&oldid=734255554. [Online; accessed 19-August-2016]. [cited on page 280]

[222] Wikipedia, 2016.   Siri — wikipedia, the free encyclopedia. URL https://en.wikipedia.org/w/index.php?title=Siri&oldid=733819791. [Online; accessed 11-August-2016]. [cited on pages 129 and 212]

[223] Wikipedia, 2016. Social choice and individual values — wikipedia, the free encyclopedia.   URL https://en.wikipedia.org/w/index.php?title=Social_Choice_and_Individual_Values&oldid=728784694. [Online; accessed 11-August-2016]. [cited on page 115]

[224] Wikipedia, 2016. Speech synthesis — wikipedia, the free encyclopedia. URL https://en.wikipedia.org/w/index.php?title=Speech_synthesis&oldid=733939839.   [Online; accessed 11-August-2016]. [cited on page 128]

[225] Wikipedia, 2016.   SPICE — wikipedia, the free encyclopedia. URL https://en.wikipedia.org/w/index.php?title=SPICE&oldid=729563868. [Online; accessed 11-August-2016]. [cited on page 101]

[226] Wikipedia, 2016. Stanford University Online High School — wikipedia, the free encyclopedia.   URL https://en.wikipedia.org/w/index.php?title=Stanford_University_Online_High_School&oldid=744878611. [Online; accessed 18-October-2016]. [cited on page 264]

[227] Wikipedia, 2016.   Teletype Model 33 — wikipedia, the free encyclopedia.   URL https://en.wikipedia.org/w/index.php?title=Teletype_Model_33&oldid=714301932. [Online; accessed 11-August-2016]. [cited on pages 14 and 81]

[228] Wikipedia, 2016.   Termcap — wikipedia, the free encyclopedia. URL https://en.wikipedia.org/w/index.php?title=Termcap&oldid=731053747.   [Online; accessed 11-August-2016].   [cited on page 63]

[229] Wikipedia, 2016.   ToolBook — wikipedia, the free encyclopedia.   URL https://en.wikipedia.org/w/index.php?title=ToolBook&oldid=754810030.   [Online; accessed 2-February-2017]. [cited on page 251]

[230] Wikipedia, 2016. TUTOR (programming language) — wikipedia, the free encyclopedia.   URL https://en.wikipedia.org/w/index.php?title=TUTOR_(programming_language)&oldid=708566916. [Online; accessed 11-August-2016]. [cited on page 97]

[231] Wikipedia, 2016.   Votrax — wikipedia, the free encyclopedia.   URL https://en.wikipedia.org/w/index.php?title=Votrax&

oldid=727935938. [Online; accessed 11-August-2016]. [cited on page 126]

[232] Wikipedia, 2016. Wolfram Mathematica — wikipedia, the free encyclopedia. URL https://en.wikipedia.org/w/index.php?title=Wolfram_Mathematica&oldid=733919600. [Online; accessed 11-August-2016]. [cited on page 119]

[233] Wikipedia, 2016. Wordperfect — wikipedia, the free encyclopedia. URL https://en.wikipedia.org/w/index.php?title=WordPerfect&oldid=732011979. [Online; accessed 11-August-2016]. [cited on page 202]

[234] Wilson, H.A. and Richard C. Atkinson, 1967. Computer-based instruction in initial reading: A progress report on the Stanford project. Psychology and Education Series 119, IMSSS. URL http://suppes-corpus.stanford.edu/techreports/IMSSS_119.pdf. [cited on page 42]

[235] Woo, Elaine, 2011. John McCarthy dies at 84; the father of artificial intelligence. Los Angeles Times. URL http://www.latimes.com/local/obituaries/la-me-john-mccarthy-20111027-story.html. October 27. [cited on page 12]

[236] Woo, Elaine, 2014. Patrick Suppes dies at 92; pioneered use of computers in classrooms. Los Angeles Times. URL http://www.latimes.com/local/obituaries/la-me-patrick-suppes-20141130-story.html. November 29, [Online; accessed 13-October-2016]. [cited on page xxiii]

Index

275, 281, 291, 293
graphics, xxv, 14, 32, 38, 42,
46, 72, 85, 89, 96, 97,
120, 138, 159, 164,
167–169, 171, 197,
201–206, 208–210,
214, 217, 221, 222,
224, 225, 227–233,
238, 240, 247, 251,
272, 281
enhanced, 216
primitive, 14
graphics presentation, 43
GRE (test), 297
Greece, 33
Gross, Michael, 84
Guatemala, 153
Guinea, 153

hackers, 279, 284
handbook, 65, 161
handhelds, 259, 284
handicapped, 10, 18, 92
Hansen, Duncan, 42, 50
Harcourt, Brace, and World,
76
Harvard University, 53, 278,
279
Haskell, Cymra, 241
Hawley, Newton, 7
Hawthorne effect, 278
Hazeltine, 85
headmaster, 264
headquarters, 175, 179, 269,
270
hearing, 59, 66, 68, 71, 92, 95,
101, 206, 283
Hearn, Tony, 237
Heathkit, 100
Hempel, Tom, 205
Hestes, Sandy, xxvii, 180
Hewlett-Packard, 84, 92

hickory stick, 164
hint, 102, 103, 117, 118, 299
histories (student data), 79,
170, 216
Hmong (language), 159
Ho, Jennifer, 151
Hofstadter, Doug, 139–140
HOMBRES (OS), 84–85
homework, 2, 3, 54, 105
Horowitz, G. R., 77
Human Ecology Research
Foundation, 153
hypothesis, 4, 118, 126, 151

IBM, 10, 12, 13, 16, 17, 24,
37–42, 44, 45, 50, 52,
56, 63, 75, 76, 78, 79,
92, 96, 166, 167, 172,
204, 208, 210, 211,
221–224, 235, 236,
240, 241, 289, 290
ILLIAC (computer), 96
IMLAC (computer), 62, 133,
136
implementation, 11, 32, 68, 75,
78, 83, 106, 107, 144,
146, 165, 177, 180,
186, 192, 193, 197,
202, 204, 237, 244,
272, 281, 290, 301
IMPLIES, 106, 108–109
IMSSS, xxx, xxxi, 1, 2, 4, 5, 9,
15, 16, 28, 38, 42, 52,
56–61, 65, 66, 72, 78,
80, 82, 85, 95–97,
102, 106, 123, 129,
136–142, 144,
152–154, 157–159,
176, 177, 214, 222,
235–237, 242, 243,
250, 257, 273–276,
279, 284, 289, 291,